VISUAL QUICKSTART GUIDE

Illustrator 6

FOR MACINTOSH

Elaine Weinmann
Peter Lourekas

Visual QuickStart Guide
Illustrator 6.0 for Macintosh
Elaine Weinmann and Peter Lourekas

Peachpit Press
2344 Sixth Street
Berkeley, CA 94710
510/548-4393
800-283-9444
510/548-5991 (fax)

Find us on the World Wide Web at: http://www.peachpit.com

Peachpit Press is a division of Addison Wesley Longman

Copyright © 1996 by Elaine Weinmann and Peter Lourekas

Cover design: The Visual Group
Interior design: Elaine Weinmann
Production: Elaine Weinmann and Peter Lourekas
Illustrations: Elaine Weinmann and Peter Lourekas, except as
  noted

Colophon
This book was created with QuarkXPress 3.3 on a Macintosh
Quadra 650 and Power Macintosh 8500. The fonts used were
Sabon and Gill Sans from Adobe Systems Inc.

ISBN 0-201-88633-2
9 8 7 6 5 4 3 2 1

Printed and bound in the United States of America

This book is dedicated to

Martine

and

Danielle

Table of Contents

Table of Contents

Table of Contents

Table of Contents

Introduction

We were delighted to have the opportunity to write a book about Adobe Illustrator because it's such a well-designed program. Illustrator has a complete set of tools for creating many different kinds of drawings, from corporate logos, symbols and labels to children's book illustrations. It has power, precision, loads of features, and a well-designed interface. It is sophisticated, yet easy to use.

Using this book, you will learn how to create, select, modify, and arrange objects. You will learn how to draw objects "from scratch" or create standard geometric objects and then reshape them. You can reshape objects "by hand" or by using commands and dialog boxes. With Illustrator you can Fill or Stroke objects with flat colors, gradients, or patterns. You can create and style type, or you can create your own letterforms by converting type into outlines and then reshaping the outlines. You can create simple illustrations or you can use features like masks, compounds, or filters to create complex illustrations composed of multiple shapes on multiple layers. Once your illustration is completed, you can print it or color separate it.

Michael Bartalos, **Technobabble**,
for Digital Equipment Corporation

This book contains hundreds of screen captures of program features. We also created hundreds of our own illustrations to illuminate key concepts and to entertain you. We've even thrown in a few tutorial-type exercises to help you practice using various features. As in our other *Visual QuickStart Guides*, the absolute, read-me-first essentials are concentrated in the early chapters. The later chapters are like a smorgasbord that you can sample in an orderly or haphazard fashion — as you wish.

If you're new to Illustrator, you'll quickly see that its features are extensive. It's not difficult to make simple drawings, though. Some of the newest features, like the filters and palettes, are actually very easy to use. We hope you have fun using this book. ■

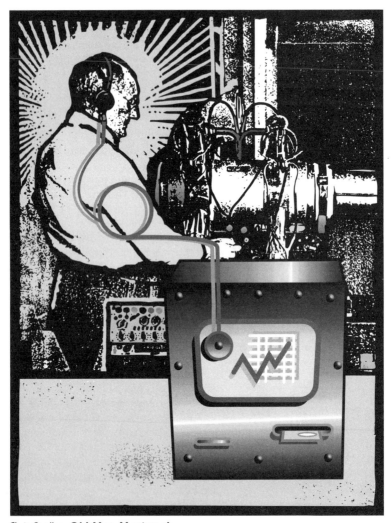

Chris Spollen, **Old Man Macintosh**

THE BASICS

This chapter is an introduction to Illustrator's tools, menus, and palettes, and it also contains a special mini-glossary to aquaint you with terms that you'll encounter throughout the book.

Chris Spollen

Hardware

Illustrator will run fastest on a Power Mac with at least 6 megabytes of application RAM (random access memory) allocated to the program. It will also run on a Macintosh II or Quadra with at least 4 megabytes of application RAM. The application also requires System 7.0 or later and a hard disk. The PowerPC edition of Illustrator will run on a PowerPC Macintosh with at least 10 to 12 megabytes of application Ram. If you're using a Mac II or Quadra, it must contain a math co-processor for all the Illustrator filters to be available and to perform intricate filter calculations.

Though most Illustrator files are small in storage size, illustrations containing placed images can be quite large and require a large hard drive for storage. You'll also probably need to purchase a removable storage device — like a SyQuest, magneto-optical, or Iomega Zip or Jaz drive — to transport files to and from a service bureau or print shop.

Color monitors display 8-bit, 16-bit, or 24-bit color, depending on the amount of Video RAM or the video card installed. With 8-bit color, 256 colors are available for on-screen color mixing. With 24-bit color or 2–4 MB of video RAM installed, 16.7 million colors are available. A 24-bit card provides optimal display, because every color can be represented exactly (and gradients will look smoother). In order to have enough room to display your illustration in a workable size and also have several palettes open, you'll need at least a 16-inch monitor, preferably larger.

You will be able to work most efficiently in Illustrator if you have the means to invest in a fast Macintosh, a large monitor, a large hard drive, and adequate RAM.

MEMORY ALLOCATION

Allocating extra RAM to Illustrator is one way to make it run faster. To learn how much RAM you have available to allocate to Illustrator, launch Illustrator and any other applications that you want to have running at the same time, click in the Finder, then choose About This Macintosh from the Apple menu. Total Memory is the amount of hardware RAM installed, and Largest Unused Block is the amount of RAM still available. The applications you launched and their RAM allotments are also displayed. Ideally, you should allocate at least 10 to 12 megabytes (MB) of RAM to Illustrator. To do this, quit Illustrator, click the Illustrator application icon in the Finder, choose Get Info from the File menu, then enter the desired amount in the Preferred size field. To enter 10MB, for example, type in "10000". Be sure to reserve enough RAM to run the System.

The Illustrator screen

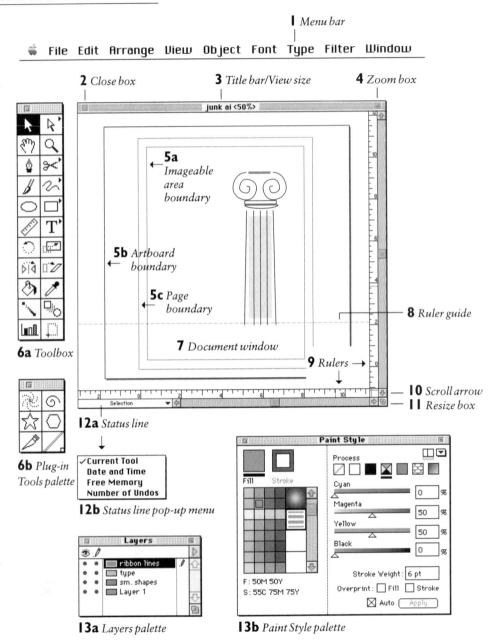

1 *Menu bar*

2 *Close box* **3** *Title bar/View size* **4** *Zoom box*

5a *Imageable area boundary*

5b *Artboard boundary*

5c *Page boundary*

6a *Toolbox*

7 *Document window*

8 *Ruler guide*

9 *Rulers →*

10 *Scroll arrow*

11 *Resize box*

12a *Status line*

6b *Plug-in Tools palette*

12b *Status line pop-up menu*

13a *Layers palette* **13b** *Paint Style palette*

Figure 1.

Key to the Illustrator screen

1 *Menu bar*
Press any menu heading to access dialog boxes, submenus, and commands.

2 *Close box*
To close a window or a palette, click its close box.

3 *Title bar/View size*
Displays the illustration's title and view size.

4 *Zoom box*
Click a document window zoom box to enlarge the window or shrink it to its previous size. Click a palette zoom box to shrink the palette or restore it to its previous size.

5a, b, c *Imageable area, Artboard, and Page boundaries*
The Imageable area — within the margin guides — is the area that will print on the currently selected printer paper size. The Artboard is the user-defined work area and the largest possible printable area. The non-printing Page boundary corresponds to the paper size for the currently selected printer. Objects can be stored in the scractch area, but they won't print.

6a, b *Toolbox, Plug-in Tools palette*
The Toolbox contains 30 drawing and editing tools. The Plug-in Tools palette contains additional tools that are supplied with Illustrator or are purchased from third-party vendors.

7 *Document window*
The illustration window.

8 *Ruler guide*
A non-printing guide used for aligning objects. Press and drag from either ruler to create a guide.

9 *Rulers*
The current position of the pointer is indicated by a mark on the horizontal and vertical rulers. Ruler and dialog box increments can be displayed in a choice of three units of measure.

10 *Scroll arrow*
Click the down arrow to move the illustration upward in the document window. Click the up arrow to move the illustration downward.

11 *Resize box*
To resize a window, press and drag its resize box diagonally.

12a, b *Status line*
Displays the name of the currently selected tool, the current Date & Time from the Macintosh Control Panel, the amount of Free Memory (RAM) available for the currently open file, or the Number of Undos/Redos available, depending on which category you select from the pop-up menu. Hold down Option and press on the Status line pop-up menu to choose special information options (try it!).

13a, b *Palettes*
Layers and Paint Style are two of eleven moveable palettes that open from the Window menu. The other palettes are Info, Character, Paragraph, Gradient, Tabs, Align, Toolbox, Plug-in Tools, and Control.

Illustrator Screen

The Toolbox

The Toolbox contains 30 tools used for object creation and modification. If the Toolbox is hidden, choose Window > Show Toolbox to open it (⌘-Control-T). Click once on a tool to select it. Double-clicking some tools will open a dialog box for that tool. Press on a tool with an arrowhead to choose a related tool from a fly-out menu. Press and drag the top bar to move the Toolbox. Press the caps lock key to turn tool pointers that are not already crosshairs into crosshairs for precise editing.

Hold down Shift and double-click a tool with an arrowhead to restore its default location on the fly-out menu.

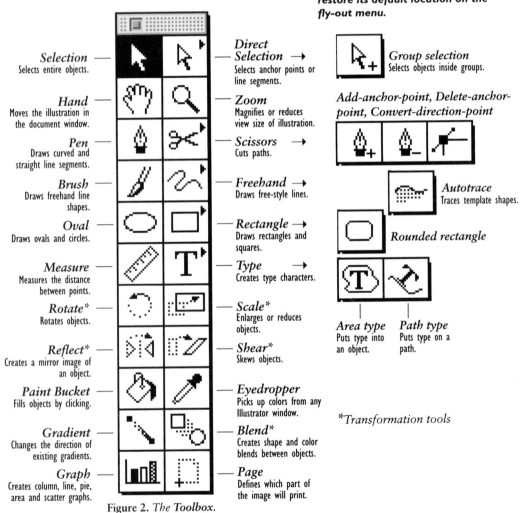

Selection — Selects entire objects.

Direct Selection → Selects anchor points or line segments.

Group selection Selects objects inside groups.

Hand Moves the illustration in the document window.

Zoom Magnifies or reduces view size of illustration.

Add-anchor-point, Delete-anchor-point, Convert-direction-point

Pen Draws curved and straight line segments.

Scissors → Cuts paths.

Brush Draws freehand line shapes.

Freehand → Draws free-style lines.

Autotrace Traces template shapes.

Oval Draws ovals and circles.

Rectangle → Draws rectangles and squares.

Rounded rectangle

Measure Measures the distance between points.

Type → Creates type characters.

Rotate* Rotates objects.

Scale* Enlarges or reduces objects.

Area type Puts type into an object.

Path type Puts type on a path.

Reflect* Creates a mirror image of an object.

Shear* Skews objects.

Paint Bucket Fills objects by clicking.

Eyedropper Picks up colors from any Illustrator window.

*Transformation tools

Gradient Changes the direction of existing gradients.

Blend* Creates shape and color blends between objects.

Graph Creates column, line, pie, area and scatter graphs.

Page Defines which part of the image will print.

Figure 2. The Toolbox.

Toolbox

The Plug-in Tools palette

Access extra tools from Adobe and third-party developers via the Plug-in Tools palette. Choose Windows > Show Plug-in Tools to display it. Plug-ins are normally installed in the Plug-ins folder in the Adobe Illustrator folder. (The Plug-ins folder itself shouldn't be moved.)

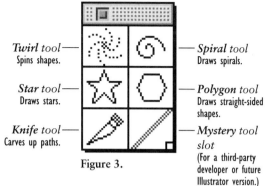

Twirl tool —
Spins shapes.

Star tool —
Draws stars.

Knife tool —
Carves up paths.

— *Spiral* tool
Draws spirals.

— *Polygon* tool
Draws straight-sided shapes.

— *Mystery* tool
slot
(For a third-party developer or future Illustrator version.)

Figure 3.

Units of measure

You can enter numbers in dialog boxes or on palettes in any of the units of measure that are used in Illustrator, regardless of the default Ruler units. You can choose a default unit of measure for the application *(see page 237)* or for a particular document *(see page 228)*. If you enter a number in a unit of measure other than the default unit, the number will be translated into the default unit. If you enter the symbol for subtraction (-), addition (+), multiplication (*), or division (/) in any entry field in Illustrator 6.0, the program will do the math for you automatically.

SYMBOLS YOU CAN USE

12 pts = 1 pica
6 picas = 1 inch

UNIT	SYMBOL
Picas	**p**
Points	**pt**
Inches	**"** *or* **in**
Centimeters	**cm**

File size units

Byte = 8 bits of digital information (approx. one black or white pixel, or one character

Kilobyte (KB) = 1,024 bytes

Megabyte (MB) = 1,024 kilobytes

Gigabyte (GB) = 1,024 megabytes

A note to our readers:

If you're familiar with the previous edition of this book, you may notice that we changed our writing format slightly so we could make more room for tips, keyboard shortcuts, and other helpful information. Where you see a configuration like this: View > Artwork, its just a less wordy way of saying "Choose Artwork from the View menu." And if you see a configuration like this: Filter > Colors > Saturate, it means you should choose Saturate from the Colors submenu under the Filter menu. This is the basic format:

Menu > command *-or-*

Menu > submenu > command

Mini-glossary

Objects

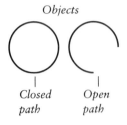

Closed path   *Open path*

Object   Any individual shape created in Illustrator.

Path   The edge of an object that defines its shape. Paths are composed of anchor points with direction lines which are joined by line segments. These elements can be modified to reshape the object. A path can be open or closed.

◆

Direction point

Direction line

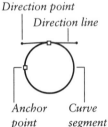

Anchor point   *Curve segment*

Straight segment

Anchor point   A corner point or a curve (smooth) point that joins two segments of a path.

Curve segment   The segment between two curve anchor points or a corner point and a curve anchor point.

Straight segment   The segment between two corner points.

Direction line   The control handle that defines the shape of a curved path segment. To reshape a segment, rotate, lengthen, or shorten a direction line by dragging its direction point.

◆

Selected object

Selected anchor point

Select   Click on an object or group with the Selection or Group Selection tool to select the whole object or group. All anchor points and segments will be highlighted.

Direct Select   Click on an anchor point or segment with the Direct Selection tool to select only that anchor point or segment.

Stroke

Stroke The color applied to the edge (path) of an object.

Fill A color, pattern or gradient applied to the inside of an object.

Gradient Fill A graduated blend between two or more colors. A Gradient Fill can be linear (side to side) or radial (radiating outward from a center point of your choice).

Linear   Radial
Gradient   Gradient

Stack The positioning of objects on top of one another within a layer. The most recently created object is placed at the top of the stack.

Layer The positioning of a stack of objects relative to other stacks. An illustration can contain multiple layers, which can be reordered.

◆

Compound Path

Compound path Two or more objects that are combined into a larger, single object. Areas where the original objects overlapped become transparent.

Mask

Mask An object that trims ("clips") away other objects that extend beyond its border. Only parts of objects that are within the confines of the mask object will display and print.

Group Individual objects that are combined so they can be moved or modified as a unit. When objects are grouped, they are moved to the layer of the top-most object.

Menus

Each menu heading provides access to related commands for modifying objects. The nine Illustrator menus are displayed on the following pages.

To choose from a menu, press and drag downward through the menu or to the right and downward through the sub-menu, then release the mouse when the desired entry is highlighted.

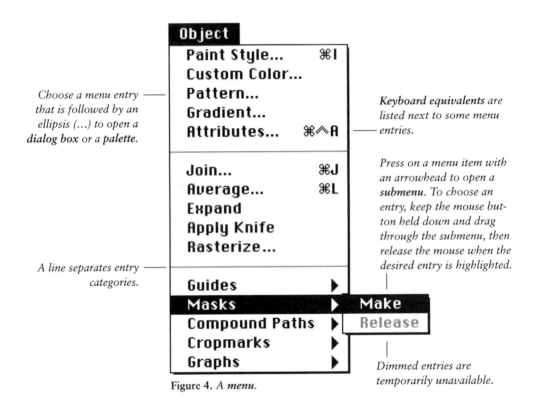

Choose a menu entry that is followed by an ellipsis (...) to open a dialog box or a palette.

Keyboard equivalents are listed next to some menu entries.

Press on a menu item with an arrowhead to open a submenu. To choose an entry, keep the mouse button held down and drag through the submenu, then release the mouse when the desired entry is highlighted.

A line separates entry categories.

Dimmed entries are temporarily unavailable.

Figure 4. *A menu.*

The File menu.

File menu commands are used to create, open, close, save, print, or color separate an illustration, import art or text from another application or paint styles from another document, choose document or printer specifications, set application and document defaults, and quit Illustrator.

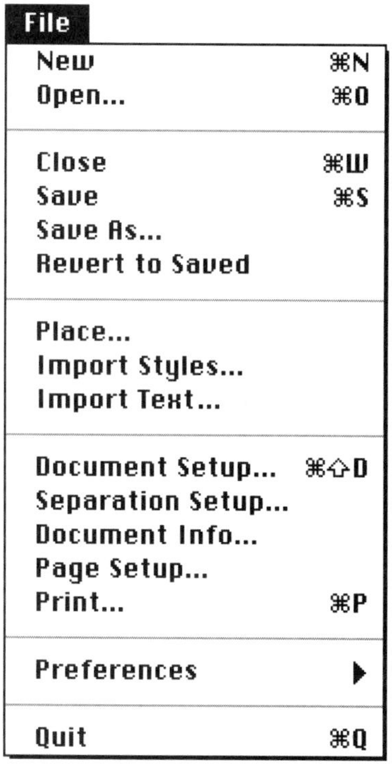

File	
New	⌘N
Open...	⌘O
Close	⌘W
Save	⌘S
Save As...	
Revert to Saved	
Place...	
Import Styles...	
Import Text...	
Document Setup...	⌘⇧D
Separation Setup...	
Document Info...	
Page Setup...	
Print...	⌘P
Preferences	▶
Quit	⌘Q

Figure 5. *The File menu.*

The Edit menu.

Edit menu commands include Undo and Redo, the Clipboard commands Cut and Copy, and Paste, the Select commands, and the Paste In Front/ Paste In Back commands, which place the current Clipboard contents in front of or behind the currently selected object.

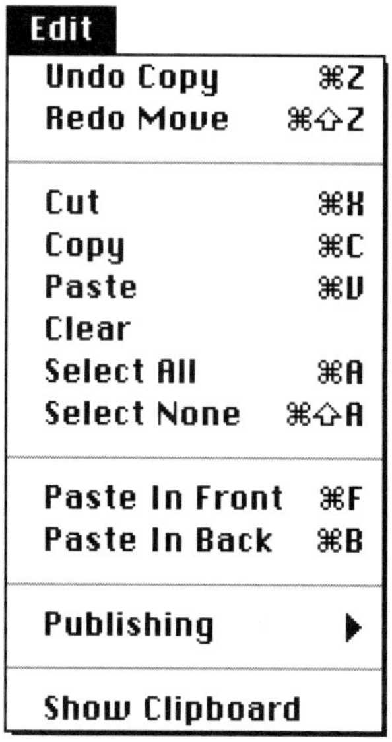

Edit	
Undo Copy	⌘Z
Redo Move	⌘⇧Z
Cut	⌘X
Copy	⌘C
Paste	⌘V
Clear	
Select All	⌘A
Select None	⌘⇧A
Paste In Front	⌘F
Paste In Back	⌘B
Publishing	▶
Show Clipboard	

Figure 6. *The Edit menu.*

About the Undo command —————

To undo an operation, choose Edit > Undo (⌘-Z). To undo the second-to-last operation, choose Edit > Undo again, etc. To reverse an undo, choose Edit > Redo (⌘-Shift-Z). You can undo after saving your document, but not if you close and reopen it.

The minimum number of undos that you can perform depends on the Undo Levels setting in the General Preferences dialog box (File menu). You can undo up to 200 operations, depending on available memory. If Illustrator requires additional RAM to perform illustration edits, it will reduce the number of undos to the minimum.

File and Edit Menus

The Arrange menu.

Arrange menu commands are used to move an object or objects, reposition an object within its stack, and group, lock, or hide objects. The Repeat Transform command repeats the last modification made with any transformation tool or with the Transform Each command.

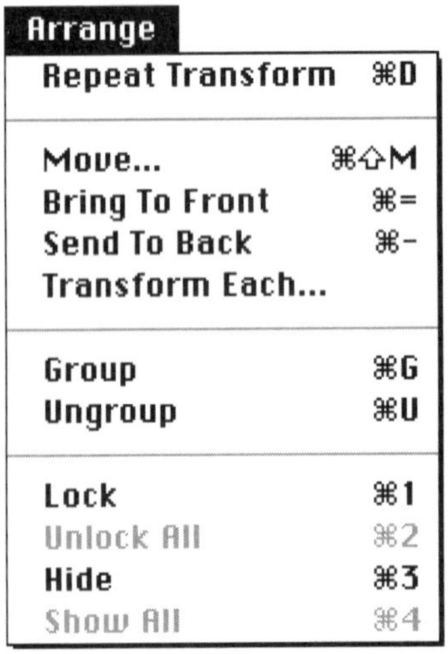

The View menu.

View menu commands affect document display. You can choose the full-color Preview view or wireframe Artwork view, show or hide rulers, tiling, edges, and guides, enlarge or reduce the view size, and create and choose custom view settings via View menu commands.

Arrange	
Repeat Transform	⌘D
Move...	⌘⇧M
Bring To Front	⌘=
Send To Back	⌘-
Transform Each...	
Group	⌘G
Ungroup	⌘U
Lock	⌘1
Unlock All	⌘2
Hide	⌘3
Show All	⌘4

Figure 7. *The Arrange menu.*

View	
✓Preview	⌘Y
Artwork	⌘E
Preview Selection	⌘⌥Y
Hide Template	⌘⇧W
Show Rulers	⌘R
Hide Page Tiling	
Hide Edges	⌘⇧H
Hide Guides	
Zoom In	⌘]
Zoom Out	⌘[
Actual Size	⌘H
Fit In Window	⌘M
New View...	⌘⌃V
Edit Views...	

Figure 8. *The View menu.*

The Object menu.

Under the Object menu are many essential commands for styling and shaping objects. They Fill and Stroke objects with colors, patterns, and gradients, join line segments, average anchor points, cut objects into smaller shapes, rasterize objects, and turn objects into guides. Separate chapters in this book are devoted to graphs, masks, and compound paths, which are created via Object menu commands.

The Font menu.

Use the Font menu to choose fonts that are currently installed and available in your System. If Adobe Type Reunion is installed, fonts are organized in families (as in this illustration), and various weights and font styles within those families are chosen from sub-menus (designated by arrowheads).

Object	
Paint Style...	⌘I
Custom Color...	
Pattern...	
Gradient...	
Attributes...	⌘⌃A
Join...	⌘J
Average...	⌘L
Expand...	
Apply Knife	
Rasterize...	
Guides	▶
Masks	▶
Compound Paths	▶
Cropmarks	▶
Graphs	▶

Figure 9. *The Object menu.*

Font	
AGaramond	▶
AGaramond Alternate	▶
AGaramond Expert	▶
American Typewriter	▶
Arcadia	▶
Avant Garde	▶
Banco	
Bank Gothic BT	▶
Bauer Bodoni	▶
Bernhard	▶
Bernhard Fashion ICG	
Birch	
Blackoak	
Bodoni	▶
Bookman	▶
Brush Script	
BSymbol	▶

Figure 10. *The Font menu.*

Object and Font Menus

The Type menu.

Character and paragraph specifications are applied via Type menu
commands or via the Character and
Paragraph palettes, which can be
opened from this menu. Other Type
menu features control text flow by
linking type blocks, wrapping type
around objects, and creating text rows
and columns. The Smart Punctuation
command produces professional
typesetting marks, and the Create
Outlines command converts type
characters into graphic objects. Word
processing features under this menu
include Check Spelling and Find.

Type
Size	▶
Leading	▶
Alignment	▶
Tracking...	⌘⇧K
Spacing...	⌘⇧O
Character...	⌘T
Paragraph...	⌘⇧P
Link Blocks	⌘⇧G
Unlink Blocks	⌘⇧U
Make Wrap	
Release Wrap	
Fit Headline	
Create Outlines	
Export...	
Check Spelling...	
Smart Punctuation...	
Find...	
Rows & Columns...	
Find Font...	
Change Case...	

Figure 11. *The Type menu.*

The Filter menu.

The various Illustrator filters recolor, create, distort, reposition, combine, select,
and stylize objects.

Filter
Free Distort	⌘⇧E
Colors	▶
Create	▶
Distort	▶
Gallery Effects: Classic Art 1	▶
Gallery Effects: Classic Art 2	▶
Gallery Effects: Classic Art 3	▶
Ink Pen	▶
Objects	▶
Pathfinder	▶
Select	▶
Stylize	▶

Figure 12. *The Filter menu.*

The Window menu.

Window menu commands create new or
activate open illustration windows and
hide and show the palettes.

Window
New Window	
Hide Toolbox	⌘⌃T
Hide Layers	⌘⌃L
Show Info	⌘⌃I
Hide Paint Style	
Show Gradient	
Show Character	
Show Paragraph	
Show Tab Ruler	⌘⇧T
Hide Align	
Hide Plug-in Tools	
Hide Control Palette	
✓test <66.67%>	

Figure 13. *The Window menu.*

Dialog boxes

Dialog boxes are like fill-in forms with multiple choices. The various ways to indicate choices are shown in Figure 14.

To open a dialog box, select any menu item followed by an ellipsis (...) or use the corresponding keyboard shortcut.

Some modifications are made by entering numbers in entry fields. Press **Tab** to highlight the next field in a dialog box. Hold down **Shift** and press **Tab** to highlight the previous field.

Click **OK** or press **Return** to accept modifications and exit a dialog box. To cancel a dialog box, use the ⌘-. shortcut.

Many Illustrator dialog boxes now have a Preview option: you can preview the effect while the dialog box is open. Take advantage of this great timesaver. For dialog boxes that have a preview option and sliders, you can hold down Option and click Reset to restore the original dialog box values.

Dialog Boxes

*Click a **radio button** to turn that option on or off.*

*Type a number into a field. Press **Tab** to move from field to field.*

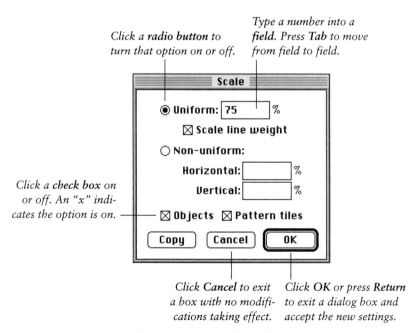

*Click a **check box** on or off. An "x" indicates the option is on.*

*Click **Cancel** to exit a box with no modifications taking effect.*

*Click **OK** or press **Return** to exit a dialog box and accept the new settings.*

Figure 14. *A sample **dialog box**.*

The Illustrator palettes

Do you like a tidy screen? Snap your palettes together top-to-bottom or side-to-side.

The Paint Style palette

The Paint Style palette is used to mix and apply Fill and Stroke colors to objects, as well as Stroke weights and styles. The palette is divided into three panels: paint swatch window *(left)*, color selection method icons and color mixing options *(right)*, and Stroke attributes *(bottom)*.

Paint Style Palette

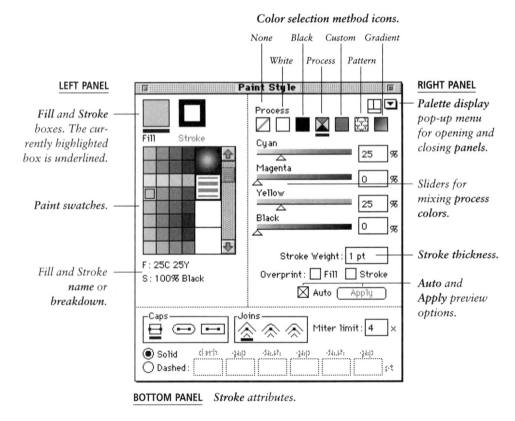

Color selection method icons.

None   Black   Custom   Gradient

White   Process   Pattern

LEFT PANEL

Fill and Stroke boxes. The currently highlighted box is underlined.

Paint swatches.

Fill and Stroke name or breakdown.

RIGHT PANEL

Palette display pop-up menu for opening and closing panels.

Sliders for mixing process colors.

Stroke thickness.

Auto and Apply preview options.

BOTTOM PANEL   *Stroke attributes.*

Figure 15. *The* **Paint Style** *palette.*

The Gradient palette

The Gradient palette is used to create and save gradient Fills using two or more colors that are mixed or selected right on the palette. The currently highlighted gradient is displayed in the color bar.

Click the palette display lever to open or close the lower panel.

Color bar.   **Midpoint** *diamond.*

UPPER PANEL

Starting color triangle.

Color selection method icons.

LOWER PANEL

Sliders for mixing process colors.

Ending color triangle.

Gradient Fill scroll list.

Name field.

Linear and **Radial Fill** buttons.

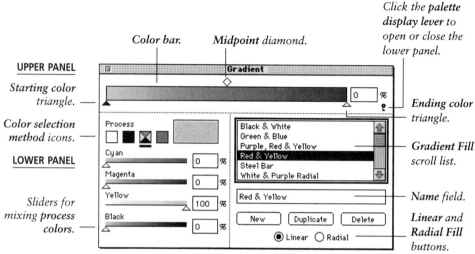

Figure 16. *The Gradient palette.*

The Character palette

The Character palette is used to apply type attributes: Font, Size, Leading, Baseline Shift, Horizontal Scale, Tracking, and Kerning. Press Return to apply specifications.

Font field.   *Weight or style field.*

UPPER PANEL

Size and Leading pop-up menus.

LOWER PANEL

Font pop-up menu.

Palette display lever to open or close the lower panel.

The Language hyphenation dictionary for the current document.

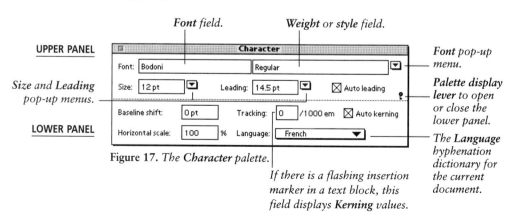

Figure 17. *The Character palette.*

If there is a flashing insertion marker in a text block, this field displays Kerning values.

Gradient and Character Palettes

The Paragraph palette

The Paragraph palette is used to apply horizontal Alignment, Indentation, Leading before ¶, Hyphenation, Word spacing and Letter spacing values. Press Return to apply specifications.

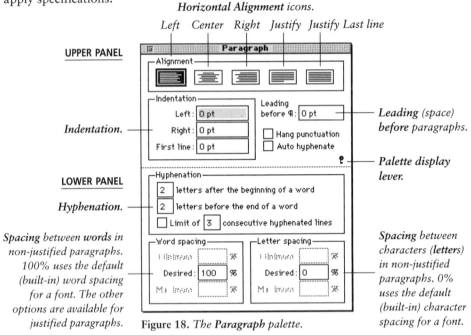

Horizontal Alignment icons.

Left   Center   Right   Justify   Justify Last line

UPPER PANEL

Indentation.

Leading (space) before paragraphs.

Palette display lever.

LOWER PANEL

Hyphenation.

Spacing between words in non-justified paragraphs. 100% uses the default (built-in) word spacing for a font. The other options are available for justified paragraphs.

*Spacing between characters (**letters**) in non-justified paragraphs. 0% uses the default (built-in) character spacing for a font.*

Figure 18. *The* **Paragraph** *palette.*

The Tabs palette

The Tabs palette is used to insert or reposition custom tab markers, which are used to align columns of text.

*Check the **Snap** box to have a tab marker snap to the nearest ruler tic mark as you insert it or drag it. Or, to temporarily turn on the Snap feature when the Snap box is unchecked, hold down **Control** as you drag a marker. Ruler increments will display in the currently chosen Ruler units (Document Setup).*

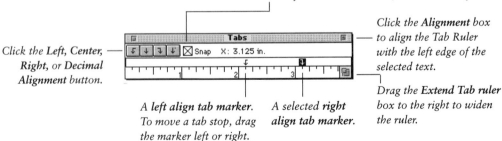

*Click the **Left, Center, Right,** or **Decimal** Alignment button.*

*Click the **Alignment** box to align the Tab Ruler with the left edge of the selected text.*

*Drag the **Extend Tab ruler** box to the right to widen the ruler.*

*A **left align tab marker.** To move a tab stop, drag the marker left or right.*

*A selected **right align tab marker.***

Figure 19. *The* **Tab Ruler.**

(sidebar) **Paragraph and Tabs Palettes**

The Layers palette

The Layers palette is used to add, delete, hide, show, and reorder layers in an illustration. You can also use this palette to control which layers are editable or move an object to a different layer.

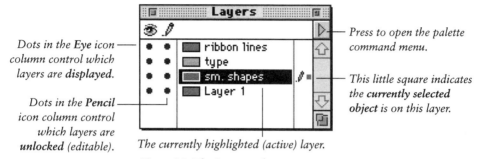

*Dots in the Eye icon column control which layers are **displayed**.*

*Dots in the **Pencil** icon column control which layers are **unlocked** (editable).*

Press to open the palette command menu.

*This little square indicates the **currently selected** object is on this layer.*

The currently highlighted (active) layer.

Figure 20. *The Layers palette.*

The Info palette

If no object is selected, the Info palette shows the horizontal and vertical position of the pointer on the illustration, as in Figure 20. If an object is selected, the palette displays the position of the object on the page and the width and height of the object. If a type tool and type are selected, the palette displays type specifications. The Info palette automatically opens when the Measure tool is used, and displays the distance and angle calculated by the tool.

*The **horizontal position** of the pointer.*

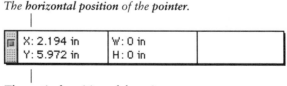

*The **vertical position** of the pointer.*

Figure 21. *The Info palette.*

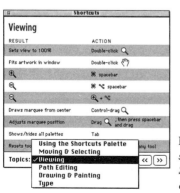

Figure 22. *If you'd like to look up shortcuts right on your screen, use the **Shortcuts** palette. Open it by chooisng Show Shortcuts from the balloon help menu, and then choose a category from the Topics pop-up menu.*

The Align palette

The Align palette is used for aligning two or more objects along their centers or along their top, left, or bottom edges, or for equalizing (distributing) the space between three or more objects.

Align centers horizontally.

Align left edges. ——

Align top edges. ——

Distribute horizontally from centers.

Distribute from left edges.

Distribute from top edges.

—— *Align right edges.*

—— *Align bottom edges.*

—— *Align centers vertically.*

—— *Distribute from right edges.*

—— *Distribute from bottom edges.*

—— *Distribute vertically from centers.*

Figure 23. *The Align palette.*

The Control palette

The Control palette displays position, width, and height information for a selected object, and the palette can be used to move, resize, or rotate a selected object (or objects).

The Reference Point Options icon. Control palette amounts are calculated from the currently selected reference point.

The x and y axes location of the currently selected object. Enter new values to move the object.

The Width and Height of the selected object.

The Scale field for resizing the whole object proportionally.

The Rotate field for rotating the object.

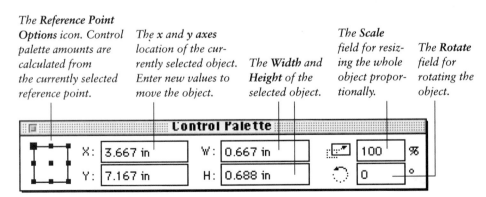

Figure 24. *The Control palette.*

HOW ILLUSTRATOR WORKS 2

Figure 1a. *An object-oriented graphic.*

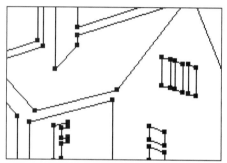

Figure 1b. *Closeup of the same object-oriented graphic in Artwork view, showing selected line segments and anchor points.*

Figure 2a. *A bitmap graphic.*

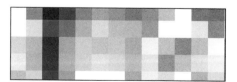

Figure 2b. *Extreme closeup of a bitmap.*

Illustrator is primarily an object-oriented program

There are two main types of picture-making applications on the Macintosh: bitmap and object-oriented. (The fancier terms "raster-based" and "vector-based" are sometimes also used.) It's important to know the strengths and weaknesses of bitmapped and object-oriented programs. Bitmap programs are great for creating soft, painterly effects; object-oriented programs are great for creating sharp, smooth-edged layered images, like logos, and for creating typographic designs. Some of the latest versions of bitmap applications — like Painter — have some vector capabilities, and in Illustrator 6.0 you can **rasterize** vector images (convert object-oriented images into bitmap images).

In an **object-oriented** program like Adobe Illustrator or Macromedia FreeHand, drawings are composed of separate, distinct objects that are positioned on one or more **layers**. Objects are drawn using free-style or precise drawing tools, and are mathematically defined. An illustrator object can be recolored, resized, and reshaped without affecting its sharpness or smoothness. It can be moved easily without affecting other objects. An object in an object-oriented drawing looks smooth and sharp regardless of the size at which it is displayed or printed (**Figures 1a–1b**).

Object-oriented files are usually relatively small in storage size, so you can save multiple versions of a file without filling up valuable hard drive space.

And object oriented drawings are **resolution independent**, which means that their print quality is dependent only on the resolution of the printer. The higher the printer resolution, the sharper and finer the printed image.

An image created in a **bitmap** program, on the other hand, is composed of a single layer of tiny squares on a grid, called pixels. If you "paint" on a bitmap image, you'll recolor pixels, not whole shapes. If you zoom in on a bitmap image, you'll see a checkerboard of tiny squares. Bitmap files tend to be quite large, and the printout quality of a bitmap image is dependent on the resolution of the image, but bitmap programs are ideal for creating soft, painterly effects (**Figures 2a–2b**).

Illustrator objects

Illustrator drawings are composed of multiple, independent elements, called **objects**. Objects are composed of **anchor points** connected by **curved** or **straight** segments (**Figure 3**). The edge of an object is called its **path**. A path can be open (with two endpoints) or closed and continuous.

Some Illustrator tools produce complete, closed paths, like the Rectangle, Oval, Polygon, and Star tools. The number and position of the anchor points on these paths is determined automatically. The Brush tool creates ribbon-like "brush stroke" shapes.

Other tools produce open *or* closed paths, like the Freehand and Pen tools. The **Freehand** tool creates open or closed freeform lines. And using the **Pen** tool, you can create as many corner or curve anchor points as you need to form an object.

Illustrator type

Illustrator has many features for creating PostScript **type**. Type can be free floating,

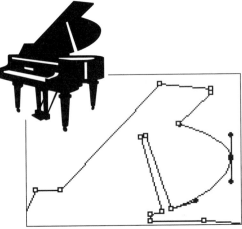

Figure 3. *Closeup of an illustration in Artwork view, showing curved and straight line segments.*

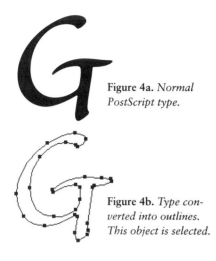

Figure 4a. *Normal PostScript type.*

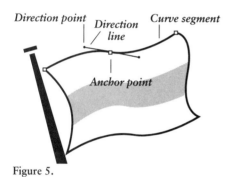

Figure 4b. *Type converted into outlines. This object is selected.*

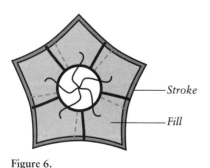

Figure 5.

Figure 6.

it can conform to the edge of an object, or it can fill the inside of an object. It can be repositioned, edited, restyled, and recolored. Or, you can convert type characters into graphic objects, called **outlines**, which can be reshaped or otherwise modified using any of Illustrator's drawing features (**Figures 4a–4b**).

Before an object can be modified…

An object must be selected before it can be modified. There are three selection tools: **Selection**, **Direct Selection**, and **Group Selection**.

How objects are modified

Objects can be modified using a variety of features, including filters and other menu commands, dialog boxes, palettes, and tools.

An object's path can be reshaped by moving its anchor points or segments or by converting curve anchor points into corner anchor points (or vice versa). A curve segment can be reshaped by rotating, lengthening, or shortening its direction lines. Because a path can be reshaped easily, you can draw a simple shape first and then develop it into a more complicated form later on (**Figure 5**).

Some tools are specifically designed for modifying paths, such as the **Add Anchor Point** tool, which adds points to a path, the **Delete Anchor Point** tool, which deletes points from a path, the **Scissors** tool, which splits a path, the **Convert Direction Point** tool, which converts points from corner to curved (or vice versa), and the new **Knife** tool, which carves out sections of an object.

Spot colors (Pantone colors) and **process colors** and can be applied to any object. You can **Fill** the inside of an object or **Stroke** the edge of an object (**Figure 6**). A Fill can be a flat color, a graduated blend of several colors, called a **gradient**, or a **pattern** of repeating shapes.

How Illustrator Works

Illustrator's **filters** modify objects in one or two easy steps. They randomly distort an object's shape, modify color, combine overlapping objects, divide areas where objects overlap into separate objects, or apply color to areas where objects overlap. The **Pathfinder** filters combine two or more objects into a new object.

Other modifications can be made using the **transformation** tools. The Scale tool enlarges or reduces an object's size; the Rotate tool rotates an object; the Reflect tool creates a mirror image of an object; the Shear tool slants an object; and the Blend tool transforms one object into another object by creating a series of transitional shapes. Multiple transformations can be performed at once using the Transform Each command or the Control palette.

Still other Illustrator commands combine individual objects into complex configurations. The **Compound Path** command, for example, "cuts" a hole through an object to reveal underlying shapes. And you can use an object as a **mask** to hide parts of other objects that extend beyond its edges.

Working tools

You can change the **view size** of an illustration as you work to facilitate editing. You can **Zoom in** to work on a small detail or **Zoom out** to see how the drawing looks as a whole. Or you can move the illustration in the document window using the **Hand** tool.

An illustration can be displayed and edited in **Preview** view, in which colors are displayed. To speed up editing and screen redraw, you can display your illustration in **Artwork** view, in which objects are displayed as "wire frame" outlines (**Figures 7a–7b**). Or, you can selectively preview individual objects in **Preview Selection** view.

Figure 7a. *Preview view.*

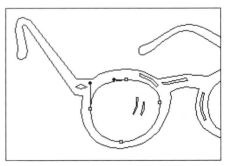

Figure 7b. *Artwork view.*

You can draw an illustration "by eye" or you can use any of Illustrator's precision tools to help you work more exactly: **rulers, guides,** the **Measure** tool, the **Move** dialog box, and the **Align** palette.

The eleven movable palettes — **Toolbox, Plug-in Tools, Paint Style, Gradient, Character, Paragraph, Layers, Info, Control, Align, Tabs Ruler** — are great time-saving features. You will probably find the Paint Style and Layers palettes to be particularly useful, and may want to leave them open while you work if your monitor is large enough (see the illustration on the next page). If you do a lot of typographic work, you'll also find the Character and Paragraph palettes indispensible.

When your illustration is finished

An Illustrator file can be **printed** on any PostScript output device. You can output an illustration on paper or produce color separations right from Illustrator; you can **import** your illustration into another application, like PageMaker or Quark-XPress; or you can use your illustration in a multimedia project or display it on the Internet's World Wide Web.

If Illustrator is brand new to you, we recommend that you read Chapter 3 first to learn how to open and save documents, and Chapter 4 to learn how to navigate around your document. Then proceed to Chapter 5, where you'll learn how to draw basic shapes. Happy illustrating!

ILLUSTRATOR
image

Color separate directly from Illustrator

Import into page layout application (QuarkXPress, PageMaker)

Export to a multimedia application (Director, Premiere)

Drag into PageMill to publish on the World Wide Web

How Illustrator Works

The Illustrator Screen.

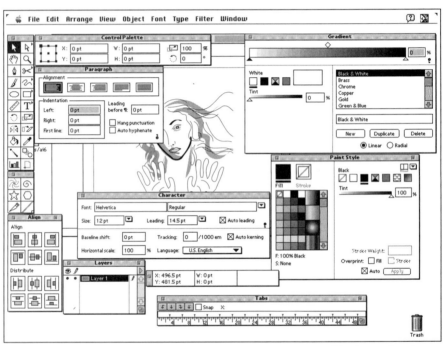

Figure 8. *You could buy a second monitor just for your palettes, but you'll be doing a lot of schlepping back and forth between monitors. See our Window Shade tip on page 41.*

How Illustrator Works

STARTUP 3

*In this chapter you will learn how to launch
Illustrator, create a new illustration with or without
a template, define the working and printable areas
of a document, save an illustration in a variety of
file formats, open an existing illustration, place a
file from another application into Illustrator, close
an illustration, and quit Illustrator.*

Figure 1. *Double-click the* **Adobe Illustrator**
icon on the **Launcher.**

To launch Illustrator:

Double-click the Adobe Illustrator folder
on the desktop, then double-click the
square Illustrator application icon.
or
If you're using System 7.5 or later, click
the Adobe Illustrator application icon on
the Launcher (**Figure 1**).
or
Double-click an Illustrator file icon
(**Figure 2**).

■ If you launch Illustrator by clicking
the application icon, a new untitled
document window will appear automatically.

Figure 2. *Or double-click an* **Illustrator file icon.**

Launch Illustrator

A **template** is a background image that you can use to trace over. For example, you can scan a hand drawn sketch, save it in the MacPaint or PICT file format, open it as a template in Illustrator, and then trace over it with the Autotrace tool or the Pen tool. You cannot select, preview, or print a template.

To create a new document without a template:

When you launch Illustrator, a new document window opens automatically. If Illustrator is already open and you want to create a new document, choose File > New (⌘-N) (**Figure 3**).

Figure 3. *Choose New from the File menu.*

To create a new document with a template:

1. With Option held down, choose File > New (⌘-Option-N) (**Figure 3**).

2. Click on a MacPaint or PICT file to use as a template, then click Open (**Figures 4–5**).
   or
   Double-click the file name. A new document window will appear with a gray template shape in the center.

■ If you reopen the document, the template will reopen with it. To reopen the document without the template or with a new template, see the second tip on page 34.

■ If you change your mind and decide to create a new document without a template, click None (⌘-N).

■ Choose View > Hide Template (⌘-Shift-W) to hide the template. Choose View > Show Template to redisplay the template.

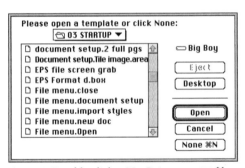

Figure 4. *Double-click a MacPaint or PICT file to use as a template.*

Figure 5. *Tracing a template with the Pen tool.*

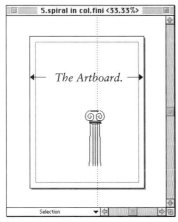

Figure 6.

Figure 7. *Choose* **Document Setup** *from the* **File** *menu.*

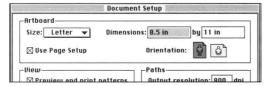

Figure 8. *In the* **Document Setup** *dialog box, choose a preset* **Artboard Size***, or enter custom* **Dimensions***, or check the* **Use Page Setup** *box to use the paper size currently selected in the Page Setup dialog box.*

In the center of every Illustrator document is a non-movable **Artboard** work area that represents the maximum printable size of the illustration (**Figure 6**). The default Artboard area is 8½ inches wide by 11 inches high. You can specify whether the Artboard will contain one printable page or facing printable pages. Or you can tile (subdivide) an oversized illustration into a grid so it can be printed in sections on standard size paper. The size of the printable page is specified in the Page Setup dialog box.

To change the Artboard dimensions:

1. Choose File > Document Setup (⌘-Shift-D) (**Figure 7**).

2. Choose a preset size from the Artboard: Size pop-up menu (**Figure 8**).
   or
   Enter numbers in the Dimensions fields. The maximum work area is 120 by 120 inches.
   or
   Check the Use Page Setup box to match the Artboard dimensions with the Paper size currently selected in the Page Setup dialog box (File menu).

3. Click OK or press Return.

■ Objects placed outside the Artboard will be saved with the illustration, but they won't print.

■ If the Page Setup Reduce or Enlarge percentage is other than 100%, the illustration will print proportionately smaller or larger. If the Use Page Setup box is unchecked in the Document Setup dialog box, the Artboard won't be affected by this Page Setup percentage; if it is checked, the Artboard dimensions will match the custom printout size. Either way, the illustration will print at the size specified in Page Setup.

Change the Artboard Dimensions

You can switch the printable area of an illustration from a vertical (portrait) to a landscape orientation, and then make the Artboard conform to the new orientation.

To create a landscape page:

1. Choose File > Page Setup.
2. Click the landscape Orientation icon (**Figure 9**).
3. Click OK or press Return (**Figure 10**).

- Press and drag with the Page tool if you want to reposition the printable area within the Artboard (**Figure 11**).
- Double-click the Hand tool to display the entire Artboard.

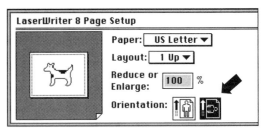

Figure 9. *Click the **landscape Orientation** icon in the Page Setup dialog box.*

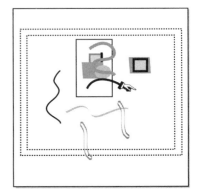

Figure 10. *The **printable page** in landscape Orientation.*

Figure 11. *The **Page** tool.*

To create a landscape Artboard:

1. Choose File > Document Setup.
2. Click the Landscape Orientation icon, if it isn't already highlighted.
3. Click OK or press Return (**Figure 12**). *(See the tips above).*
4. If the entire page isn't visible in the document window, reopen Document Setup and enter new Dimensions to enlarge the Artboard to accommodate the new orientation.

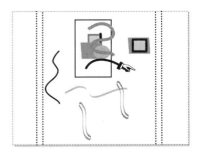

Figure 12. *The **Artboard** in landscape Orientation. The printable page doesn't extend beyond the Artboard.*

Create a Landscape Artboard

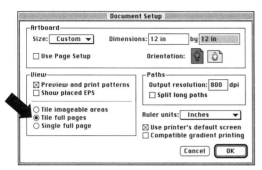

Figure 13. *Click the* **Tile full pages** *button in the* **Document Setup** *dialog box.*

By default, a new document contains a single page, but you can turn it into a multi-page document. If you turn on the Tile Full Pages option, as many full page borders as can fit in the current size of the Artboard will be drawn. Changing the Artboard size will increase or decrease the number of page borders.

To divide the Artboard into multiple pages:

1. Choose View > Fit in Window.
2. Choose File > Document Setup.
3. Click the View: "Tile full pages" button (**Figure 13**).
4. Click OK or press Return.
5. *Optional:* Choose the Page tool (**Figure 14**), then click near the left edge of the Artboard. New page borders will be drawn (**Figure 15**). (If the tile lines are not visible, choose View > Show Page Tiling.)

■ To Tile full pages in landscape mode, click the landscape Orientation icon in the Document Setup dialog box, and choose Size: Tabloid. If necessary, click with the Page tool near the top or bottom of the Artboard to cause the new page borders to be drawn (**Figure 16**).

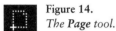

Figure 14.
The **Page** *tool.*

Parts of objects that fall within this "gutter" area will not print.

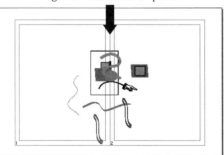

Figure 15. *The* **Artboard** *divided into two pages.*

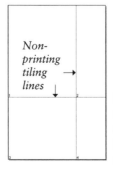

Non-printing tiling lines →

Figure 16. *An oversized illustration tiled into sections for printing (see page 242)*

Divide the Artboard

A file saved in the native Illustrator format will be smaller in file size than the same file saved in the EPS format. However, if you want to open an Illustrator file in another application other than Photoshop, you must save it in the Illustrator EPS format (instructions on the next page) or in another file format that your target application can read (see pages 32–33).

To save a new illustration in the native Illustrator format:

1. Choose File > Save (⌘-S) (**Figure 17**).

2. Enter a name in the "Save this document as" field (**Figure 18**).

3. Click Desktop.

4. Highlight a drive, then click Open.

5. Highlight a folder in which to save the file, then click Open. Or, to create a new folder, choose a location in which to save the new folder, click New, enter a name for the folder, then click Create.

6. Leave the Format as Illustrator 6, and click Save or press Return.

Figure 17. *Choose **Save** from the **File** menu.*

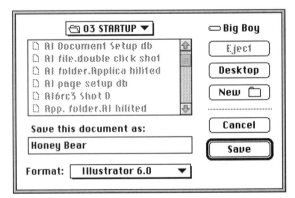

Figure 18. *Enter a name in the **Save this document as** field, click **Desktop**, open a drive and folder, then click **Save**.*

Save a New Document: Illustrator Format

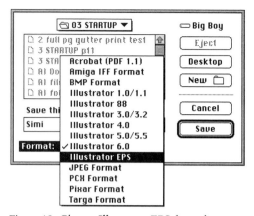

Figure 19. *Choose **Illustrator EPS** from the Format pop-up menu in the Save or Save as dialog box.*

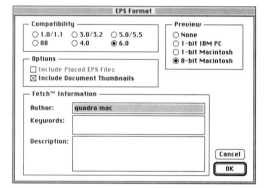

Figure 20. *Click an illustrator version (**Compatibility**) and a **Preview** option in the **EPS Format** dialog box.*

An EPS file icon.

A file in the native Illustrator 6 format has a no preview option, so it can only be opened and modified in Illustrator. To import an Illustrator file into QuarkXPress, save it in the Illustrator EPS format. Other file formats for other applications are discussed on page 33.

To save an illustration as an EPS:

1. Follow steps 1–6 on the previous page. If the file has already been saved, choose File > Save As for Step 1.

2. Choose Illustrator EPS from the Format pop-up menu (**Figure 19**).

3. Click Save or press Return.

4. Click a Compatibility option (**Figure 20**). If you choose an earlier version, some elements of your illustration may be altered.

5. Click Preview: None to save the illustration with no preview. The EPS won't display on screen in any other application, but it will print.
   or
   Click 1-bit IBM PC or 1-bit Macintosh to save the illustration with a black-and- white preview.
   or
   Click 8-bit Macintosh to save the illustration with a color preview. This option produces the largest file storage size.

   Note: Regardless of which preview option you choose, color information will be saved with the file and the illustration will print normally from Illustrator or any application you import it into.

6. *Optional:* Check the Include Placed EPS Files box to save a copy of any placed files within the illustration.

7. *Optional:* If you use the Fetch application to catalog and locate files, check the Include Document Thumbnails box and enter Author, Keywords (separate by commas), and Decription info.

8. Click OK or press Return.

Save an Illustration as an EPS

The prior version of a file is overwritten when the **Save** command is executed. Don't be shy — save frequently!

To save an existing file:

Choose File > Save (⌘-S).

You can use the Save or Save As dialog box to save your illustration in a different file format or to convert it to an earlier Illustrator version. Or use Save As to save the illustration under a new name so you can work on the new version of it while preserving the original.

Note: If you save an illustration in an earlier version, but it was created using features that are not present in the earlier version, the illustration may be altered or information may be deleted from it to make it compatible with the earlier version. For example, a gradient Fill may be reduced into a black Fill or it may be converted into a blend. The earlier the Illustrator version, the more the illustration may change.

To save a file in a different format or Illustrator version number:

1. With the file open, choose File > Save As (**Figure 21**).

2. Choose from the Format pop-up menu (**Figure 22**). For Illustrator EPS format, see the previous page.

3. *Optional:* To save the file in an earlier version or the same version and preserve your original illustration with all its Illustrator 6 features, enter a new name or change the name in the "Save this document as" field.

4. Choose a location in which to save the new version. If you'd like to create a new folder, click New, enter a name, then click Create.

Figure 21. *Choose Save As from the File menu.*

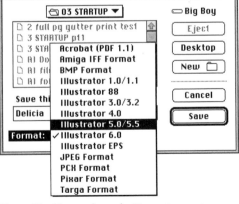

Figure 22. *Choose from the Format pop-up menu.*

Save a File in a Different Format or Illustrator Version

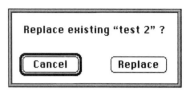

Figure 23. *The Replace warning prompt.*

CHOOSE FROM THESE FORMATS TO EXPORT AN ILLUSTRATOR 6.0 FILE

Prior Illustrator versions
1/1.1, 88, 3/3.2, 4 (for Windows), and 5/5.5.

Illustrator EPS
Use to export your Illustrator file to another application, like QuarkXPress or PageMaker, or a non-Adobe, pixel-based application.

If you double-click on an Illustrator EPS in a PageMaker document, the EPS will open in Illustrator. If you then modify the EPS in Illustrator, the file will automatically update in your PageMaker document.

Acrobat PDF 1.1
Use to transfer your Illustrator file to another application or another computer platform that reads PostScript-based Acrobat PDF files, or use the Acrobat format to save your Illustrator file for the World Wide Web. To view a file in Acrobat (PDF) format, use Acrobat Reader. To view and edit a PDF file, use Acrobat Exchange.

Amiga IFF
Use to transfer your Illustrator file to the Amiga format, which is supported by a few Macintosh graphics applications.

BMP
Windows bitmap graphics format.

PCX
A popular DOS and Windows graphics file format.

Targa
Use for high-end DOS-based graphics applications.

Pixar
Use for Macintosh 3-D modeling and rendering programs.

5. Click Save or press Return.

■ If you don't alter the name of the file and you click Save, a warning prompt will appear (**Figure 23**). Click Replace to save over the original file or click Cancel to return to the Save As dialog box.

■ An Illustrator 5.5 file can be opened in Aldus Freehand 5.5, but some elements — like pattern Fills and rasterized object — won't translate.

■ If you save a file in a raster file format like Photoshop JPEG, BMP, PCX, Pixar, or TARGA, the resulting image resolution will be 72 pixels per inch. Use these formats for multimedia or Web projects — not for print projects.

■ As of yet you can't save to the GIF file format from Illustrator. To export an Illustrator file to the GIF format, open the file in Photoshop 3.0.5 and use the GIF export option.

To publish on the World Wide Web via a different route, you can drag or copy Illustrator objects into Adobe PageMill.

Save a File in a Different Format or Illustrator Version

Acquiring images in Illustrator

You can use Illustrator 6.0 to open, import, or save an illustration in a variety of file formats, so you can work with imagery created in other applications as well as prepare your Illustrator files for other applications and other platforms. Methods for acquiring images from other applications include the Open command, the Place command, the Copy-and-Paste method, and the drag-and-drop method. The method you choose to use depends on which formats the original application can save to and how you want to use the imagery in Illustrator.

When you open a document from another object-oriented application using the **Open** command, a new Illustrator file is created and objects can be manipulated using any Illustrator tool, command, or filter. If you open a document from a bitmap-based program like Photoshop or Painter using the Open command, the image won't convert into workable paths; it will stay in an outlined box.

The **Place** command inserts imagery into an existing Illustrator document. EPS is a particularly good format for saving a file for placing into Illustrator, because it preserves the color, detail, and resolution of the original image, and because you can dim a placed EPS image in Illustrator if you're planning to trace it.

You can use the **Clipboard** (Copy and Paste commands) to copy objects between Illustrator and any other Adobe program. A pasted object will become a path object if the program the image is coming from is object-oriented, or a rasterized image within an outlined box if the program the image is coming from is pixel-based.

If you're using System 7.5, you can **drag-and-drop** a Photoshop selection into Illustrator, where it will be placed into an outlined box. (If you drag-and-drop a path object from Illustrator into Photoshop, it will appear as a selection on the current target layer.)

Note: Objects that are rasterized via the Rasterize command in Illustrator can't be copied-and-pasted or dragged-and-dropped into Photoshop.

Bitmap imagery placed in Illustrator can be moved, placed on a different layer, masked, or modified using any transformation tool and some filters.

A TIFF or PICT opened or placed into Illustrator 6.0 will downsample to 72 ppi, which is an acceptable resolution for a multimedia or Web project, but not for printing. To acquire an image for a print project, use Illustrator's Place command with its Placed EPS option.

Formats you can open using the Open command
Illustrator versions 1.0 through 6.0, Illustrator EPS, EPS Level 1, PICT, TIFF, Photoshop 2.5 or later (single-layer only), Photoshop JPEG, PDF (Acrobat Portable Document Format), Kodak Photo CD, Filmstrip, Amiga IFF, BMP, PCX, Pixar, PixelPaint, MacPaint, and Targa.

Formats you can open using the Place command
Illustrator EPS, EPS Level 1, Amiga IFF, BMP, PCX, Photoshop 2.5 and 3.0, Photoshop JPEG, TIFF, PICT, Pixar, Kodak PhotoCD, MacPaint, PixelPaint, Filmstrip, and Targa.

Acquiring Images in Illustrator

Figure 24. *Choose* Open *from the* File *menu.*

Figure 25. *Highlight a file name in the Open dialog box, then click* Open.

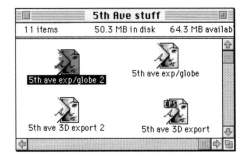

Figure 26. *Double-click a* file icon.

A list of file formats that can be opened in Illustrator appears on the previous page.

To open an illustration from within Illustrator:

1. Choose File > Open (⌘-O) (**Figure 24**).

2. Check the Show Preview box to display a preview of the illustration, if the file contains a preview that Illustrator can display.

3. Locate and highlight a file name, then click Open.
or
Double-click a file name (**Figure 25**).

■ If you open a parsed EPS that contains a mask or a clipping path, select the outlined box using the Selection tool to select both the image box and the mask. Use the Direct Selection tool to select only the mask.

■ A new untitled document opens when you launch Illustrator. It will close and be deleted automatically if you have not created anything in it and you then open an existing Illustrator document.

■ To open a document that was saved with a template with a different template, hold down Option and choose File > Open, locate and open the document, then locate and open the template you want to use. (Click None to open the document without a template.)

To open an illustration from the Finder:

Double-click an Illustrator file icon in the Finder (**Figure 26**). Illustrator will launch if it is not already open.

Open an Illustration

A PICT file created in an object-oriented drawing program — like MacDraw, DeltaGraph, or a CAD program — can be opened in Illustrator 5.5 or later and used as path objects. A PICT file from Photoshop 3.0 will open as 72 ppi raster art.

To open a PICT image in Illustrator:

1. Choose File > Open.
2. Highlight the file you want to import.
3. Click Open.
4. Click PICT Image to open the PICT as placed art (**Figure 27**).
   or
   Click Illustrator Template (PICT) to open the PICT as a template.

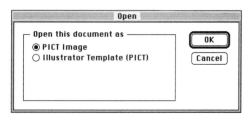

*Figure 27. In the **Open** dialog box for a PICT, click **PICT Image** to open the PICT as placed art or click **Illustrator Template** (PICT) to open it as a non-editable image for tracing.*

A placed picture can be moved, placed on a different layer, masked, or modified using any transformation tool. A list of file formats that can be placed into Illustrator appears on page 34.

To place a file from another application into an Illustrator document:

1. Open an Illustrator file.
2. Choose File > Place (**Figure 28**).
3. Locate and highlight a file name, then click Place.
   or
   Double-click a file name (**Figure 29**).
4. For an EPS file, click Parsed EPS or Placed EPS (**Figure 30**). A parsed EPS will appear as 72 ppi, with any mask or clipping path as an editable object, separate from the image box itself. Bitmap filters and some Colors filters can be applied to it.

   A placed EPS will appear in Illustrator in an outlined box. No Illustrator filters can be used on it. When using the Placed EPS option, the actual, original image will remain separate from the Illustrator file with its original resolution. If you modify and resave the image in its original

*Figure 28. Choose **Place** from the **File menu**.*

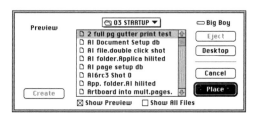

Figure 29. Double-click an EPS file.

Figure 30. *In the* **Open** *dialog box for an EPS, click* **Parsed EPS** *or* **Placed EPS**.

Figure 31. *This warning dialog box will appear if you choose the* **Place** *command when an existing placed EPS image is selected.*

program, it will automatically update in your Illustrator document.

5. Click OK or press Return.

■ See the first tip on page 35.

■ Fonts used in a placed EPS that are not installed in your system will print in Courier.

■ If a placed EPS is moved from the location it was in when the Illustrator file it was placed in was last saved, you will be prompted to locate and place the EPS when you reopen the Illustrator document. When prompted to locate a placed EPS image, if you click Continue, the file will open but the placed EPS won't be present, and the Save command won't be available, but you can use the Save As command to save over the file or create a new version.

■ If you place a Photoshop EPS file with a clipping path into Illustrator, the area around the image will be transparent, and will remain so if you move, scale, reflect, rotate, shear or apply a bitmap filter to it.

If you replace one placed image with another image of the same format, any transformations made to the original placed image will be applied to the newly placed image.

To replace one placed image with another of the same format:

1. Select a placed image outlined box.

2. Choose File > Place.

3. Locate and highlight a file name, then click Place.
    or
    Double-click a file name.

4. For an EPS, click Placed EPS.

5. Click OK or press Return (**Figure 31**).

6. Click Replace. (Click Ignore if you change your mind and want to place the new image in its own outlined box.)

By default, a placed EPS image will display as an empty outlined box with an "x" through it in Artwork view. Follow these instructions to display a black-and-white version of the image in the outlined box in Artwork view. If it was saved in its original application with an EPS preview that Illustrator recognizes, the full version of a placed EPS image will display in Preview view, regardless of the "Show placed images" setting in the Document Setup dialog box.

To display a placed EPS in Artwork view:

1. Choose File > Document Setup.
2. Check the "Show placed EPS" box (**Figure 32**).
3. Click OK or press Return (**Figures 33a–c**).

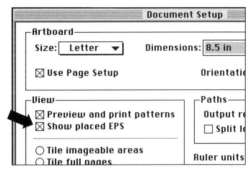

Figure 32. *Check the* **Show placed EPS** *box in the* **Document Setup** *dialog box.*

Figure 33a. *Placed EPS, Artwork view.*

Figure 33b. *Placed EPS, Artwork view, "Show placed EPS" checked.*

By default, a placed EPS will not be saved with the Illustrator file into which it is placed. Only a screen version of the picture will save with the file, with a reference to the actual EPS file for printing. Follow these instructions to save a copy of a placed EPS file with an illustration.

Figure 33c. *Placed EPS, Preview view.*

To save a copy of a Placed EPS file with an illustration:

1. With the Illustrator document that contains the placed image open, choose File > Save As.
2. Choose Illustrator EPS from the Format pop-up menu.
3. Click Save.
4. Check the "Include Placed EPS Files" box (**Figure 34**).
5. Click OK or press Return. If you reopen the document and the EPS file was moved from its original location, you'll get a prompt to locate the EPS.

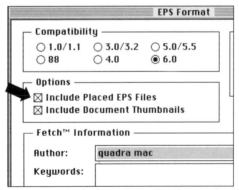

Figure 34. *Check the* **Include Placed EPS Files** *box in the* **EPS Format** *dialog box.*

Figure 35. *Choose Object > Attributes.*

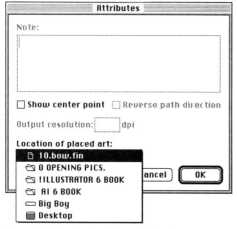

Figure 36. *In the Attributes dialog box, press and hold on the Location of placed art pop-up menu to see the file's location.*

To locate the actual Placed EPS file:

1. Choose a selection tool.

2. Click on the placed image.

3. Choose Object > Attributes (⌘-Control-A) (**Figure 35**).

4. Press on the "Location of placed art" pop-up menu (**Figure 36**). The drive and folder location of the actual placed image file will be listed.

5. Click OK or click Cancel.

■ Hold down Option and double-click a placed image to launch the application in which it was created, if the application is available on your system. If you then modify the original placed image and save it, the placed image in the Illustrator document will be updated automatically. *Note:* If the original application is available but doesn't open, try rebuilding the Desktop first.

■ To display or save a list of all the placed files in an illustration, make sure no objects are selected, choose File > Document Info, then choose Placed EPS from the Info pop-up menu. For a list of Parsed EPS or Raster art files, choose Raster Art from the Info pop-up menu.

Locate a Placed EPS File

TO ACQUIRE A FRACTAL DESIGN PAINTER IMAGE IN ILLUSTRATOR

A Painter 4 file can be opened or placed into Illustrator if it is saved in a file format Illustrator can read. For example, you can place or open a Painter TIFF or PICT; it will appear as a raster image. The Painter EPS format can be opened or placed, but you may not be able to use any filters on it. Illustrator can't read Painter's native RIFF format. You can open or place a Painter Photoshop 3 file into Illustrator, but you can't preview the image, so this format is of little value.

To export Painter shapes into Illustrator 6 to use as vector objects, use Painter 4.0's File >

Export command. In Illustrator, choose File > Open, and in the Open dialog box, choose the Illustrator option.

To acquire an Illustrator object in Painter 4.0

Copy the object in Illustrator, and in Painter 4, use the Edit > Paste > Normal command. The objects will become editable Painter shapes.

Or, in Painter, choose File > Acquire, then locate and open the Illustrator file. You will be given the option to have Illustrator gradient fills become Painter blends. The acquired objects will become editable Painter shapes.

To revert to the last saved version:

Choose File > Revert to Saved (**Figure 37**).

Figure 37. *Choose **Revert to Saved** from the **File** menu.*

To close an illustration:

Click the Close box in the upper left corner of the document window.

or

Choose File > Close (⌘-W).

■ If you attempt to close a picture and it was modified since it was last saved, a warning prompt will appear (**Figure 38**). You can close the file without saving, save the file, or cancel the close operation.

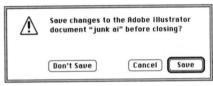

Figure 38. *If you try to close a picture that was modified since it was last saved, this prompt will appear.*

To quit Illustrator:

Choose File > Quit (⌘-Q) (**Figure 39**).

■ If you quit Illustrator, all open Illustrator files will close. If changes have been made to an open file since it was last saved, a warning prompt will appear. You can save the file before quitting or cancel the quit operation.

Figure 39. *Choose **Quit** from the **File** menu.*

Revert to Saved; Close; Quit

DISPLAY 4

In this chapter you will learn how to change view sizes, change views (Preview or Artwork), create custom view settings, move an illustration in its window, and display the same illustration in two windows.

The current *view size.*

Figure 1.

Figure 2. *Choose Zoom In or Zoom Out from the View menu.*

Within the document window, you can display the entire Artboard, the illustration at actual size, an enlarged detail of an illustration, or any view size in between.

The display size is indicated as a percentage on the title bar (**Figure 1**), and can range from 6.25% to 1600%. 100% is actual size. The display size does not affect the printout size.

To magnify an illustration:
Choose View > Zoom In (⌘-]) (**Figure 2**).

To reduce the view size of an illustration:
Choose View > Zoom Out (⌘-[) (**Figure 2**).

- If you're using Illustrator 6.0 and System 7.5 or later, you can use the WindowShade option (turn it on from the Control Panels submenu under the Apple menu). With WindowShade on, you can double-click any window or palette title bar to shrink it to a title bar. Double-click again to enlarge it.

41

To change the view size using the Zoom tool:

1. Choose the Zoom tool (**Figure 3**).

2. Click on the illustration in the center of the area you want to reduce or drag a marquee across an area to magnify that area (**Figure 4**).
or
Hold down Option and click on the illustration to reduce the display size (**Figure 5**).
or
Drag a marquee, then, without releasing the mouse, press and hold down Space bar and drag the marquee over the area you wish to magnify, then release.

■ Double-click the Zoom tool to display an illustration at Actual Size (100%). Or, choose Actual Size from the View menu (⌘-H).

If you double-click the Zoom tool when your illustration is in a small display size, the white area around the Artboard may appear in the document window, instead of the center of the illustration appearing in the window. Click the left or right scroll arrow to reposition the illustration in the window, if desired.

■ To magnify the illustration when another tool is selected, hold down Command (⌘) and Space bar and click in the document window. To reduce the display size, hold down Command (⌘), Option, and Space bar and click.

■ You can click to change the view size while the screen is redrawing.

■ The smaller the marquee you drag with the Zoom tool, the greater the level of magnification.

■ Choose View > Fit in Window (⌘-M) or double-click the Hand tool to scale the Artboard to fit the window.

Figure 3.
Zoom tool.

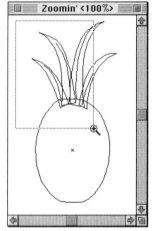

Figure 4. *Press and drag with the* **Zoom** *tool.*

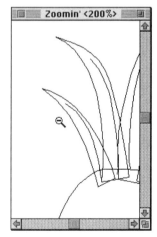

Figure 5. *Hold down* **Option** *and click to reduce the view size.*

Zoom In or Zoom Out

Preview	⌘-Y
Artwork	⌘-E
Preview Selection	⌘-Option-Y

View

✓Preview   ⌘Y
Artwork   ⌘E
Preview Selection   ⌘⌥Y

Hide Template   ⌘⇧W
Show Rulers   ⌘R
Hide Page Tiling
Hide Edges   ⌘⇧H
Hide Guides

Zoom In   ⌘]
Zoom Out   ⌘[
Actual Size   ⌘H
Fit In Window   ⌘M

New View...   ⌘^V
Edit Views...

Figure 6. *Choose* **Preview,** *Artwork,* or **Preview Selection** *from the* **View** *menu.*

An illustration can be displayed and edited in three different views: Preview, Artwork, or Preview Selection.

To change the view:
From the View menu, choose **Preview** to display all the objects with their Fill and Stroke colors and all printable placed images (**Figures 6–7**).
or
Choose **Artwork** to display all the objects as "wire frames" with no Fill or Stroke colors (**Figure 8**). Editing is faster in Artwork view. *Note:* A placed EPS will display as a box with an "x" in the middle in Artwork view if the Show Placed Images box is unchecked in the Document Setup dialog box (File menu). If Show Placed Image is checked, the image will display as a rough 1-bit preview.
or
Choose **Preview Selection** to display any currently selected object or objects in Preview view, and all other objects in Artwork view. To preview an object, click on it with any selection tool (**Figure 9**).

■ Use the Layers palette to choose a view for an individual layer *(see page 139)*.

■ In all three views, the other View menu commands — Hide/Show Templates, Page Tiling, Edges, and Guides — are accessible, and any selection tool can be used.

Change the View (Artwork or Preview)

Figure 7. *Preview view.*

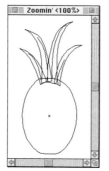

Figure 8. *Artwork view.*

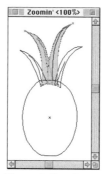

Figure 9. *Preview Selection view.*

You can define and save up to 25 custom view settings that you can switch to quickly using an assigned shortcut. You can specify whether your illustration will be in Preview view or Artwork view for each setting that you define.

To define a custom view setting:

1. Follow the instructions on page 39 or page 40 to display your illustration at the desired view size, and choose scroll bar positions.

2. Choose View > Preview or View > Artwork.

3. Choose View > New View (⌘-Control-V) (**Figure 10**).

4. Enter a name for the new view in the Name field (**Figure 11**).

5. Click OK or press Return.

■ If you choose a custom view setting for which you've chosen Artwork view and you want to display your illustration in Preview view, choose a custom view with the Preview setting or choose View > Preview.

Figure 10. *Choose* **New View** *from the* **View** *menu.*

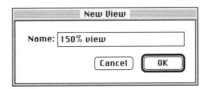

Figure 11. *Enter a* **Name** *for the view setting in the* **New View** *dialog box.*

To choose a custom view setting:

Choose the view name from the bottom of the View menu (**Figure 12**).
or
Hold down Command (⌘) and Control and press the number that was automatically assigned to the view setting. The shortcut will be listed next to the view name under the View menu.

Figure 12. *Choose a custom view setting from the* **View** *menu.*

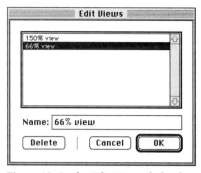

Figure 13. *In the Edit Views dialog box, highlight a view, then change the Name or click Delete.*

To rename or delete a custom view setting:

1. Choose View > Edit Views.

2. Click on the name of the view you want to alter (**Figure 13**).

3. Type a new name in the Name field.
   or
   Click Delete to delete the view setting.

4. Click OK or press Return. The View menu will update to reflect your changes.

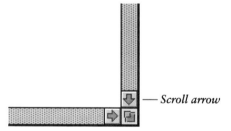
— *Scroll arrow*

Figure 14.

 Figure 15.
Hand tool.

To move an illustration in its window:

Click the up or down scroll arrow (**Figure 14**).
or
Choose the Hand tool, then drag the illustration to the desired position (**Figure 15**).

- Double-click the Hand tool to fit the entire Artboard in the document window.

- Hold down Space bar to turn the currently selected tool temporarily into the Hand tool.

Move an Illustration in its Window

The number of Illustrator documents that can be open at a time is limited only by the amount of RAM (Random Access Memory) currently available to Illustrator (**Figure 16**). Open windows are listed under and can be activated via the Window menu (**Figure 17**).

You can open the same illustration in two windows: one in a large display size, such as 200%, to edit small details, and the other in a smaller view size so you can see the whole illustration. In one window you could hide individual layers or display individual layers in Artwork view and in another window you could Preview all the layers together.

Note: The illustration in the window for which Preview view is selected will redraw each time you modify the illustration in the window for which Artwork view is selected, which means you won't save processing or redraw time when you work in the Artwork window.

To display an illustration in two windows:

1. Open an illustration.

2. Choose Window > New Window. A new window of the same size will appear on top of the first window, with the same title followed by ":2".

3. Reposition the new window by dragging its title bar so the original and new windows are side by side, and resize one or both windows (**Figure 18**).

    If you close and reopen the file, both windows will display again.

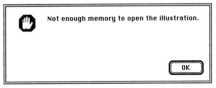

Figure 16. *This warning will appear if there is insufficient RAM to open another file.*

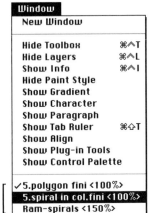

Currently open documents.

Figure 17. *The Window menu.*

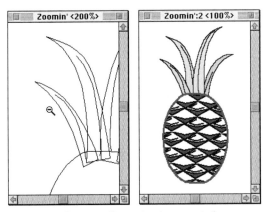

Figure 18. *The same illustration in two windows.*

One Illustration in Two Windows

CREATE OBJECTS 5

An object is a shape that is composed of anchor points connected by straight and/or curved line segments. An object can be open or closed. A path is the edge of an object that defines its shape. Rectangles and ovals are closed paths because they have no endpoints. A line is an open path.

In this chapter you will learn how to use the creation tools to draw rectangles and ovals. How to round the corners of any existing object. How to delete an object. How to use the Brush tool to create filled shapes that look like brush strokes. How to use the Freehand tool to create hand-drawn lines. How to use the Plug-in Tools — Polygon, Star, and Spiral — to create geometric shapes. And finally, how to turn an Illustrator object into a bitmap image using the Rasterize command.

(The Pen tool, which produces curved and straight line segments, is covered in Chapter 8.)

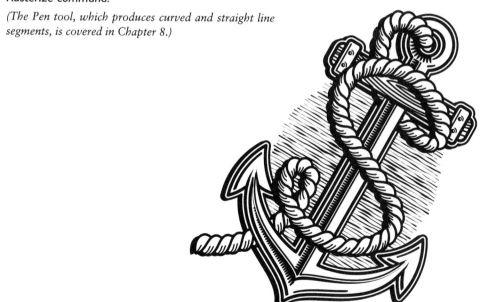

Daniel Pelavin, **Anchor**

To create a rectangle or oval by dragging:

1. Choose the Rectangle or Oval tool (**Figure 1**).

2. Press and drag diagonally (**Figure 2**). As you drag, you'll see a wireframe representation of the rectangle or oval. When you release the mouse, the rectangle or oval will be selected and colored with the current Fill and Stroke settings.

■ Hold down Option while dragging to draw a rectangle or oval from the center. Or, double-click the Rectangle or Oval tool before dragging to draw from the center (**Figure 3**). Double-click the tool again to restore its default setting.

■ Hold down Shift while dragging to create a square with the Rectangle tool or a circle with the Oval tool.

To create a rectangle or oval by specifying dimensions:

1. Select the Rectangle or Oval tool.

2. Click on the Artboard where you wish the object to appear.

3. In the Rectangle or Oval dialog box, enter dimensions in the Width and Height fields (**Figure 4**). To create a circle or square, enter a number in the Width field, then click the word Height to copy the width value into the Height field.

4. *Optional:* To create a rectangle with rounded corners, enter a value greater than 0 in the Corner radius field. If the radius is equal to or greater than the height or width, an oval will be created.

5. Click OK or press Return.

■ Values in dialog boxes are displayed in the unit of measure selected in the General Preferences dialog box (File > Preferences > General).

Oval tool. — *—Rectangle tool.*
Figure 1.

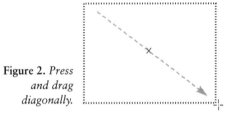

Figure 2. *Press and drag diagonally.*

The draw-from-center pointer.

Figure 3. *Double-click the Rectangle or Oval tool to draw from the center.*

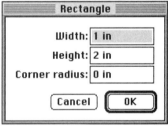

Rectangle

Width: 1 in

Height: 2 in

Corner radius: 0 in

Cancel   OK

Figure 4. *Enter Width and Height dimensions in the Rectangle (or Oval) dialog box.*

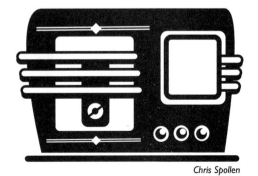

Chris Spollen

Create a Rectangle or Oval

Figure 5. *Rounded Rectangle tool.*

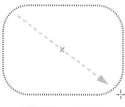

Figure 6a. *Press and drag diagonally.*

Figure 6b. *The rectangle is automatically painted with the current Fill and Stroke settings.*

To create a rounded rectangle:

1. Choose the Rounded Rectangle tool (**Figure 5**).

2. Press and drag diagonally. As you drag, you'll see a wireframe representation of the rounded rectangle (**Figure 6a**). When you release the mouse, the rounded rectangle will be selected and colored with the current Fill and Stroke settings (**Figure 6b**).

■ You can also create a rounded rectangle using the Rounded Rectangle dialog box. Choose the Rounded Rectangle tool, click on the Artboard, then enter values in the Width, Height, and Corner radius fields.

■ The current Corner radius value in the General Preferences dialog box, which determines how rounded the corners of the rectangle will be, is entered automatically in the Corner radius field in the Rounded Rectangle dialog box, and vice versa.

Figure 7. *Top row: the original objects; second row: after applying the Round Corners filter (30pt).*

To round the corners of an existing object:

1. Select the object.

2. Choose Filter > Stylize > Round Corners.

3. Enter a Radius value (the radius of the curve, in points).

4. Click OK or press Return (**Figure 7**).

To delete an object:

1. Select the object.

2. If all the anchor points on the object are selected, press Delete once.
   or
   If only some points are selected, press Delete twice.

You can use the Brush tool to produce hard-edged brush strokes in a uniform thickness if you're using a mouse, or variable thicknesses if you're using a stylus and pressure sensitive tablet (the harder you press on the tablet, the wider the shape). You can also use the Brush tool to create calligraphic strokes (see the next page). A stroke created with the Brush tool will actually be a closed path with Stroke and Fill attributes, as opposed to a line, which is an open path with end-points and a Stroke color, but no Fill.

To use the Brush tool:

1. Double-click the Brush tool (**Figure 8**).

2. Enter the desired stroke thickness in the Width field. If you're using a stylus and pressure-sensitive tablet, click Variable and enter a Minimum and Maximum stroke Width (**Figure 9**).

3. Click the round or square-cornered Caps button for the shape of the stroke ends.

4. Click the smooth or square-cornered Joins (bends) button.

5. Click OK or press Return.

6. Press and drag to draw a stroke (**Figures 10–11**). When you release the mouse, the stroke will be painted with the current Fill and Stroke settings.

Figure 8.
Brush tool.

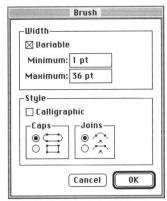

Figure 9. *Enter a* **Width** *in the* **Brush** *dialog box.*

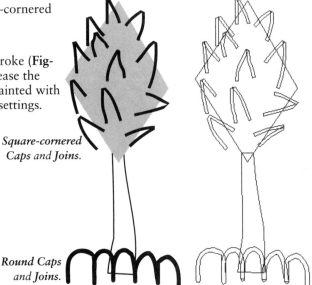

Square-cornered Caps and Joins.

Round Caps and Joins.

Figure 10.

Figure 11. *The same image in Artwork view. The strokes are actually closed paths.*

Use the Brush Tool

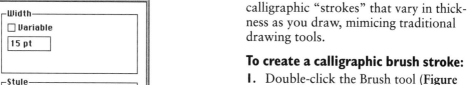

Figure 12. *Check the* **Calligraphic angle** *box.*

The Brush tool can be used to create calligraphic "strokes" that vary in thickness as you draw, mimicking traditional drawing tools.

To create a calligraphic brush stroke:

1. Double-click the Brush tool (**Figure 8**).
2. Check the Calligraphic angle box (**Figure 12**).
3. Enter a number in the Calligraphic angle field. The Calligraphic angle controls the thickness of the horizontal and vertical strokes relative to each other. A 0° angle will produce a thin horizontal stroke and a thick vertical stroke. A 90° angle will produce the opposite effect. Other angles will produce different effects.
4. Click OK or press Return.
5. Press and drag to draw a stroke. The stroke will preview as you drag, and will be painted with the current Fill and Stroke settings when you release the mouse (**Figures 13–15b**).

■ To make a line calligraphic after it's created, apply the Calligraphy filter (Filter > Stylize > Calligraphy) *(see page 209).*

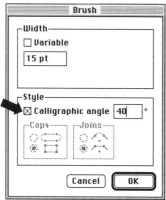

Figure 13.

Figure 14.

Figure 15a. *A calligraphic stroke in Preview view...*

Figure 15b. *...and in Artwork view.*

Create a Calligraphic Brush Stroke

Lines drawn with the Freehand tool look hand drawn or quickly sketched.

Note: The Freehand tool tends to create bumpy curves, and it doesn't create straight lines. Use the Pen tool to create straight lines and smooth curves.

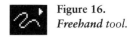

Figure 16. *Freehand* tool.

To draw a line using the Freehand tool:

1. Choose the Freehand tool (**Figure 16**).

2. *Optional:* Click the Stroke box on the Paint Style palette, then enter a new number in the Stroke Weight field.

3. Press and drag to draw a line. A dotted line will appear as you draw. When you release the mouse, the line will be colored with the current Fill and Stroke settings and its anchor points will be selected (**Figure 17**). In Artwork view, you'll see only a wireframe representation of the line (**Figure 18**).

■ If the current Fill setting is other than None, curves on the line path will be filled in. To remove the Fill and leave only a Stroke along the path of the line, choose a Fill of None and a Stroke color of your choice from the Paint Style palette *(see pages 101–102)*.

Diane Margolin

Figure 17. *Blue-footed booby, drawn with the Freehand tool.*

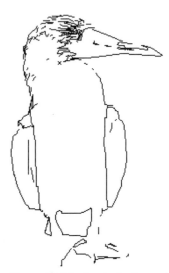

To erase part of a line as you draw with the Freehand tool:

1. Keep the mouse button down, then hold down Command (⌘) and drag with the erasure pointer over any section of the dotted line preview you wish to erase.

2. Release Command (⌘), position the point of the pencil right on the dotted line, and continue to draw.

Figure 18. *The booby in Artwork view.*

Draw a Line — Freehand Tool

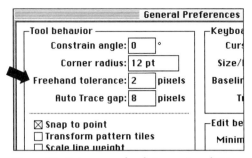

Figure 19. *Enter a number between 0 and 10 in the Freehand tolerance field.*

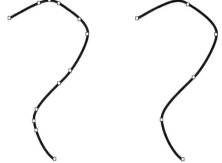

Figure 20. *A line drawn with a Freehand tolerance of 2.*

Figure 21. *A line drawn with a Freehand tolerance of 8.*

The number of anchor points produced with the Freehand tool is determined by the Freehand tolerance setting in the General Preferences dialog box. The fewer the anchor points, the smoother the line. If you change the Freehand Tolerance, only subsequently drawn lines will be affected, not existing lines.

To specify the amount of anchor points the Freehand tool produces:

1. Choose File > Preferences > General.

2. Enter a number between 0 and 10 in the Freehand tolerance field (**Figure 19**). A Freehand tolerance of 0 will produce many anchor points (**Figure 20**). A higher Freehand tolerance will produce anchor points only at sharp line direction changes (**Figure 21**).

3. Click OK or press Return.

- You can remove anchor points from a line using the Delete-anchor-point tool. You can reposition points on a line using the Direct Selection tool.

Diane Margolin

Freehand Tolerance

To add to a line:

1. Select the Freehand tool (**Figure 16**).

2. Position the pencil pointer directly over either end of the line. The pencil icon will change to a white point with a black eraser tip when it is positioned over an endpoint (**Figures 22–23**).

3. Press and drag the mouse to create an addition to the line. When you release the mouse, the completed line path and its anchor points will be selected and the addition will be connected to the existing line.

■ If the new and existing lines did not connect, delete the new line and try again or use the Join command to join the two lines *(see page 79)*.

Figure 22. *Continue-a-line pointer.*

Figure 23. *Start-a-new-line pointer.*

Figure 24. *In the Polygon dialog box, choose a Radius distance and a number of Sides.*

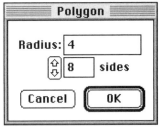

Using the **Polygon**, **Spiral**, and **Star** plug-in tools, you can easily create perfect geometric objects without having to draw with the mouse. The current Fill and Stroke settings are automatically applied to objects produced using these tools.

To create a polygon by clicking:

1. Choose the Polygon tool from the Plug-in Tools palette (Window > Show Plug-in Tools).

2. Click where you want the center of the polygon to be.

3. Enter a value in the Radius field (the distance in the current Ruler units from the center of the object to the corner points) (**Figure 24**).

4. Choose a number of sides for the polygon by clicking the up or down arrow or entering a number between 3 and 1000. The sides will be of equal length.

5. Click OK or press Return.

Miriam Schaer

Add to a Line; Create a Polygon

Figure 25. *The Polygon tool.*

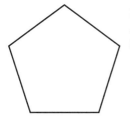

Figure 26. *The polygon used as a starting point for Figure 27a.*

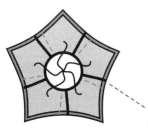

Figure 27a. *To refine the large shape, a curve anchor point was added between each pair of existing points and then dragged inward.*

Diane Margolin

Figure 27b. *The final shape used as an element in an overall pattern.*

To create a polygon by dragging:

1. Choose the Polygon tool from the Plug-in Tools palette (Window > Show Plug-in Tools) (**Figure 25**).

2. Press and drag, starting from where you want the center of the polygon to be (**Figure 26**).

3. While dragging, use any of the following options:

   Drag away from or towards the center to increase or decrease the size of the polygon, respectively.

   Drag in a circular fashion to rotate the polygon.

   Hold down Shift while dragging to constrain the bottom side to the horizontal axis.

   With the mouse still held down, press the up or down arrow key to add or delete sides from the polygon.

   Hold down Space bar while dragging to move the polygon.

4. When you release the mouse, the polygon will be selected and colored with the current Fill and Stroke settings.

Create a Polygon

To create a spiral by clicking:

1. Choose the Spiral tool from the Plug-ins toolbox (Window > Show Plug-in Tools) (**Figure 28**).

2. Click where you want the center of the spiral to be.

3. Enter a number in the Radius field (the distance in the current Ruler units from the center of the spiral to the outermost point) (**Figure 29**).

4. Enter a percentage between 5 and 150 in the Decay field to specify how tightly the spiral winds).

5. Choose a number of segments for the spiral (the number of quarter revolutions around the center point) by clicking the up or down arrow or entering a number.

6. Click the Counterclockwise or Clockwise button (the direction the spiral will wind from the center point).

7. Click OK or press Return (**Figures 30a–c**).

8. Apply a Stroke color to the spiral *(see pages 101–102)*.

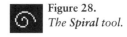

Figure 28.
The Spiral tool.

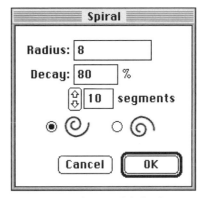

Figure 29. *In the Spiral dialog box, enter numbers in the Radius and Decay fields, choose a number of segments, and click the clockwise or counterclockwise button.*

Figures 30a–c.

Create a Spiral

A spiral.

After applying Filters > Distort > Punk and Bloat (Bloat 15%)...

...and reversing the Fill and Stroke colors.

To create a spiral by dragging:

1. Choose the Spiral tool from the Plug-in Tools palette (Window > Show Plug-in Tools) (**Figure 28**).

2. Press and drag, starting from where you want the center of the spiral to be.

3. While dragging, use any of the following options:

   Drag away from or towards the center to increase or decrease the size of the spiral, respectively.

   Hold down Option while dragging to add or delete segments from the spiral as you change its size.

   Drag in a circular fashion to rotate the spiral.

   Hold down Shift while dragging to constrain the rotation of the entire spiral to 45° increments.

   With the mouse still held down, press the up or down arrow key to add to or delete segments from the spiral.

   Hold down Space bar while dragging to move the spiral.

   Hold down Control and drag away from/towards the center to control how tightly the spiral winds. (The Control key affects the Decay value.)

4. When you release the mouse, the object will be selected and colored with the current Fill and Stroke colors.

■ Don't hold down Control before dragging with the Spiral tool — you'll end up with a very low Decay value and only one segment. Click with the Spiral tool to enter a higher Decay value.

Create a Spiral

To create a star by clicking:

1. Choose the Star tool from the Plug-in Tools palette (Window > Show Plug-in Tools) (**Figure 31**).

2. Click where you want the center of the star to be.

3. Enter a number in the Radius 1 field (the distance from the center of the object to the outer points in the current Ruler units) (**Figure 32**).

4. Enter a number in the Radius 2 field (the distance from the center of the object to the inner points, where the segments bend inward).

5. Choose a number of points for the star by clicking the up or down arrow or entering a number between 3 and 1000.

6. Click OK or press Return (**Figures 33–34**).

■ The distance from the center to the outer points of the star shape will always be the larger of the two Radius values, regardless of which field contains the larger value.

■ The greater the difference between the Radius 1 and Radius 2 values, the longer the arms of the star.

■ You can use the Rotate tool to rotate the completed star.

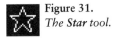

Figure 31.
The Star tool.

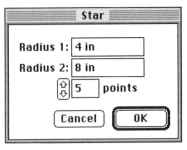

Figure 32. *In the Star dialog box, enter numbers in the **Radius 1 and Radius 2** fields, and choose a number of **points**.*

Figure 33.

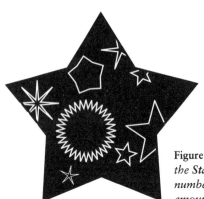

Figure 34. *Stars created using the Star tool, with different numbers of points and Radius amounts.*

Create a Star

Stars created by dragging with the Star tool with "W" held down, and then twirled using the Twirl filter.

To create a star by dragging:

1. Choose the Star tool from the Plug-in Tools palette (Window > Show Plug-in Tools) (**Figure 31**).

2. Press and drag, starting from where you want the center of the star to be.

3. While dragging, use any of the following options:

   Drag away from or towards the center to increase or decrease the size of the star, respectively.

   Drag in a circular fashion to rotate the star.

   Hold down Shift while dragging to constrain one or two points to the horizontal axis.

   With the mouse still held down, press the up or down arrow key to add or delete sides from the star.

   Hold down Space bar while dragging to move the star.

   Hold down Option to make shoulders (opposite segments) parallel.

   Hold down Control and drag away from/towards the center to increase/decrease the difference between the two radii of the star, making the arms of the star longer or shorter.

4. When you release the mouse, the object will be selected and colored with the current Fill and Stroke settings.

   ■ Hold down "W" while dragging with the Star or Polygon tool to create progressively larger copies of the shape. Drag quickly. Apply a Stroke color to distinguish the different shapes. Try using the Twirl tool to spread out the shapes around their center.

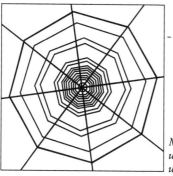

Multiple polygons drawn with the Polygon tool with "W" held down.

Using the Rasterize command, you can convert a vector-based path object into pixel-based image right in Illustrator, and then apply any Gallery Effects, Photoshop, or other bitmap filter to it.

To convert a path object into a pixel image:

1. Select an object.

2. Choose Object > Rasterize.

3. Choose a Color Model for the image: RGB for video or on-screen display (GE filters available); CMYK for print output; Grayscale for shades of black and white (GE filters available); or Bitmap for only black-and-white (**Figure 35**).

4. Click a Resolution setting or enter a Resolution value in the Other field.

5. Check the Anti-Alias box to have Illustrator softly fade the edge of the rasterized shape.

6. Check the Create Mask box to include a mask with the image that follows the contours of the object.

7. Click OK or press Return. A selection box will surround the path object. If the Create Mask option was unchecked, the background of the box will be opaque white (**Figures 36a–d**).

■ You can't apply Gallery Effects or Photoshop plug-in filters to a rasterized object in the Bitmap Color Model, and you can't apply Gallery Effects filters to an image in the CMYK Color Model.

■ If you rasterize an object containing a pattern Fill, the pattern color and line weight may change somewhat. If the object had a pattern Fill with a transparent background, the transparent background will turn solid white. Try rasterizing an object containing a pattern Fill using the Bitmap Color Model — you'll get interesting results. You can also appy a Fill color to a rasterized object.

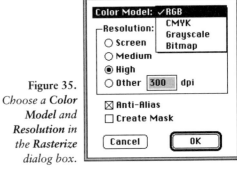

Figure 35. Choose a Color Model and Resolution in the Rasterize dialog box.

Figure 36a. *A rasterized object with a mask after applying the GE Splatter filter. The effect is limited to the object shape by the mask.*

Figure 36b. *A rasterized object without a mask after applying the GE Splatter filter. The effect extends beyond the object's original edge.*

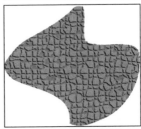

Figure 36c. *A rasterized object with a mask after applying the GE Mosaic filter. The effect is limited to the object shape by the mask.*

Figure 36d. *A rasterized object without a mask after applying the GE Mosaic filter. The effect extends beyond the object's original edge.*

Rasterize an Object

SELECT/MOVE 6

In chapter 5 you learned how to create various objects. In later chapters you will learn many methods for modifying objects, such as reshaping, recoloring, and transforming. An object must be selected before it can be modified, however, so selecting objects is an essential Illustrator skill to learn. In this chapter you will learn how to use the selection tools and filters to highlight objects for modification. You'll also learn how to hide an object's anchor points and direction lines, how to hide, lock, or deselect whole objects, and how to copy and move objects within the same file or between files.

Diane Margolin

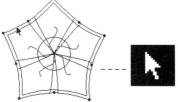

THE THREE SELECTION TOOLS:

The **Selection** tool is used to select all the anchor points on an object or path. If you click on the edge or the fill of an object with the Selection tool, you will select all the points on the object.

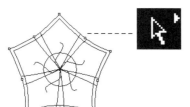

The **Direct Selection** tool is used to select one or more anchor points or segments of a path. If you click on the edge of an object with the Direct Selection tool, you will select only that segment, and the segment's direction lines and direction points will become visible. (Straight line segments don't have direction lines — they only have anchor points.) If you click on the Fill of an object in Preview view using this tool, you will select all the points on the object.

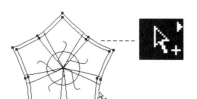

The **Group Selection** tool can be used to select all the anchor points on a path, but its primary use is to select groups within a group in the order in which they were added to the larger group. Click once to select an object; click twice to select that object's group; click three times to select the next group that was added to the larger group, etc.

Select by Clicking

To select an object or objects:

1. Choose the Selection tool or Group Selection tool (**Figures 1–2**), then click on the path of the object (**Figure 3**).
   or
   If your illustration is in Preview view and the Area Select option is on *(see the info at right),* click on the object's Fill.
   or
   Position the pointer outside the object or objects you want to select, then drag the pointer diagonally across them (a dotted marquee will define the area as you drag over it). The whole object or objects will be selected, even if only a portion of the object is marqueed (**Figure 4**).

2. *Optional:* Hold down Shift and click to select additional objects or deselect any selected objects.

■ Hold down Option to use the Group Selection tool while the Direct Selection tool selected.

THE AREA SELECT OPTION ────────

If the Area Select box is checked in the General Preferences dialog box (File > Preferences > General Preferences), you can click on an object's Fill when your illustration is in Preview view to select the object's entire path. If the Area Select box is unchecked or the object has no Fill, you must click on the edge of the object to select it. If your illustration is in Preview Selection view, you must click on the edge of an object to select it, regardless of the Area Select setting. (Fill and Stroke are defined in Chapter 9.)

Figure 1.
Selection tool.

Figure 2. *Group Selection tool.*

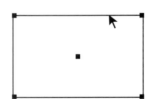

Figure 3. *A path and all its anchor points selected with the Selection tool.*

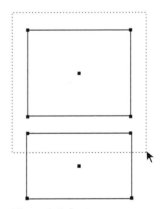

Figure 4. *Selecting two objects by marqueeing them with the Selection tool.*

To select anchor points or segments:

1. Choose the Direct Selection tool (**Figure 5**).

2. Click on the anchor point(s) or segment(s) (**Figures 6–7**).
   or
   Position the pointer outside the object or objects you want to select, then drag the pointer diagonally across them (a dotted marquee will define the area as you drag over it). Only the anchor points or segments you marquee will be selected (**Figures 8**).

3. *Optional:* Hold down Shift and click to select additional anchor points or segments or deselect selected anchor points or segments.

■ Hold down Command (⌘) to use the last highlighted selection tool when another tool is selected. With Command (⌘) held down, you can click to select or deselect an object.

■ If you select or move curve segments without moving their corresponding anchor points, you will reshape the curves and the anchor points will remain stationary (more about reshaping curves in the next chapter).

Figure 5. *Direct Selection tool.*

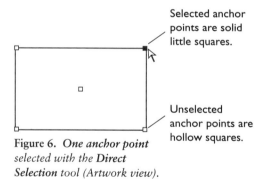

Selected anchor points are solid little squares.

Unselected anchor points are hollow squares.

Figure 6. *One anchor point selected with the **Direct Selection** tool (Artwork view).*

Figure 7. *A **segment** selected with the **Direct Selection** tool.*

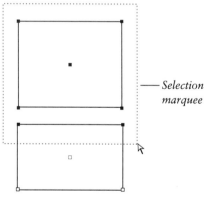

— Selection marquee

Figure 8. *A marquee selection being made with the **Direct Selection** tool. Only anchor points within the marquee are selected.*

To select all the objects in an illustration:

Choose Edit > Select All (⌘-A) (**Figure 9**). All unlocked objects in your illustration will be selected, whether they are currently showing in the document window or not.

Use the **Select filters** to select objects with similar characteristics to a currently selected object. Each filter is named for the attributes it searches for.

To select using a filter:

1. Choose any selection tool.
2. Click on an object with characteristics you wish to search for in other objects (look at the submenu in **Figure 10**).
3. Choose from the Select submenu under the Filter menu:

   Same Fill Color to search for Fill attributes only.

   Same Paint Style (Fill and Stroke color and stroke weight) to search for all paint attributes.

   Same Stroke Color to search for Stroke attributes only.

   Same Stroke Weight to search for Strokes of the same weight.

   Select Inverse to select currently deselected objects and deselect currently selected objects.

   Select Masks to select masking objects. This filter is useful because the edges of a masking object display in Preview view only when the object is selected.

   Select Stray Points to select single points that are not part of any paths so they can be deleted easily.

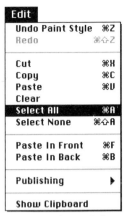

Figure 9. *Choose Select All from the Edit menu.*

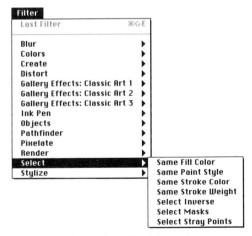

Figure 10. *Choose from the Select submenu under the Filter menu.*

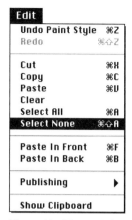

Figure 11. *Choose Select None from the Edit menu.*

To prevent an object from being modified, it must be deselected.

To deselect an object or objects:

1. Choose a selection tool.
2. Click outside the selected object or objects.
   or
   Choose Edit > Select None (⌘-Shift-A) (**Figure 11**).

■ To deselect an individual object within a multiple selection, hold down Shift and click on the object or press and drag over the object.

■ To deselect all selected objects and select all unselected objects, choose Filter > Select > Select Inverse.

Use the Hide Edges command to hide an object's anchor points, and direction lines while still keeping the object selected and editable. Use this command when you want to see how different Stroke colors or widths look on an object in Preview view, or to hide distracting points when you're working in Artwork view.

To hide the anchor points and segments of an object or objects:

1. Select the object or objects.
2. Choose View > Hide Edges (⌘-Shift-H) (**Figure 12**).

■ To redisplay the anchor points and segments, choose View > Show Edges.

■ To display or hide a selected object's center points, choose Object > Attributes, then click or unclick the "Show center point" box.

Figure 12. *Choose Hide Edges from the View menu.*

The Hide command can help you isolate objects to work on. If your illustration is complex, you'll find this command to be particularly useful both for selecting the objects you want to work on more easily and to speed up screen redraw. A hidden object will be invisible in both Artwork and Preview views, and will not print. If you close and reopen the file, hidden objects will redisplay.

To hide an object:

1. Select the object or objects to be hidden.

2. Choose Arrange > Hide (⌘-3) (**Figure 13**).

■ Individual hidden objects cannot be selectively redisplayed. To redisplay *all* hidden objects, choose Arrange > Show All (⌘-4). You can use the Layers palette to hide or lock objects on an individual layer *(see pages 138–140)*.

■ To hide all *unselected* objects, hold down Option and choose Arrange > Hide (⌘-Option-3).

A locked object cannot be selected or modified. If you close and reopen the file, locked objects will remain locked.

To lock an object:

1. Select the object or objects to be locked.

2. Choose Arrange > Lock (⌘-1) (**Figure 14**).

■ To lock all *unselected* objects, hold down Option and choose Arrange > Lock (⌘-Option-1).

■ Locked items can't be unlocked individually. To unlock all locked items, choose Arrange > Unlock All. All previously locked objects will be selected and previously selected objects will be deselected.

■ Lock whole layers using the Layers palette.

LOCK/HIDE TIPS

■ You can't lock or hide *part* of an object or a path.

■ To unlock or show only one of several locked or hidden objects, choose Unlock All or Show All from the Arrange menu, choose the Selection tool, hold down Shift and click on the object you wish to unlock or show, then choose Lock or Hide for the remaining selected objects.

■ If you chose Lock or Hide for an object within a group, you can unlock or show just that object. Select the group, then hold down Option and choose Unlock All or Show All from the Arrange menu.

Figure 13. *Choose **Hide** from the **Arrange** menu.*

Figure 14. *Choose **Lock** from the **Arrange** menu.*

Hide Objects; Lock Objects

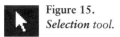

Figure 15.
Selection tool.

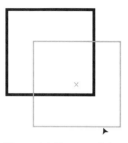

Figure 16. *Press and drag
the object's edge.*

To align objects to custom x/y axes ———

Choose File > Preferences > General, then enter a new number in the Constrain Angle field (0° is the default). Any new object you draw will rest on the new axes, and any object you move or transform with Shift held down will snap to the new axes.

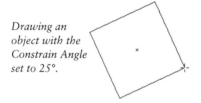

*Drawing an
object with the
Constrain Angle
set to 25°.*

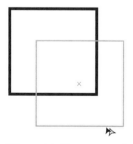

Figure 17. *To copy an object,
hold down **Option** and press
and drag the object. Note the
double arrowhead pointer.*

To move an object by dragging:

1. Choose the Selection tool (**Figure 15**).
2. If your illustration is in Artwork view, press and drag the object's edge (**Figure 16**).
   or
   If your illustration is in Preview view, press and drag the object's edge or the object's Fill (if there is one, and the Area Select option is on in General Preferences). This can also be done with the Direct Selection tool.

■ Press any arrow key to move a selected object the current Cursor key increment (which is specified in the General Preferences dialog box). Precise methods for moving and aligning objects are discussed in Chapter 21, Precision Tools.

■ If the Snap to Point box is checked in the General Preferences dialog box, the part of the object directly underneath the pointer will snap to the nearest guide or to a point of another object if it comes close to it (the pointer will turn white when it's over a guide or the point of another object).

■ Hold down Shift while dragging to constrain the movement to the x or y axis.

To move a copy of an object by dragging:

1. Choose the Selection tool.
2. Hold down Option and press and drag the Fill or the edge of the object you want to copy (the pointer will turn into a double arrowhead) (**Figure 17**).
3. Release the mouse, then release Option. A copy of the object will appear in the new location.

■ To create additional copies of the object, choose Arrange > Repeat Transform (⌘-D) as many times as you like.

Move an Object; Move a Copy of an Object

Note: If you are using System 7.5 or later, you can drag-and-drop objects between documents or even drag-aware applications. Drag-and-drop requires fewer steps than using the Clipboard (instructions on the next page).

If you select an object or group and then choose the **Cut** or **Copy** command, that object or group is placed onto the **Clipboard**, a temporary storage area in memory. The previous contents of the Clipboard are replaced when you choose Cut or Copy.

The **Paste** command places the current Clipboard contents in the center of the currently active document window. The Clipboard contents can be pasted an unlimited number of times.

To move an object or a group from one document to another:

1. Choose the Selection tool.

2. Click on the object or group.

3. Choose Edit > Cut (⌘-X) (**Figure 18**).

   The object or group will be removed from the current document.

4. Click in the "destination" document window.

5. Choose Edit > Paste (⌘-V) (**Figure 19**).

■ To move a copy of an object or a group, choose Edit > Copy (⌘-C) for step 3 above.

■ You can place an object created in Illustrator into a document in another Adobe PostScript application using the Clipboard commands (Cut, Copy, Paste).

■ To place a bitmap PICT version of an object on the Clipboard, hold down Option when you choose Cut or Copy.

Moving grouped objects ────────

If you copy an object in a group by dragging (use the Direct Selection tool with Option held down), the copy will be *part of* that group. If you use the Clipboard to copy and paste an object in a group, the object will paste *outside* the group (the Group command is discussed on page 132).

Figure 18. *Choose Cut from the Edit menu.*

Figure 19. *Choose Paste from the Edit menu.*

Move an Object to a Different Document

Notes: To drag-and-drop, you must be using System 7.5 or later or install the Drag Manager Extension for System 7.1.x. In order to drag-and-drop between Illustrator and Photoshop, you must have Photoshop 3.0.4 or later.

To drag-and-drop a copy of an object (Illustrator-to-Illustrator or between Photoshop and Illustrator):

1. Select the object you want to drag-and-drop in an Illustrator or Photoshop document.

2. Open the Illustrator or Photoshop document that you want to copy the object to.

3. Drag the object into the destination document window, and presto, a copy of the object will appear in the new location!

■ If you copy an Illustrator object to a Photoshop document, the object will appear as a new floating selection. Pause while the Photoshop image redraws. If you drag-and-drop Illustrator text into Photoshop, it will appear as a floating anti-aliased type selection.

■ To convert an Illustrator object into paths in Photoshop, hold down Command as you drag-and-drop.

■ If you drag-and-drop from Photoshop to Illustrator, the image will drop as an RGB PICT, 72 dpi. If you're going to print the image, Adobe recommends saving the Photoshop file as a CMYK EPS instead, and then using the Place command in Illustrator to acquire it.

WHAT YOU CAN'T DRAG-AND-DROP

You can't drag-and-drop, from Illustrator to Photoshop, a pattern-filled object or an object that was rasterized in Illustrator. You can, however, save a file with a pattern Fill in the Photoshop JPEG format using Illustrator's Save As command and then open the file in Photoshop.

Drag-and-Drop

The Offset Path filter copies a path shape and offsets the copy from the original by a specified distance, and it also reshapes the copy slightly so it fits neatly next to the original path — which doesn't happen if you simply duplicate a path using the Option-drag method or the Scale tool.

We recommend that you use this filter on a line or an open path that has a Stroke but no Fill. On an object that contains a Fill color, you're better off using the Scale tool.

To offset a copy of a path:

1. Select an object.

2. Choose Filter > Objects > Offset Path.

3. In the Offset field, enter a positive number to place the offset path above the edge of the original path or a negative value to place the copy below the original path (**Figure 20**). Be sure the Offset value you enter is larger than the stroke weight, if any, so the offset won't overlap the original path.

4. Choose a Line join (bend) style: miter (pointed), round (semicircular), or bevel (square-cornered).

5. *Optional:* Enter a new Miter limit. The Miter limit represents the maximum amount the path's line weight can be enlarged before the miter join becomes a bevel join.

6. Click OK or press Return (**Figure 21**).

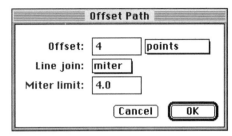

Figure 20. *In the Offset Path dialog box, enter an Offset amount and choose a Line join style.*

Figure 21. *The original path — the darkest gray line — with an offset path above it (positive Offset value) and an offset path below it (negative Offset value).*

Offset a Copy of a Path

RESHAPE PATHS 7

As you learned in Chapter 5, a path is the edge of an object that defines its shape. In this important chapter, you will learn how to change the profile of an object by changing the number, position or type of anchor points on its path. Using these techniques, you'll be able to draw just about any shape imaginable.

You will learn how to move anchor points or path segments to reshape a path, how to convert a corner anchor point into a curve anchor point (or vice versa) to reshape the segments that it connects, how to add or delete anchor points, and how to carve away parts of a path using the Knife tool or the Apply Knife command.

You will also learn how to split a path, how to align anchor points, how to join endpoints, how to combine paths using the Unite filter, and how to trace a template or a placed image automatically or manually. Also included in this chapter are two practice exercises.

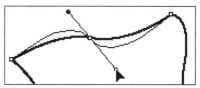

The angle of a direction line affects the slope of the curve into the anchor point.

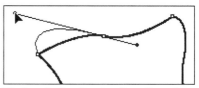

The length of a direction line affects the height of the curve.

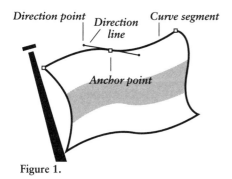

Figure 1.

What is a Bézier curve?

In Illustrator, a curve segment is also called a Bézier curve. A Bézier curve consists of two anchor points connected by a curve segment, with at least one direction point and direction line attached to each anchor point (**Figure 1**). If an anchor point connects a curve and a straight line segment, it will have one common direction line. If an anchor point connects two curve segments, it will have a pair of direction lines.

If you move an anchor point, segments connected to it will reshape. If you move a curve segment, connecting anchor points will not move along with it. If you move a straight line segment, connecting anchor points will also move.

To move an anchor point or a segment:

1. Choose the Direct Selection tool (**Figure 2**).

2. Press and drag the anchor point or segment (**Figures 3a–b**).

■ Hold down Shift to constrain the movement of an anchor point to 45°, 90°, 135°, or 180°.

■ If all the anchor points on a path are selected, you will not be able to move an individual point or segment. Deselect the object, then reselect an individual point.

■ Hold down Shift and click to select more than one anchor point at a time.

In the previous instructions, you learned that you can drag a curve segment or an anchor point to reshape a curve. A more precise way to reshape a curve is to lengthen, shorten, or change the angle of its direction lines.

To reshape a curve segment:

1. Choose the Direct Selection tool.

2. Click on an anchor point (**Figure 4**).

3. Press and drag a direction point (the end of the direction line) toward or away from the anchor point (**Figure 5**).

   or

   Rotate the direction point around the anchor point (**Figure 6**). The anchor point will remain selected when you release the mouse.

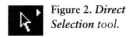

Figure 2. *Direct Selection tool.*

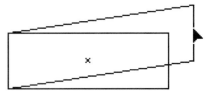

Figure 3a. *Moving a segment.*

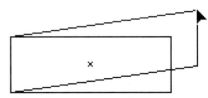

Figure 3b. *Moving an anchor point.*

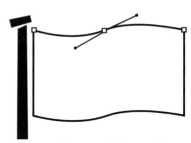

Figure 4. *The original shape with an anchor point selected.*

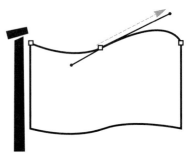

Figure 5. *A direction point is dragged away from the anchor point.*

Move a Point or Segment; Reshape a Curve

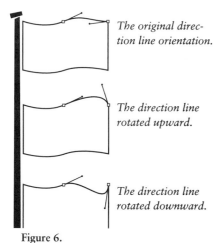

The original direction line orientation.

The direction line rotated upward.

The direction line rotated downward.

Figure 6.

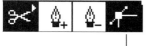

Figure 7. *Convert-direction-point tool.*

To convert a corner anchor point into a curve anchor point:

1. Choose the Direct Selection tool (**Figure 2**).

2. Click on the edge of the object. The anchor points will be hollow.

3. Choose the Convert-direction-point tool (**Figure 7**) or hold down Control with any selection tool.

4. Press on an anchor point, then drag away from it. Direction lines will be created as you drag. The further you drag, the rounder the curve will become (**Figure 8**).

5. *Optional:* To further modify the curve, choose the Direct Selection tool, then drag the anchor point or a direction line.

■ Direction lines on a smooth curve form a straight line in relationship to each other even if one direction line is moved or the curve segment or anchor point they are connected to is moved.

■ If the new curve segment twists around the anchor point as you drag, keep the mouse button down, rotate the direction line back around the anchor point to undo the twist, then continue to drag in the new direction (**Figure 9**).

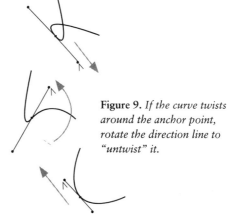

Figure 9. *If the curve twists around the anchor point, rotate the direction line to "untwist" it.*

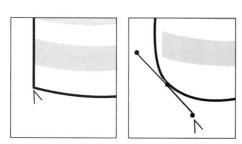

Figure 8. *To convert a corner anchor point into a curve anchor point, click with the* **Convert Direction Point** *tool on the anchor point, then drag away from it.*

To convert a curve anchor point into a corner anchor point:

1. Choose the Direct Selection tool (**Figure 2**).

2. Click on the edge of the object to display its anchor points.

3. Choose the Convert-direction-point tool (or hold down Control) (**Figure 7**).

4. Click on a curve anchor point. Don't drag! Its direction lines will be deleted (**Figure 10**).

Figure 10. *Click with the Convert Direction Point tool on a curve anchor point to convert it into a corner anchor point.*

The direction lines in a pinched curve rotate independently of each other — they don't stay in a straight line.

To pinch a curve inward:

1. Choose the Direct Selection tool (**Figure 2**).

2. Click on the edge of an object to display its anchor points.

3. Choose the Convert-direction-point tool (or hold down Control) (**Figure 7**).

4. Press and drag a direction point at the end of one of the direction lines. The curve segment will reshape as you drag (**Figure 11**).

5. Choose the Direct Selection tool. Click on the anchor point.

6. Drag the other direction line for that anchor point.

■ To revert an independent-rotating direction line pair back to its previous straight-line alignment and produce a smooth, un-pinched curve segment, choose the Convert-direction-point tool, then click on either direction point.

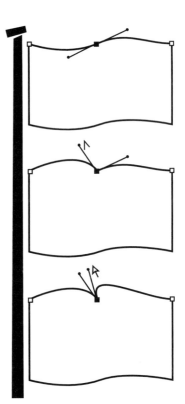

Figure 11. *Direction lines are moved independently to pinch the curve.*

Another way to reshape an object is to manually add or delete anchor points from its path using the Add-anchor-point or Delete-anchor-point tool. Adding or deleting points from a path will not split or open it; the path will remain closed. A new anchor point on a curve segment will be a curve anchor point with direction lines. A new anchor point on a straight line segment will be a corner anchor point.

Figure 12. *Add-anchor-point* tool.

To add anchor points to a path manually:

1. *Optional:* Select an object to display its anchor points *(see page 62)*.

2. Choose the Add-anchor-point tool (**Figure 12**).

3. Click on the edge of the object. A new, selected anchor point will appear (**Figure 13**). Repeat, if desired, to add more points.

4. *Optional:* Use the Direct Selection tool to move the new anchor point (**Figure 13**).

■ If you don't click precisely on a segment of an object, a warning prompt will appear. Click OK, then try again.

■ Hold down Option to use the Delete-anchor-point tool when the Add-anchor-point tool is selected and is over an anchor point.

■ Hold down Command (⌘) and Control to use the Add-anchor-point tool when the Freehand tool is selected and is over a segment.

■ Hold down Control to use the Add-anchor-point tool when the Pen tool is selected and is over a segment.

Click on a segment with the Add-anchor-point tool to create a new anchor point...

...then move the anchor point, if you like.

Figure 13.

Add Anchor Points to a Path

The **Add Anchor Points** filter inserts one anchor point midway between every two existing anchor points.

To add anchor points to a path using a filter:

1. Select an object or objects.

2. Choose Filter > Objects > Add Anchor Points (**Figures 14–17**).

3. *Optional:* Reapply the filter to add more points (⌘-Shift-E).

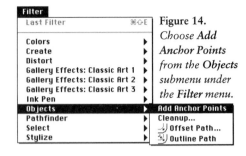

Figure 14. *Choose Add Anchor Points from the Objects submenu under the Filter menu.*

Figure 15. *The original object.*

Figure 16. *After adding anchor points and applying the Punk and Bloat filter, Bloat 70%.*

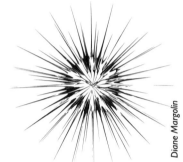

Diane Margolin

Figure 17. *After adding anchor points to the original object applying the Punk and Bloat filter, Punk 70%.*

Figure 18. *Delete-anchor-point tool*

To delete anchor points from a path:

1. Select an object *(see page 56)*.

2. Choose the Delete-anchor-point tool (**Figure 18**).

3. Click on an anchor point. The point will be deleted and an adjacent point will become selected (**Figure 19**). Repeat to delete other anchor points, if desired.

■ If you do not click precisely on an anchor point, a warning prompt will appear. Click OK and try again.

■ Hold down Option to use the Add-anchor-point tool when the Delete-anchor-point tool is selected and is over a segment.

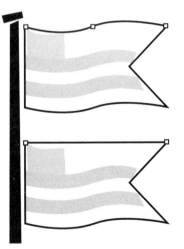

Figure 19. *To delete an anchor point, click on it with the Delete-anchor-point tool. The path will reshape.*

Figure 20.
Scissors tool.

An open path can be split into two paths and a closed path can be opened using the **Scissors** tool. A path can be split at an anchor point or in the middle of a segment.

To split a path:

1. Choose any selection tool.
2. Click on an object to display its anchor points.
3. Choose the Scissors tool (**Figure 20**).
4. Click on the object's path (**Figure 21a**). If you click on a closed path, it will turn into a single, open path. If you click on an open path, it will be split into two paths. If you click on a segment, two new endpoints will appear, one on top of the other. If you click on an anchor point, a new anchor point will appear on top of the existing one. The new endpoints will be selected and will overlap each other.

To move the new endpoints apart:

5. Choose the Direct Selection tool.
6. Click away from the object to deselect it (**Figure 21b**).
7. Click on the object's path.
8. Click on the new endpoint (**Figure 21c**), then drag it away to reveal the endpoint underneath (**Figure 21d**).

■ You can apply a Fill color to an open path. If you apply a Stroke color, you will be able to see where the missing segment is (**Figure 22**).

■ You cannot split an open path if it has text on it or inside it.

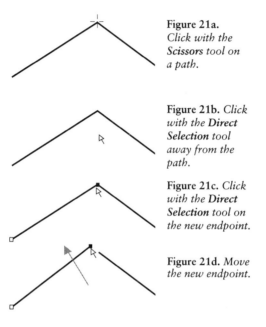

Figure 21a.
Click with the Scissors tool on a path.

Figure 21b. *Click with the **Direct Selection** tool away from the path.*

Figure 21c. *Click with the **Direct Selection** tool on the new endpoint.*

Figure 21d. *Move the new endpoint.*

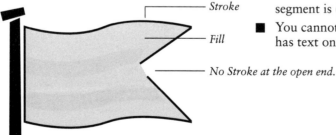

Stroke

Fill

No Stroke at the open end.

Figure 22. *An open path can have a Fill and a Stroke.*

The **Average** command reshapes one or more paths by precisely realigning their endpoints or anchor points to the horizontal and/or vertical axis.

To average anchor points:

1. Choose the Direct Selection tool.

2. Hold down Shift and click on two or more anchor points. You might want to zoom in on the objects so you can clearly see the selected points.

3. Choose Object > Average (⌘-L) (**Figure 23**).

4. Click **Both** to overlap the points along both the horizontal and vertical axes. Choose this option if you want to join them later into one point *(instructions on the following page)*.
   or
   Click **Horizontal only** to align the points along the horizontal (*x*) axis.
   or
   Click **Vertical only** to align the points along the vertical (*y*) axis (**Figure 24**).

5. Click OK or press Return (**Figure 25**).

Average Anchor Points

Figure 23. *Choose Average from the Object menu.*

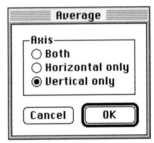

Figure 24. *Click an Axis button in the Average dialog box.*

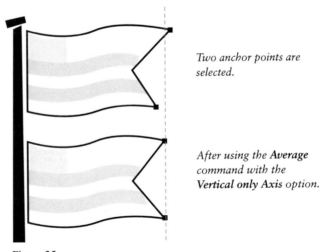

Two anchor points are selected.

After using the **Average** command with the **Vertical only Axis** option.

Figure 25.

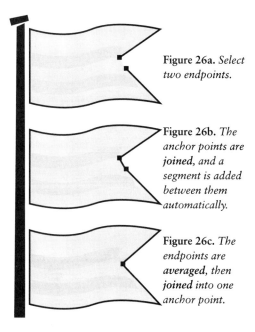

Figure 26a. *Select two endpoints.*

Figure 26b. *The anchor points are joined, and a segment is added between them automatically.*

Figure 26c. *The endpoints are averaged, then joined into one anchor point.*

Figure 27. *Choose Join from the Object menu.*

Figure 28. *Click Corner or Smooth Points in the Join dialog box.*

If you align two endpoints on top of each other and then execute the **Join** command, they will combine into one anchor point. If the endpoints are not on top of each other, a new straight line segment will be created between them. The Join command will not add direction lines to the new anchor point.

To join two endpoints:

1. Choose the Direct Selection tool.

2. *Optional:* If you want to combine two endpoints into one, move one endpoint on top of the other manually or use the Average command (Axis: Both) to align them *(instructions are on the previous page)*.

3. Hold down Shift and click on two endpoints or marquee them (**Figure 26a**).

4. Choose Object > Join (⌘-J) (**Figure 27**). If the endpoints are not on top of each other, the Join command will connect them with a straight line segment (**Figure 26b**). If the endpoints are aligned on top of each other, the Join dialog box will open. In the Join dialog box (**Figure 28**):

   Click **Corner** to join corner points into one corner point with no direction lines or to connect two curve points (or a corner point and a curve point) into one curve point with independent-moving direction lines. This is the default setting (**Figure 26c**). *or*
   Click **Smooth** to connect two curve points into a curve point with direction lines that move in tandem.

5. Click OK or press Return.

■ To average and join two selected endpoints via one keystroke, hold down Command (⌘) and Option and press "J".

Filters under the Pathfinder submenu combine multiple objects into one new object. The **Unite** filter is used in these instructions.

To combine two objects into one using the Unite filter:

1. Position two or more objects so they overlap (**Figure 29**).

2. Choose the Selection tool.

3. Press and drag a marquee around all the objects.

4. Choose Filter > Pathfinder > Unite (**Figure 30**). The individual objects will combine into one closed object (**Figures 31–33b**), and will be colored with the top object's paint attributes.

■ If you apply a Sroke color to the new object, you will see that its previously overlapping segments were removed.

■ You can use the new closed object as a masking object. (You could not create a mask with the original objects before they were united.)

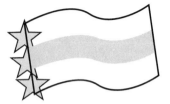

Figure 29. *Overlap two or more objects, then select them all.*

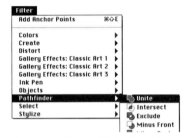

Figure 30. *Choose* **Unite** *from the* **Pathfinder** *submenu under the* **Filter** *menu.*

Figure 31. *The individual shapes are combined into a single shape.*

Figure 32. *These numbers were converted to outlines before applying the Unite filter.*

Figures 33a–b.

Figure 34. *The outer shape of this tag was created by placing a rectangle over a circle and then applying the Unite filter.*

Peter Fahrni

Add-anchor-point *tool*

Convert-direction-point *tool*

Figure 35.

Delete-anchor-point *tool*

Exercise

Change a square into a star (or a clover):

1. If the rulers are not displayed, choose Show Rulers from the View menu.

2. Choose the Rectangle tool.

3. Click on the Artboard.

4. In the Rectangle dialog box, enter 3'' in the Width and Height fields, then click OK.

5. Choose the Selection tool.

6. Press and drag a guide from the horizontal ruler. Release the mouse when the guide is over the rectangle's center point.

7. Press and drag a guide from the vertical ruler. Release the mouse when the guide is over the rectangle's center point (**Figure 36**).

8. Choose the Add-anchor-point tool (**Figure 35**).

(Continued on the following page)

Exercise

Exercise *(continued)*

9. Position the pointer over the inter-
    section of a ruler guide and the edge
    of the rectangle, then click to add a
    point in the middle of the segment
    (**Figure 37**).

10. Add points to the other segment
    midpoints.

11. Choose the Direct Selection tool.

12. Drag each of the midpoints inward
    toward the center point (**Figure 38**).
    You should now have a star with
    four narrow spokes (**Figure 39**).

13. Choose the Convert-direction-point
    tool.

14. Drag from the outer anchor points
    to convert the corners into smooth
    curves (**Figure 40**).

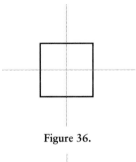

Figure 36.

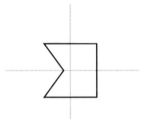

Figure 37.

Figure 38.

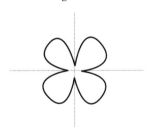

Figure 39.

Change the star back into a square:

1. If the star is not selected, select it
    with a selection tool.

2. Choose the Convert-direction-point
    tool.

3. Click on the curve points to convert
    them back into corner points.

4. Choose the Delete-anchor-point tool.

5. Click on each of the inner anchor
    points. The outer points will be
    reconnected by a single segment,
    and the object will be square again.

Figure 40.

Exercise

Exercise

Create the flag shown in Figure 1:

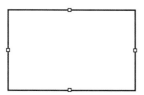

1. *Draw a rectangle. Apply a White Fill and a Black Stroke. Add points to the middle of the segments using the Add-anchor-point tool.*

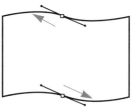

2. *Drag with the Convert-direction-point tool from the top and bottom midpoints.*

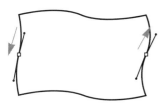

3. *Drag with the Convert-direction-point tool from the side midpoints.*

4. *Using the Direct Selection tool, move the left midpoint inward, then rotate the direction lines. Drag the right midpoint direction lines away from their anchor point.*

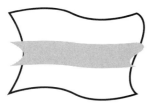

5. *Select the whole object, then double-click the Scale tool. Enter Non-uniform: Horizontal 100%, Vertical 30%, then click Copy. Apply a Gray Fill and a Stroke of None.*

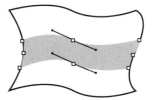

6. *Rotate the top and bottom midpoints' direction lines to match the flag's curves. Move the left and right anchor points to fit into larger shape as closely as possible.*

7. *To cover the edges of the gray shape with a copy of the flag, select the large flag shape, choose Edit > Copy. Select the gray shape, then Choose Edit > Paste in Front. Apply a Fill of None and a Black Stroke in a thick Weight. Marquee all the shapes with the Selection tool, then choose Arrange > Group.*

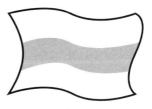

The **Autotrace** tool automatically traces a path over a PICT image opened as a template. Unfortunately, this tool is not as magical as it sounds because it can create extraneous anchor points and place points in inappropriate locations. Also, it doesn't create perfect rectangles, circles, or straight lines. Autotraced shapes usually need to be cleaned up (use the tools discussed in this chapter).

The exactness with which the Autotrace tool traces a path is determined by the Auto Trace gap and Freehand tolerance settings in the General Preferences dialog box (File menu). The Auto Trace gap is the minimum width in pixels of gaps in linework that will be traced. A high Auto Trace gap setting may result in the creation of a lot of extraneous points. The higher the Freehand tolerance, the less exactly an object will be traced, and the fewer anchor points will be created.

Adobe's Streamline program traces more accurately and offers more options than Illustrator's Autotrace tool. You can also adjust a bitmapped image in Streamline before using the program to trace it.

To use the Autotrace tool:

1. Hold down Option and choose File > New.

2. Locate and highlight a PICT file, then click Open (**Figure 41**).

3. Choose a Fill of None and a Stroke of Black from the Paint Style palette.

4. Choose the Autotrace tool (**Figure 42**).

5. Click on the edge of the template shape. The shape will be traced automatically (**Figures 43–44**).
   or
   Press and drag to define an area to be traced.

6. Click on any other white areas within the template shape (**Figures 45–46**).

■ Hold down Control to use the Pen tool when the Autotrace tool is selected.

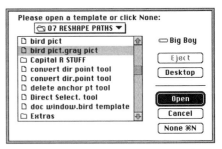

Figure 41. *In the open template dialog box, highlight a PICT file, then click* **Open***.*

Figure 42. *Autotrace tool.*

Figure 43. *The template in the document window.*

Figure 44. *The outer path traced.*

Figure 45. *The outer and inner paths traced.*

Figure 46. *The final objects after applying Black and White Fills.*

Figure 47. *The final label.*

Figure 48. *A closeup of the PICT template.*

Figure 49. *A closeup of an Autotrace of the letters. Note the non-systematic distribution of anchor points and direction lines.*

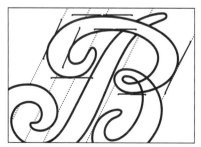

Figure 50. *The letters drawn manually (the template is hidden). Direction lines are horizontal or on the same diagonal.*

To trace letters manually:

The Autotrace tool traces quickly and is useful if the feel of the relatively coarse rendering it produces is appropriate for your particular project (**Figure 49**). If you need to create smoother shapes, however, you can refine the Autotrace tool paths or trace the template manually. The following is a description of how designer Peter Fahrni uses Illustrator to produce his own letterforms. **Figure 47** is a label that he produced.

1. *Scan the artwork*

To make sure the baseline of your letter-work template squares with the horizontal guidelines in Illustrator, trim the edge of your drawing parallel to the baseline, then slide it against the glass frame of the scanner. Scan your artwork at a resolution of 72 ppi if you usually work in 100% or 150% view in Illustrator, or choose a higher resolution — like 300% — if you need the image to look sharp at 300% view. Save it as a PICT, TIFF or EPS.

2. *Manual trace*

Use the Place command to open the image in Illustrator if you want to be able to move it around on the Artboard, or open it as a template if it's a PICT. If it's an EPS, you can dim its layer using Layer Options to make tracing easier. Most round shapes can be drawn using four anchor points to support the path. In upright letters, place anchor points on the topmost, bottommost, leftmost, and rightmost points of the curve. Hold down Shift if you want to draw out the direction lines horizontally or vertically.

To create the inclined letter shown in **Figure 50**, a line was drawn following the inclination of a stem, (in this case the lower case "t"), and then it was copied and converted into a guide for positioning the direction lines (choose Object > Guides > Make. The direction lines of

(Continued on the following page)

the leftmost and rightmost points were drawn out to align with the guides.

3. *Fine tune the flow of curves*

Select an anchor point, then move it by pressing the arrow keys (the length and the angle of the direction lines will not change). Select a curve segment, and press the arrow keys to adjust its shape (the length, but not the angle, of the direction lines will change).

The manually traced "B" consisted of two closed crisscrossing paths (**Figure 51**). The Filter > Pathfinder > Unite filter was applied to combine the two paths into one (**Figure 52**). ■

Figure 51. *The hand drawn "B."*

Figure 52. *The final "B" after applying the Unite filter.*

A comparison between an Autotraced character and an Adobe font character.

Figure 53a. *The PICT template in Illustrator.*

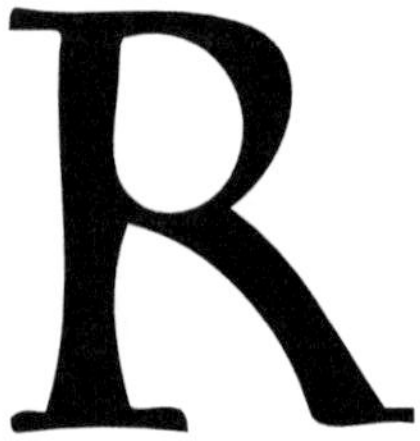

Figure 53b. *The character Autotraced.*

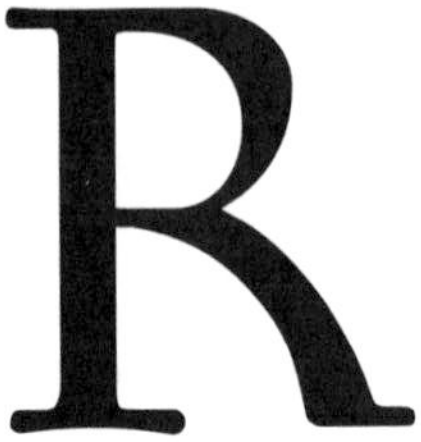

Figure 54. *A character in the Goudy 100 Adobe PostScript font, created as type in Illustrator.*

Using the Pen tool or the Freehand tool, you manually trace over any TIFF, PICT, or EPS placed image. When you manually trace an image, you can organize and simplify path shapes as well as control their stacking order. If you like, you can even place different path shapes on different layers as you trace. (The Autotrace tool won't trace a placed image.)

To manually trace over a placed image:

1. Choose File > Place, and place a TIFF, PICT or EPS image (**Figure 55**). *(See page 36)*

2. On the Layers palette, click on the layer name for the placed image, then click the lock icon so the image won't move when you trace over it.

3. If the image is a placed EPS, double-click its layer name on the Layers palette, check the Dim placed EPS box, then click OK. This will allow your pen paths to stand out clearly. Placed TIFFs and PICTs can't be dimmed.

4. Choose the Pen tool or the Freehand tool.

5. Trace the placed image (**Figure 56**).

■ You can move the placed image anywhere on your Artboard (unlike a template, which can't be moved from the center of the Artboard). You can also transform a placed image before you trace it.

Figure 55. *A placed PICT image.*

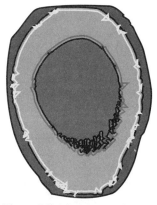

Figure 56. *After tracing the PICT using the Pen tool, filling and stroking the paths with various shades of black, and applying the Roughen filter with low Size and Detail settings to give the path strokes a more handmade appearance.*

Manually Trace a Placed Image

The Knife tool reshapes paths like a carving knife, and is a wonderful tool for artists who have a freehand drawing style.

Figure 57.
Knife tool.

To cut an object into separate shapes:

1. Choose the Knife tool from the Plug-in Tools palette (Window > Show Plug-in Tools) (**Figure 57**).

2. Starting from outside the object's edge, drag the Knife tool completely across an object to divide it, or end up outside the object again to reshape it (**Figures 58a–c**). Hold down Shift while dragging to cut in a straight line.

■ Choose Arrange > Group to group separate shapes into one object, and then use the Direct Selection tool when you need to select separate shapes within the group.

■ If you drag the Knife tool only inside the object (and not outside-to-inside the object), the resulting shape will be a compound. If you choose Artwork view, you'll see a cutout shape and a copy of the cutout shape directly behind the object.

If you draw a straight line within an object with the Knife tool, you will create a tear in the object. To open the tear, select the inner line shape of the compound path and pull the direction lines.

■ The Knife tool won't cut a line or an open path. If a Stroked line is among the stack of objects cut by the Knife tool, the line will be sent backward in the stack.

■ If the Knife tool cuts through a mask, any objects within the mask that the Knife tool passes over will be released from the mask and will be cut by the Knife. The the mask and any remaining masked objects won't be affected.

Figure 58a. *The original mother and child elephants.*

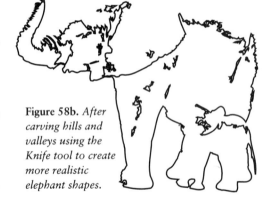

Figure 58b. *After carving hills and valleys using the Knife tool to create more realistic elephant shapes.*

Figure 58c. *The final image, after applying a black Fill.*

Diane Margolin

The Apply Knife command cuts objects into individual object shapes. It uses the topmost object shape to determine how and where underlying objects will be cut.

To cut objects using the Apply Knife command:

1. Create or select an object to be used as the cutting shape. Place it on top of the objects you want to cut.

2. Select **only** the topmost cutting object.

3. Choose Object > Apply Knife. The topmost shape will be deleted and the underlying objects will be cut apart along the edge of the formerly topmost object.

■ To keep the topmost cutting object, make a copy of it first.

■ Using Apply Knife on top of objects within a mask will release those objects from the mask.

■ The Apply Knife command gathers objects from different layers onto one layer. To prevent objects from being affected by Apply Knife, either hide the objects or place them on a non-editable layer.

Figure 59. *The cutting object is the black circle.*

Figure 60. *After using* **Apply Knife.** *The cutting object is deleted, and the remaining objects are cut apart along the circle's edge. For this illustration, the hidden areas were then deleted and a pattern-filled rectangle was placed behind the trimmed objects.*

Figure 61. *To create this cutout shape, a brush stroke was drawn with the Brush tool, the Apply Knife command was chosen, and then the resulting cut shape was selected using the Direct Selection tool and deleted.*

Apply Knife

The Zig Zag filter adds anchor points to a path or line and then moves those points to produce zigzags or waves.

To create a zigzag or wavy line:

1. Select a path.

2. Choose Filter > Distort > Zig Zag.

3. Click the Preview box (**Figure 62**).

4. Click Smooth to create a wavy line or click Corner to create a zigzag line.

5. Choose an Amount for the distance added anchor points will move.

6. Choose a number of Ridges for the number of anchor points to be added between existing points. If you enter a number, press Tab or check and then uncheck the Preview box to preview.

7. Click OK or press Return (**Figure 63**).

Figure 62. *In the **Zig Zag** dialog box, click the **Preview** box, click **Smooth** or **Corner**, and choose an **Amount** and number of **Ridges**.*

Figure 63:

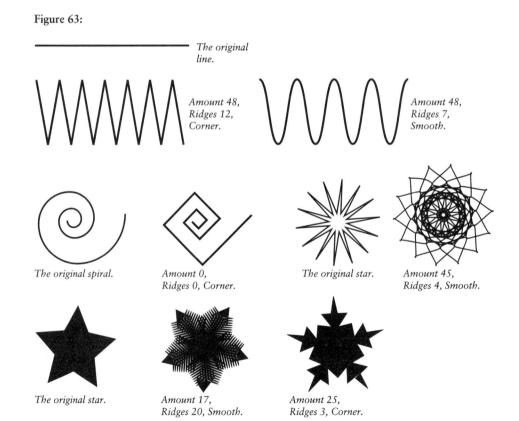

The original line.

Amount 48, Ridges 12, Corner.

Amount 48, Ridges 7, Smooth.

The original spiral.

Amount 0, Ridges 0, Corner.

The original star.

Amount 45, Ridges 4, Smooth.

The original star.

Amount 17, Ridges 20, Smooth.

Amount 25, Ridges 3, Corner.

PEN TOOL 8

The Pen tool creates precise curved and straight line segments connected by anchor points. If you click with the Pen tool, you will create corner points and straight line segments with no direction lines. If you drag with the Pen tool, you will create smooth curve points and curve segments with direction lines. The distance and the direction in which you drag the mouse determines the shape of the curve segment.

The Pen tool is the most difficult tool in Illustrator to master. Patience and practice are required to become comfortable and adept using it. If you find the Pen tool too difficult to use, remember that you can transform a simple shape into a complex shape using the point and path editing tools, as shown in Chapter 7, Paths. You'll also want to look at Chapter 7 to learn how to reshape paths you create using the Pen tool.

The true story behind Systems Crash: Along with the pictures of beautiful women that Spollen downloaded from Holland on his foreign server came a little monster virus that destroyed everything on his hard drive.

Chris Spollen, **Systems Crash**

Click with the Pen tool to create an open or closed straight-sided polygon.

To create a straight-sided object using the Pen tool:

1. Choose the Pen tool (**Figure 1**).
2. Click to create an anchor point.
3. Click to create a second anchor point. A straight line segment will connect the two points.
4. Click to create additional anchor points. They will be also connected by straight line segments.
5. To complete the shape as an **open path**:
   Click the Pen tool or any other tool on the Toolbox.
   or
   Hold down Command (⌘) and click outside the new shape to deselect it.
   or
   Choose Edit > Select None.

   To complete the shape as a **closed path**, position the Pen pointer over the starting point (a small circle will appear next to the pointer), then click (**Figure 2**).

■ If you use the Pen tool when your illustration is in Preview view and a Fill color is selected on the Paint Style palette, the Pen path will be filled as soon as three points are created. To create segments that appear as lines only, choose a Fill of None and choose a Stroke color before using the Pen tool *(see pages 101-102)*.

■ Hold down Shift while clicking with the Pen tool to the nearest 45° increment.

Figure 1.
Pen tool.

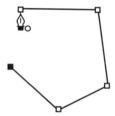
Figure 2. *The Pen tool pointer positioned over the starting point. Note the small circle next to the pointer.*

Figure 3. *Teacup created using both straight and curved segments.*

Miriam Schaer

Figure 4a. *Press and drag to create the first anchor point.*

Figure 4b. *Release and reposition the mouse, then drag in the direction you wish the curve to follow.*

Figure 4c. *Continue to reposition and press-and-drag.*

Figure 4d. *Continue to reposition and press-and-drag. To complete the object as an open path, click the* **Pen** *tool on the toolbox.*

Follow these instructions to create continuous curves — smooth anchor points connected by smooth curve segments, each with a pair of direction lines that move in tandem. The longer the direction lines, the larger the curve. You can practice drawing curves by tracing a template. The Fundamentals folder in the Tutorial folder in the Illustrator application folder contains files with shapes that you can use.

To create continuous curves using the Pen tool:

1. Choose the Pen tool (**Figure 1**).

2. Press and drag to create the first anchor point (**Figure 4a**). The angle of the pair of direction lines that you create will be determined by the direction you drag.

3. **Release the mouse and move it away from the last anchor point,** then press and drag in the direction you want the curve to go to create a second anchor point (**Figure 4b**). A curve segment will connect the first and second anchor points, and a second pair of direction lines will be created. The shape of the curve segment will be defined by the length and direction you drag the mouse. Remember, you can always reshape the curves later (see Chapter 7).

4. Drag to create additional anchor points and direction lines (**Figures 4c–d**). The anchor points will be connected by curve segments.

(Continued on the following page)

Create Continuous Curves

5. To complete the object as an **open path**:

Click the Pen tool on the Toolbox.
or
Click a selection tool, then click away from the new object to deselect it.
or
Choose Edit > Select None.

To complete the object as a **closed path**, position the Pen pointer over the starting point (a small circle will appear next to the pointer) (**Figures 5a–e**), drag, then release the mouse.

■ The fewer the anchor points, the smoother the shape. Too many anchor points will produce bumpy curves.

■ Hold down Command (⌘) to use the Selection tool or Direct Selection tool (whichever was last highlighted) while the Pen tool is selected.

■ If the last created anchor point was a curve point and you want to convert it into a corner point, click on it with the Pen tool, and continue to draw. One direction line will disappear.

If the last created anchor point was a corner point and you want to convert it into a curve point, position the Pen tool pointer over the last anchor point, then press and drag. A direction line will appear.

Figures 5a–e. *Another path being created, finishing as a closed path.*

Figure 5a.

Figure 5b.

Figure 5c.

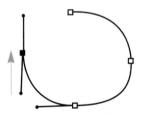
Figure 5d.

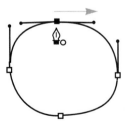
Figure 5e. *To close the path, press and drag over the starting point.*

Figure 6a. *Press and drag to create the first anchor point.*

Figure 6b. *Release and reposition the mouse, then press and drag to create a second anchor point.*

Figure 6c. *Hold down* **Option** *and press and drag from the last anchor point in the direction you wish the new curve to follow. Note that the direction lines are on the same side of the curve segment.*

Figure 6d. *Press and drag to create another anchor point, etc.*

You can use the Pen tool to create non-continuous curves — segments that curve on only one side of an anchor point, like a series of archways (**Figure 6d**). (In a continuous curve, segments curve on both sides of an anchor point.) The anchor point that connects non-continuous curves is called a corner point. If you move one direction line from a corner point, only the curve on the same side of the point will reshape. Continuous and non-continuous curves can be combined in the same path.

Two methods for producing non-continuous curves follow. In the first set of instructions, you will press and drag to create an anchor point first, then hold down Option to redraw the direction line for that anchor point.

To create non-continuous curves (Pen tool method):

1. Choose the Pen tool (**Figure 1**).

2. Press and drag to create the first anchor point (**Figure 6a**).

3. **Release the mouse and move it away from the last anchor point,** then press and drag to create a second anchor point (**Figure 6b**). A curve segment will connect the first and second anchor points, and a second pair of direction lines will be created. The shape of the curve segment will be determined by the length and direction you drag.

4. Hold down Option and press and drag from the last anchor point in the direction you wish the new curve to follow (**Figure 6c**). A new direction line will be created.

5. Repeat steps 3 and 4 to create a series of anchor points and curves (**Figure 6d**).

Create Non-Continuous Curves

To create non-continuous curves (Convert-direction-point tool method):

1. Follow the steps on page 93 to create an open path with smooth curves.

2. Choose the Direct Selection tool (**Figure 7**).

3. Click on the path (**Figure 8a**).

4. Click on the anchor point to be modified (**Figure 8b**).

5. Hold down Control to temporarily use the Convert-direction-point tool and rotate the direction line so it forms a "V" shape with the other direction line (**Figure 8c**). The curve segment will be on the same side of the anchor point as the previous curve segment.

6. Release Control.

7. Repeat steps 4–6 to convert other anchor points (**Figure 8d**).

■ Hold down Option and Control to use the Convert-direction-point tool to move a direction line when the Pen tool is selected.

■ To convert a pair of direction lines back into a smooth curve, choose the Direct Selection tool, click on the anchor point, choose the Convert-direction-point tool (or hold down Control), then click on a direction line point.

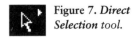

Figure 7. *Direct Selection tool.*

Figure 8a. *Click on the path.*

Figure 8b. *Click with the Direct Selection tool on the anchor point you wish to modify.*

Figure 8c. *Hold down* **Control** *and rotate the direction line, then release Control.*

Figure 8d. *Repeat steps 4–6 for other anchor points you wish to convert.*

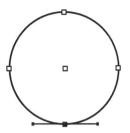

Figure 9. *Click on the bottom edge of the circle.*

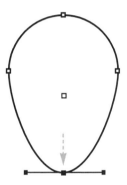

Figure 10. *Move the bottom anchor point downward.*

Exercise
Convert a circle into a heart:

1. Draw a perfect circle with the Oval tool (hold down Shift while dragging).
2. Choose the Direct Selection tool.
3. Click away from the object to deselect it.
4. Click on the bottom edge of the circle (**Figure 9**).
5. Select the bottom anchor point, start dragging it downward, hold down Shift, then continue to drag (**Figure 10**).
6. Hold down Control to temporarily use the Convert-direction-point tool and press and drag one of the direction lines upward to form a non-continuous curve (**Figure 11**).
7. Release Control.
8. Click on the bottom anchor point to reselect it, then drag the second direction line upward. The bottom of the circle will become a corner point with handles (**Figure 12**). Deselect.
9. Hold down Shift and drag the anchor point from the top of the circle downward (**Figure 13**).

(Continued on the following page)

Exercise

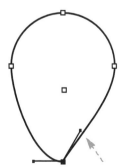

Figure 11. *Hold down **Control** and move one of the direction lines upward.*

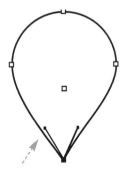

Figure 12. *Reselect the bottom anchor point, then drag the second direction line upward.*

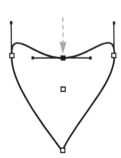

Figure 13. *Move the top anchor point downward.*

10. Hold down Control to temporarily use the Convert-direction-point tool and drag a direction line connected to the top anchor point upward to form a non-continuous curve (**Figure 14**).

11. Release Control.

12. Click on the top anchor point to reselect it, then drag the second direction line upward. The top of the circle will become a corner point with handles (**Figure 15**). ■

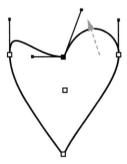

Figure 14. *Hold down* **Control**, *drag one of the top direction lines upward, then release Control.*

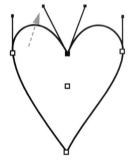

Figure 15. *Click on the top anchor point, then drag the second direction line upward.*

Figure 16. *The completed heart.*

PAINT STYLE 9

*In this chapter you will learn to Fill the inside or
Stroke the edge of an object with a color or shade,
choose Stroke styles like dashes and arrowheads,
mix process colors, append paint styles from another
document, use the Eyedropper tool to sample colors
from any Illustrator document window, use the
Paint Bucket tool to apply Fill and Stroke colors at
the same time, and saturate/desaturate, invert, or
blend colors using filters. Gradients and patterns
are covered in the next two chapters, respectively.*

Chris Spollen

FOR THE INSTRUCTIONS IN THIS CHAPTER

▪ Open the Paint Style palette (choose Object >
Paint Style or choose Window > Show Paint
Style or use the ⌘-I shortcut). Display both
the left and right panels of the palette (instruc-
tions are on the following page), and check the
Auto box to apply colors immediately.

▪ Work with your illustration in Preview view so
you can see colors on screen as you apply them
(choose View > Preview).

Colors are applied using the **Paint Style**
palette. You can choose a Fill or Stroke
color from premixed swatches, mix your
own gray percentage, mix a process color
from Cyan, Magenta, Yellow and Black,
or choose a Pantone or other named
color swatch. You can also Fill a shape
with a pattern or gradient and store any
custom color, pattern, or gradient Fill on
the Paint Style palette. Custom colors are
saved with the illustration in which they
are created or applied.

The Paint Style palette can also be used
to set line style characteristics, such as
Stroke color, Stroke thickness, and Stroke
style (dashed or solid).

A Fill and/or Stroke can be applied to a
closed or open path. Any new object you
create will automatically be painted with
the current Paint Style palette Fill and
Stroke settings, which can be changed at
any time. When an object is selected, the
Paint Style palette displays its paint characteristics.

The Paint Style palette

The palette is divided into three panels: Paint swatches on the left panel, color selection method icons and the Stroke Weight field on the right panel, and Stroke attribute options on the bottom panel (**Figure 1**).

You can control which panel or combination of panels are open using the pop-up panel display menu in the upper right corner of the palette. Or, click the section on the miniature palette that corresponds to the panel you wish to display or hide.

■ To open the left and right panels at the same time, click on the line between the left and right panels on the miniature palette.

■ When the Auto box on the right panel is checked, color attributes apply immediately to any currently selected object or objects. To apply colors when the Auto box is unchecked, click the Apply button, or double-click a color swatch, or press Enter.

(Overprinting is discussed in Chapter 24)

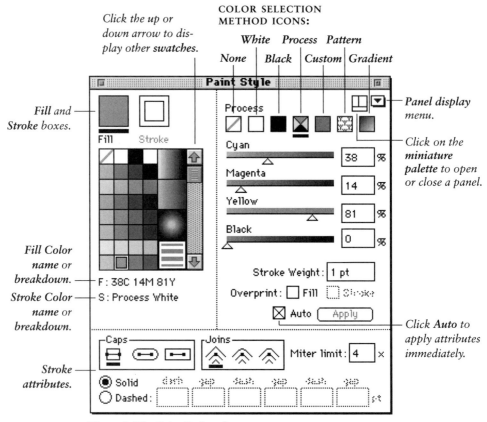

Click the up or down arrow to display other swatches.

COLOR SELECTION METHOD ICONS:

White   Process   Pattern

None   Black   Custom   Gradient

Fill and Stroke boxes.

Panel display menu.

Click on the miniature palette to open or close a panel.

Fill Color name or breakdown.

Stroke Color name or breakdown.

Stroke attributes.

Click Auto to apply attributes immediately.

Figure 1. *The Paint Style palette.*

Note: Instructions for applying a custom (named) color are on page 103, instructions for applying a gradient Fill are in Chapter 10, *Gradients,* and instructions for applying pattern Fills and Strokes are in Chapter 11, *Patterns.*

To apply a Fill or Stroke color (None, Black, White, or Process):

1. Select an object (not all the anchor points need to be solid). To select multiple objects with the same paint attributes, use a Select filter *(see page 64).*

2. If the Paint Style palette is not displayed, choose Object > Paint Style (⌘-I) or choose Window > Show Paint Style. Check the Auto box.

   The palette will display the current paint attributes of the selected object.

3. Click the Fill box at the top of palette. *or* Click the Stroke box at the top of the palette.

4. To Fill or Stroke with **None,** click the color selection method icon with the slash. The Fill or Stroke box will also have a slash through it and any previously applied Fill or Stroke color will be removed from the object.

   To Fill or Stroke with **White,** click the White color selection method icon. A slider will appear below the Color selection boxes. Leave it all the way to the left to apply white.

   To Fill or Stroke with **Black** or **gray,** click the Black color selection method icon. A slider will appear below the color selection boxes. Move the slider to mix a shade of gray. Or, enter a number in the percentage field, then press Return.

   To Fill or Stroke with a **Process** color, click the process color selection method icon. Four sliders will appear below the color selection boxes. Move

(Continued on the following page)

MORE ABOUT SWATCHES ——————

▓ You can save up to 255 swatches with a document.

▓ If you click on a paint swatch, the color name or the CMYK breakdown of that color will be displayed just below the swatch scroll window.

▓ To store a custom color, pattern, gradient, or new process color in the swatch window, first click the swatch window scroll arrow to display the empty squares. Then drag a color name from the right panel onto an empty square, or drag from the Fill or Stroke box onto an empty square, or hold down Option and click on an empty square to fill that square with the current FIll or Stroke color (whichever is currently highlighted). To replace a swatch, drag a new swatch or color name over it instead of onto an empty square.

▓ To move a swatch, Option-drag it.

▓ To delete a swatch, Command-click on the swatch, then click Delete when the warning prompt appears. To delete several swatches with a warning prompt, hold down command and drag over them. To delete several swatches without a warning prompt, drag over them with Option and Command held down. You can't restore a deleted swatch with the Undo command.

the sliders. Or, enter numbers in the percentage fields, pressing Tab after each entry.
or
Click a swatch on the left side of the palette.

■ A Gradient can't be applied as a Stroke color.

■ To make the Fill color the same as the Stroke color, or vice versa, drag one box over the other.

■ Hold down Shift and drag the Cyan, Magenta, Yellow, or Black slider to change its amount while preserving its relationship to the other colors.

■ You can paint multiple selected objects. If their Fill or Stroke colors differ, a question mark will appear in the corresponding Fill or Stroke box, but you can apply a new Fill and/or Stroke color to all the objects.

■ To recolor type, use the selection method described on page 153. But don't apply a large Stroke Weight to small type — it will distort the letter-forms.

Fair warning

For a print job, don't mix process colors or choose spot (Pantone) colors based on how they look on the screen (unless you're working on a very carefully calibrated monitor, which most people aren't). Screen colors — which are seductively bright and luminous — don't accurately simulate printed colors. To avoid an embarassing and costly on-press surprise, use matching books to choose spot colors or mix process colors, and run color proofs of your job.

An object with a Fill color and a Stroke of None.

An object with a Fill color and a Stroke color.

Type with a Fill color and a Stroke of None.

Figure 2.

Type with a Stroke color and a Fill of None.

What is a Custom Color? —————

A custom color is a color that you mix or name yourself or a color from a matching system, such as Pantone or Trumatch. In order to access a custom color in an Illustrator document, you must mix and name it or copy it from one of the color matching system files that are supplied with Illustrator (instructions are on the next two pages). Matching system colors aren't automatically available in a document.

*Click the **Custom** color selection icon to display the custom color scroll window.*

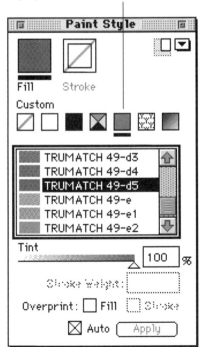

Figure 3. *The right side of the **Paint Style** palette.*

To Fill or Stroke with a custom (named) color:

1. Select an object or objects.

2. Click the Fill or Stroke box at the top of the Paint Style palette (the attribute of the object you wish to modify).

3. On the right panel, click the Custom color selection method icon (**Figure 3**). A scroll window will appear.

4. Click a custom color name or type the first few characters or the number of the color (for example, type "10-b" for TRUMATCH 10-b). The new color will appear in the Fill or Stroke box and in the selected object.

5. *Optional:* For a spot color, move the tint slider or enter a number in the Tint field.

■ To display the process color break-down of a color, highlight the color name, then click the Process color selection method icon.

■ To convert a process color into a custom color, drag the process color swatch or the Fill or Stroke box onto the Custom color selection method icon or drag a swatch onto the custom color scroll list. Click OK when the Custom Color dialog box opens. (You can also change the color name before you click OK.)

■ If you modify a named color, it will automatically be modified in all the objects to which it has already been applied.

Apply a Custom Color

To create or modify a process color:

1. Choose Object > Custom Color (**Figure 4**).
   or
   On the Paint Style palette, click the Custom color selection method icon, then double-click a color name on the custom color scroll list.

2. For a new color, click New, then enter a name for the color in the "Change name to" field (**Figure 5**).

3. Click the Black color selection method icon, then choose a shade by moving the slider.
   or
   Click the Process color selection method icon, then move the sliders, or enter numbers in the percentage fields, pressing Tab after each entry.

4. Click OK or press Return. If you created a new color, the color name will appear on the Paint Style palette.

▪ To delete a custom color, double-click the color name, then click Delete. Objects painted with that color will be painted Black. The color will be deleted from all open documents in which it has been saved. (To retrieve a deleted custom color after closing the Custom color dialog box, choose Undo from the Edit menu.)

▪ Beware: if you click Select All Unused and then click Delete, all unused custom colors will be deleted from the custom color list of all open documents.

Figure 4. *Choose* **Custom Color** *from the* **Object** *menu.*

3) Click a color selection method icon.

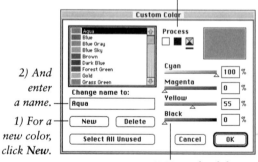

2) And enter a name.

1) For a new color, click **New**.

4) Move the sliders (or enter percentages).

Figure 5. **Custom Color** *dialog box.*

Figure 6. *Choose Open from the File menu.*

You can choose colors from the Focoltone, Pantone, Toyo, and Trumatch color matching systems.

To add matching system colors to a document:

1. Choose File > Open (**Figure 6**).

2. Locate and highlight the desired matching system file in the Color Systems folder, which is in the Utilities folder in the Adobe Illustrator folder (**Figure 7**).

3. Click Open.

4. Choose your document name from the Window menu (**Figure 8**).

5. Click the Custom color selection method icon (fifth icon) on the Paint Style palette. The matching system color names will appear on the scroll list (click the scroll arrow to display them, if necessary).

6. Press and drag any color name you want to save onto a blank square in the paint swatch window (scroll, if necessary, to display blank swatches).

7. Choose the matching system document from the Window menu, then click on that document's close box. Don't save over a matching system file if it has been altered. If a warning prompt appears, click Don't Save.

   The selected matching system colors will be saved with your document, and can be accessed from the custom color swatch window and scroll list.

■ If you use Import Styles to append matching system colors, the document to which they are appended will contain all the colors from that matching system file, and its file storage size will increase.

Figure 7. *Click on a matching system name, then click Open.*

Figure 8. *Choose your document name from the Window menu.*

Add Matching System Colors to a Document

Use the **Import Styles** command to append custom colors, patterns, and gradients from another Illustrator document or from the Illustrator Gradients, Fill Patterns, or Color Systems folder to your current document.

To append colors, patterns or gradients:

1. Choose File > Import Styles (**Figure 9**).
2. Locate the document or open the folder containing the color styles you want to append.
3. Click Import. If you append a color (or pattern or gradient) with the same name as a color in the current document, it will replace the color in the current document.

■ Paint swatches on the Paint Style palette in the document from which styles are imported won't append.

TO APPEND MORE SELECTIVELY ──────

To import colors, patterns, or gradients one at a time, choose Open from the File menu, then locate and open the document you wish to append from. Click on your "destination" document, then drag any individual color, pattern, or gradient name you want to append from the Paint Style palette scroll list onto a swatch square.

Figure 9. *Choose* **Import Styles** *from the* **File** *menu.*

You can change a Stroke's color, weight (thickness), and style (dashed or solid, rounded or sharp corners, and flat or rounded ends).

To change the thickness of a Stroke:

1. Select an object.
2. Click the Stroke box at the top of the Paint Style palette.
3. Enter a width in points in the Stroke Weight field (**Figure 10**). Half the Stroke will be applied inside the object, the other half will be applied outside the object (**Figure 11**).

■ A line weight of 0, output on a high resolution printer, will be a one-pixel wide hairline.

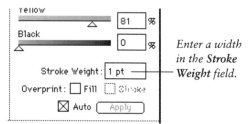

Enter a width in the Stroke Weight field.

Figure 10. *The right panel of the* **Paint Style** *palette.*

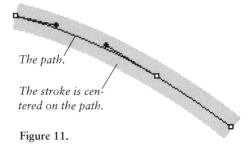

The path.

The stroke is centered on the path.

Figure 11.

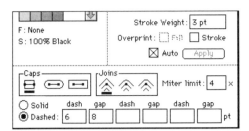

Figure 12. *Click the Dashed button and enter dash and gap amounts on the bottom panel of the **Paint Style** palette.*

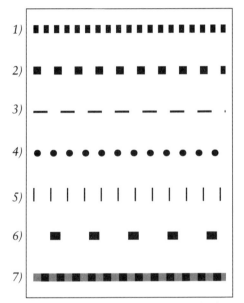

Figure 13. *A variety of dashed lines (the first Caps icon was selected for all except #4):*

1) stroke 6, dash 4, gap 4.

2) stroke 6, dash 6, gap 10.

3) stroke 1.5, dash 11, gap 10.

4) stroke 5, dash 0, gap 12 (round caps).

5) stroke 10, dash 1, gap 12.

6) stroke 6, dash 0, gap 10, dash 8, gap 10.

7) stroke 6, dash 6, gap 6 (pasted in front of a 6-point gray Stroked line).

To create a dashed Stroke:

1. Select an object.
2. Click the Stroke box on the Paint Style palette.
3. Choose a Stroke color and Weight.
4. Click a Caps icon (the dash shape).
5. Click the Dashed button on the bottom panel of the Paint Style palette (**Figure 12**).
6. Enter a number in the first dash field (the length of the first dash, in points), then press Tab or Return to apply (**Figure 13**).
7. *Optional:* To create dashes of varying lengths, enter other amounts in the other dash fields. If you enter an amount only in the first dash field, that amount will be repeated for all the dashes.
8. Enter an amount in the gap field (the length of the first gap after the first dash), then press Tab or Return to apply.
9. *Optional:* Enter other amounts in the other gap fields to create gaps of varying lengths. If you enter an amount only in the first gap field, that amount will be repeated for all the gaps.

■ To create a dotted line, click the second Caps icon, enter 0 for the Dash value, and enter a Gap value that is greater than or equal to the Stroke Weight.

Create a Dashed Line (Stroke)

To modify Stroke caps and/or joins:

1. Select an object.

2. Click the Stroke box at the top of Paint Style palette.

3. Make sure the bottom panel of the palette is displayed (**Figure 14**).

4. To modify the endpoints of a solid line or all the dashes in a dashed line:

   Click the left **Caps** icon to create square-cornered ends or square-cornered dashes in which the Stroke stops at the endpoints. Use this option to align paths precisely.

   Click the middle **Caps** icon to create round ends or round-ended dashes with a more hand-drawn appearance.

   Click the right **Caps** icon to create square-cornered ends or square-cornered dashes in which the Stroke extends beyond the endpoints.

5. To modify the line bends:

   Click the left **Joins** icon to produce pointed bends (miter joins) (**Figure 15**).

   Click the middle **Joins** icon to produce semicircular bends (round joins).

   The right **Joins** icon to produce square-cornered bends (bevel joins).

To create arrowheads:

1. Select an open path.

2. Choose Filter > Stylize > Add Arrowheads.

3. Click the scroll icon to choose from the various head and tail designs (**Figure 16**).

4. *Optional:* Resize the arrowhead by entering a different Scale percentage.

5. Click the Start, End, or Start-and-End button for the location of the arrowhead, according to the order in which the path anchor points were created .

6. Click OK or press Return.

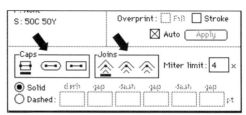

Figure 14. *The* Caps *and* Joins *icons on the* Paint Style *palette.*

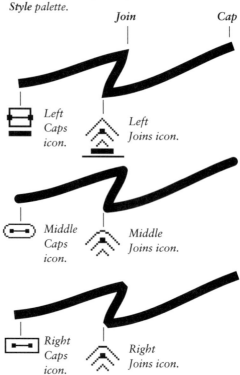

Figure 15.

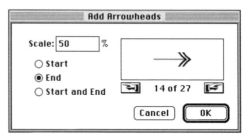

Figure 16. *Choose a* Scale, *location (*Start, End, *or* Start and End*) and style in the* Add Arrowheads *dialog box.*

Figure 17.
Paint Bucket tool.

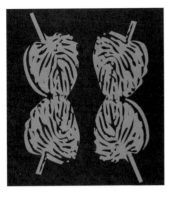

Figure 18a.
*The original
illustration.*

Diane Margolin

Figure 18b. *After
using the Paint
Bucket to apply a
white Fill and a
dashed Stroke to the
leaves on the left.*

If you click with the **Paint Bucket** tool on an object, that object will be Filled and Stroked using the current Paint Style palette settings. The Paint Style palette does not have to be displayed for you to use the Paint Bucket tool.

To use the Paint Bucket tool:

1. Choose the Paint Bucket tool (**Figure 17**).

2. Choose Fill and Stroke colors from the Paint Style palette.
   or
   Hold down Option and click on a color anywhere in any open Illustrator window (temporary Eyedropper).

3. Click on an object (the object does not have to be selected). The object will become selected and colored with the current Paint Style palette attributes (**Figures 18a–b**). For an object without a Fill color, click the black spill of the Paint Bucket cursor on the path outline.

Paint Bucket Tool

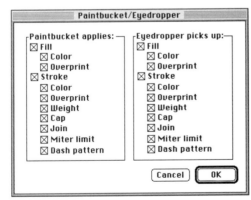

Figure 19. *Click check boxes on or off in the
Paintbucket/Eyedropper dialog box.*

Use the Paintbucket/Eyedropper dialog box to change the default attributes for either or both tools.

To choose paint attributes the Eyedropper picks up or the Paint Bucket applies:

1. Double-click the Paint Bucket or Eyedropper tool.

2. Click check box options on or off (**Figure 19**).

3. Click OK or press Return.

If you click on an object with the Eyedropper tool, it will pick up the object's paint attributes and display them on the Paint Style palette.

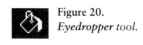

Figure 20.
Eyedropper tool.

To use the Eyedropper tool:

1. *Optional:* Select an object or objects if you want to recolor them immediately with the attributes you pick up with the Eyedropper.

2. Choose the Eyedropper tool (**Figure 20**).

3. Click once on any object in any open Illustrator window to display that object's paint attributes on the Paint Style palette. You can then apply them to any newly selected object. (To pick up a color from type, click on the type itself or its baseline.)
or
Double-click a selected object or non-selected object. In either case, the paint attributes of the object you click on will be applied to all the selected objects.

■ Hold down Option to use the Paint Bucket tool while the Eyedropper is selected. The Paint Style palette does not have to be open to do this.

■ To preserve the color to use again, drag from the Fill or Stroke box onto a swatch square.

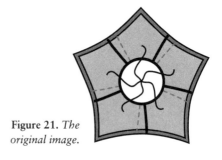

Figure 21. *The original image.*

The Invert Colors filter converts colors into their four-color opposites. 0% yellow, for example, will become 100%, 20% yellow will become 80% yellow, and watch out — 0% K will become 100% black. Custom colors and gradients cannot be inverted.

To invert colors:

1. Select the object or objects whose colors you want to invert.

2. Choose Filter > Colors > Invert Colors (**Figures 21–22**).

Figure 22. *After applying the Invert Colors filter.*

Diane Margolin

Eyedropper Tool; Invert Colors

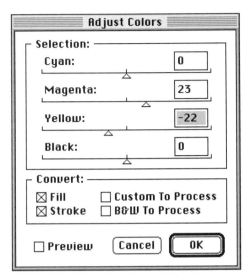

Figure 23. *In the Adjust Colors dialog box, enter Cyan, Magenta, Yellow, or Black percentages or move the sliders.*

Use the **Adjust Colors** filter to manually adjust colors in one or more selected objects, including text objects.

To adjust colors:

1. Select the object or objects whose colors you want to adjust.

2. Choose Filter > Colors > Adjust Colors.

3. *Optional:* Click Preview to preview color adjustments in your illustration with the dialog box open (**Figure 23**).

4. Move the Cyan, Magenta, Yellow, or Black sliders, or enter percentages in those fields (the amount of those colors that you want to increase or decrease).

5. *Optional:* Click the Fill and or Stroke box, then click the Custom To Process box to convert custom Fill and/or Stroke colors into CMYK (process) colors and/or click the B&W To Process box to convert 100% black into CMYK (four-color) black. For a process black, adjust the C, M, or Y percentages after you click OK.

6. Click OK or press Return.

A 1-bit TIFF image opened or placed in Illustrator can be colorized via the Paint Style palette. Black areas in the TIFF image will recolor; white areas will remain transparent. *Notes:* The Clipboard commands (Copy and Paste) can't be used to import a 1-bit TIFF. And a 1-bit-TIFF copied using the drag-and-drop method can't be colorized.

To colorize a 1-bit TIFF image:

1. Use File > Open or File > Place to open a 1-bit TIFF image in Illustrator.

2. Select the TIFF.

3. Apply a Fill color *(see pages 101-102)*.

■ To make transparent areas in a 1-bit TIFF look as if it's colorized, create an object with the desired background color and send it behind the TIFF.

Adjust Colors; Colorize a 1-Bit TIFF

Use the Saturate filter to deepen or fade colors in selected objects by a specified percentage.

To saturate or desaturate colors:

1. Select the object(s) whose colors you want to saturate or desaturate.

2. Choose Filter > Colors > Saturate.

3. Check the Preview box to preview color changes immediately in your illustration (**Figure 24**).

4. Move the Saturate slider or enter a percentage between 100% and –100% for the amount you want to intensify or fade the color.

5. Click OK or press Return.

To blend colors between objects:

1. Select three or more objects. The two objects that are farthest apart should not contain custom colors, gradients, or patterns.

2. Choose one of these three blend filters from the Colors submenu under the Filter menu:

   Blend Front to Back to create a color blend using the Fill colors of the frontmost and backmost objects as the starting and ending colors (**Figure 25**). Objects will stay on their original, respective layers.

   Blend Horizontally to create a color blend using the Fill colors of the leftmost and rightmost objects as the starting and ending colors (**Figures 26a–b**).

   Blend Vertically to create a color blend using the Fill colors of the topmost and bottommost objects as the starting and ending colors.

   Any selected objects that are stacked between the front most and backmost objects (or positioned between the leftmost and rightmost or topmost and bottommost objects) are assigned intermediate blend colors.

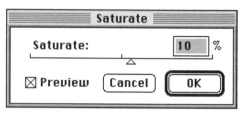

Figure 24. *In the* **Saturate** *dialog box, choose a positive percentage to saturate or a negative percentage to desaturate.*

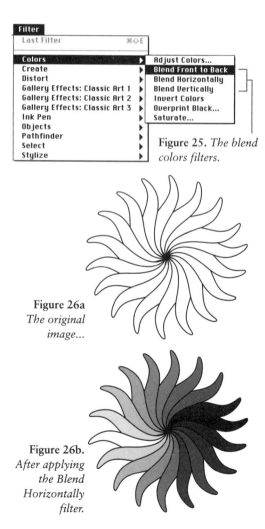

Figure 25. *The blend colors filters.*

Figure 26a
The original image...

Figure 26b.
After applying the Blend Horizontally filter.

Saturate or Desaturate; Blend Colors Between Objects

GRADIENTS 10

A gradient Fill is a gradual blend between two or more colors. In this chapter you will learn how to create two-color and multi-color gradients and how to use the Gradient tool to change the angle or order of gradient colors.

Chris Spollen, **New York Retro**

The simplest gradient Fill consists of a starting and ending color, with the point where the colors are equally mixed together midway between the two colors. A gradient can be linear (side-to-side) or radial (out-from-center). You can apply a gradient Fill to one object or across several objects. Illustrator comes with predefined gradients, but you can also create your own gradients using the Gradient palette. The Paint Style palette is used to apply a gradient to an object.

Once an object is filled with a gradient, you can use the Gradient tool to modify how the Fill is distributed within the object: the direction of the gradient, how quickly one color blends into another, or the placement of the center of a radial gradient Fill.

Follow these instructions to apply a predefined gradient Fill, which can be a gradient supplied with Illustrator or a custom gradient that you have already created. To create your own gradient Fill, follow the next set of instructions.

To Fill with a gradient:

1. Select an object.
2. On the Paint Style palette (⌘-I), check the Auto box (**Figure 1**).
3. Click the Fill box on the palette.
4. On the right panel, click the Gradient color selection method icon.
5. Click a gradient name on the scroll list or click on a swatch (**Figure 1**). (To append other Illustrator gradients or gradients from another document, see page 106.)
6. *Optional:* Enter a new angle for a linear Fill in the Angle field (press Return).

- To apply a gradient to a Stroke, first apply Filter > Objects > Outline Path to convert the Stroke into a closed object, then follow steps 2–5 above.

- To Fill type with a gradient, you must first convert it into outlines (Type > Create Outlines).

- You can also use the Paint Bucket tool to apply a gradient to an object.

To create a two-color gradient Fill:

1. Choose Window > Show Gradient (**Figure 2**).
   or
   Choose Object > Gradient.
   or
   Double-click a gradient name on the Paint Style palette (**Figure 1**).
2. If the bottom panel of the Gradient palette is not displayed, click the palette display lever.
3. Click the New button (**Figure 3**).
4. Type a new name for the gradient in the highlighted field so you don't save over an existing gradient.

3) Click the Gradient color selection method icon.

4) Click a gradient name.

2) Click the Fill box.

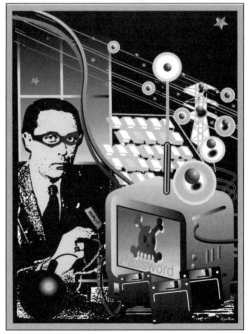

1) Check the Auto box.

Figure 1. *The Paint Style palette.*

*Chris Spollen, **Internet Theft***

Fill with a Gradient; Two-Color Gradient Fill

Figure 2. *Choose* ***Show Gradient*** *from the* ***Window*** *menu.*

Click here to shrink or enlarge the palette.

Starting color triangle

Midpoint diamond *(where the starting and ending colors are half-and-half).*

Ending color triangle

Enter a unique ***name*** *for the Gradient.*

Click the ***Linear*** *or* ***Radial*** *button.*

Figure 3. *The* ***Gradient*** *palette. The* ***midpoint diamond*** *was moved to the left. The gradient Fill now contains more of the ending color than the starting color.*

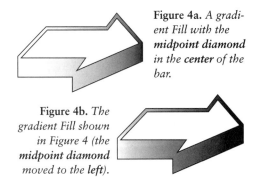

Figure 4a. *A gradient Fill with the* ***midpoint diamond*** *in the* ***center*** *of the bar.*

Figure 4b. *The gradient Fill shown in Figure 4 (the* ***midpoint diamond*** *moved to the* ***left***).

5. Press Return.

6. Click the starting color triangle under the left side of the color bar.

7. Click the White or Black color selection icon. Move the slider to choose a shade of gray.
   or
   Click the Process color selection icon, then move the sliders to mix a color.
   or
   Click the Custom color selection icon, click a name on the scroll list, and, if desired, move the Tint slider.

8. Click the ending color triangle under the right side of the color bar.

9. Repeat step 7.

10. Click the Linear or Radial button.

11. *Optional:* Move the midpoint diamond (above the color bar) to the right to produce more of the starting color than the ending color, or to the left to produce more of the ending color than the starting color (**Figures 4a–b**).

The new gradient name will appear on the Gradient and Paint Style palette scroll lists and will save with the document.

■ To color separate a gradient containing more than one custom color, assign a different screen angle to each color using Separation Setup, and uncheck the Convert to Process box. Or click the Process color icon on the Gradient palette to translate the custom color into a process color. See the Illustrator User Guide for more information, and ask your service bureau for help.

■ To color separate a gradient from a custom color to white on one piece of film, make the gradient the custom color to 0% of the same color.

■ To swap the starting and ending colors, drag one triangle over the other.

Two-Color Gradient Fill

A gradient Fill can contain up to 32 colors.

To create a multicolor gradient Fill:

1. Follow steps 1–10 on the previous page to produce a two-color gradient Fill.
   or
   Click a gradient name on the Gradient palette.

2. Click on the bottom of the color bar where you wish to place the new color. A new triangle will appear (**Figure 5**).

3. Mix a new color.

Steps 4–6 are optional:

4. Move the new triangle left or right to change the location of that color in the gradient (**Figure 5**).

5. Move the midpoint diamond to the left or right of the new color to change the location where the new color is evenly blended with either of the colors adjacent to it.

6. Repeat steps 2–5 to add more colors (**Figure 6**).

- ■ To produce a sharp transition between colors, drag the midpoint diamond close to a color triangle or move the color triangles close together.

- ■ To remove a color triangle, drag it downward off the color bar.

- ■ To create a variation of a gradient Fill, click the Duplicate button on the Gradient palette, rename the gradient, then modify it.

- ■ To delete a gradient Fill name from the Gradient palette, click on it, then click Delete. All objects filled with that gradient in any open document will be filled with Black.

- ■ To switch a pair of colors, just drag one triangle on top of the other.

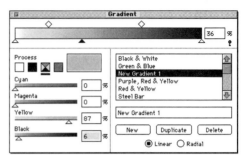

Figure 5. *To add a color to a gradient, click under the color bar to add a new triangle, click a color selection method icon, then mix a process color or click on a custom color name.*

Figure 6. *Six new shades of black have been added to this gradient. Move the* **midpoint diamond** *between a pair of colors to change the location where those colors are evenly blended, or move a* **triangle** *to move that individual color.*

Figure 7. *Multi-color gradients.*

Figure 8.
Gradient tool.

Figure 9a. *A linear gradient Fill applied using the Paint Style palette only.*

Figure 9b. *The Gradient tool dragged a short distance from **right to left** across the same gradient.*

Once an object is filled with a gradient, you can use the **Gradient tool** to manually change the angle of the Fill, the order of the starting and ending colors, or the location of the center of a radial gradient Fill.

To use the Gradient tool:

1. Follow the instructions on page 100 to apply a gradient Fill to an object. Keep the object selected.

2. Choose the Gradient tool (**Figure 8**).

3. To modify a **linear** gradient Fill, you can press and drag across the object in a new direction (right-to-left or diagonally) (**Figures 9a–b**). To blend the colors quickly, drag a short distance; to blend the colors slowly across a wider span, drag a long distance.

   To modify a **radial** gradient Fill, position the pointer where you want the center of the fill to be, then press and drag (**Figures 10a–b**).

■ Repeat step 3 — drag in a different direction to produce a different result. The new gradient will replace the old.

■ Drag in the opposite direction to reverse the order of the Fill colors.

■ If you start to drag or finish dragging outside the edge of an object with the Gradient tool, the colors at the beginning or end of the gradient Fill won't appear in the object.

Gradient tool

Figure 10a. *A radial gradient Fill before using the Gradient tool.*

Figure 10b. *After dragging the Gradient tool across the same radial gradient Fill.*

Extend a Gradient Across Multiple Objects

To extend a gradient across multiple objects:

1. Select the objects.
2. Fill them with a gradient *(instructions on page 114)* (**Figure 11**).
3. Choose the Gradient tool (**Figure 8**).
4. Drag over the objects in the direction and angle you wish the gradient Fill to appear (**Figure 12**). Hold down Shift while dragging to draw on the nearest 45° increment.

■ Once multiple objects are filled with the same gradient, don't combine them into a compound path — it may become too complex to print.

Figure 11. *A gradient Fill applied using the **Paint Style palette** only. Each type object is filled with its own gradient.*

Figure 12. *The gradient adjusted using the **Gradient** tool. The arrow shows the direction the mouse was dragged. A single gradient blends across all the type outlines.*

To convert gradient shades into separate objects, use the Expand command (see page 129).

An object containing the Steel Bar gradient Fill.

*The **Expand** command applied with a setting of 12 steps.*

After deleting the resulting mask object. A few objects were pulled apart for illustration purposes.

Figure 13.

Peter Fahrni

PATTERNS 11

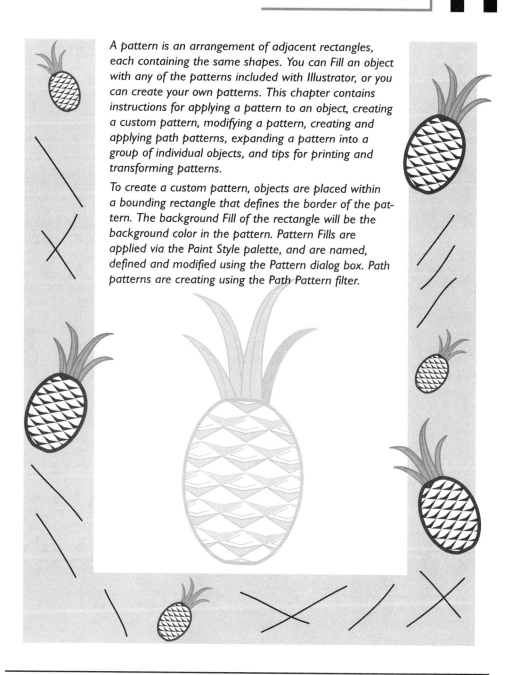

A pattern is an arrangement of adjacent rectangles, each containing the same shapes. You can Fill an object with any of the patterns included with Illustrator, or you can create your own patterns. This chapter contains instructions for applying a pattern to an object, creating a custom pattern, modifying a pattern, creating and applying path patterns, expanding a pattern into a group of individual objects, and tips for printing and transforming patterns.

To create a custom pattern, objects are placed within a bounding rectangle that defines the border of the pattern. The background Fill of the rectangle will be the background color in the pattern. Pattern Fills are applied via the Paint Style palette, and are named, defined and modified using the Pattern dialog box. Path patterns are creating using the Path Pattern filter.

Follow these instructions to apply a predefined pattern or an existing custom pattern.

To Fill with a pattern:

1. Select an object.
2. Check the Auto button on the Paint Style palette.
3. Click the Fill box at top of the palette (**Figure 1**).
4. Click the Pattern color selection method icon on the right panel.
5. Click a pattern name on the scroll list (**Figures 2a–c**).

■ To append additional Illustrator patterns or patterns from another document, follow the instructions on page 106. Patterns currently on the Paint Style palette will save with your document. To delete all unused patterns from all open documents, choose Object > Pattern, click Select All Unused, then click Delete.

■ If you've used a pattern in your illustration but you no longer need to preview it on screen, you can speed up redraw and printing by choosing File > Document Setup and unchecking the "View: Preview and print patterns" box. Remember to re-check this option before printing.

*1) Click the **Fill** box.* *2) Click the **Pattern** color selection method icon.*

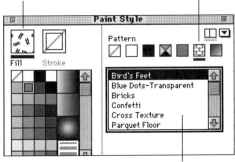

*3) Click a **pattern name**.*

Figure 1. *The **Paint Style** palette.*

Fill with a Pattern

Figure 2a.
Congo Stripes.
(All Adobe patterns.)

Figure 2b.
Haida arrows.

Figure 2c.
Mali.

Figure 3. *Draw objects for the pattern. Simple shapes are least likely to cause printing errors.*

Figure 4. *Draw a bounding rectangle around the objects, then send the rectangle to the back.*

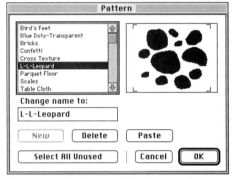

Figure 5. *In the* **Pattern** *dialog box, click* **New**, *then enter a name in the* **Change name to** *field.*

Figure 6. *Our L-L-Leopard pattern Fill.*

To create a pattern:

1. Draw an object or objects to be used as the pattern (**Figure 3**).

2. Choose the Rectangle tool.

3. Draw a half-inch to one-inch square around the objects. Fit the square closely around the objects if you don't want an empty border to be part of the pattern (**Figure 4**). If the pattern is complex, make the rectangle small (about a half inch square) to facilitate printing.

4. Choose Edit > Send to Back. The bounding rectangle must be behind the pattern objects.

5. Apply a Fill and Stroke of None to the rectangle.
   or
   Apply a Fill color to be the background color in the pattern.

6. Choose the Selection tool.

7. Position the cursor outside all the objects, then press and drag diagonally across them.

8. Choose Object > Pattern.

9. Click New. The pattern tile will preview in the dialog box (**Figure 5**).

10. Enter a name in the "Change name to" field.

11. Click OK (**Figure 6**). The pattern will save with your document.

■ A pattern can't contain a mask, an object filled with a pattern, or a gradient.

■ Simple shapes are least likely to cause printing errors.

■ To reposition the pattern within the object, deselect then reselect the object with the Selection tool, then hold down "P" and press and drag inside the object.

Create a Pattern

You can create a geometric pattern by arranging straight-sided objects around a common center point.

To create a geometric pattern:

1. Create a geometric object (**Figure 7**). Use the Polygon, Spiral, or Star tool to create an object easily, if you wish *(see pages 54–59)*.

2. Choose a selection tool.

3. Hold down Option and press and drag a copy of the object so it abuts the original. Hold down Shift while dragging to constrain the movement horizontally or vertically.

4. Repeat step 3 with other objects to create a symmetrical arrangement (**Figure 8**).

5. *Optional:* Apply different Fill colors to add variety to the pattern.

6. Choose the Rectangle tool.

7. Press and drag a rectangle around the objects. Make sure the symmetry is preserved (**Figure 9**).

8. Follow steps 4–11 on page 121. (**Figure 10**)

■ You can use the Crop filter to see exactly what the pattern tile will look like *(see page 215)*.

■ To create a pattern that repeats seamlessly, follow the instructions in the Illustrator User Guide.

Figure 7. *Draw a geometric object.*

Figure 8. *Copy the object and arrange the copies symmetrically.*

Figure 9. *Draw a bounding rectangle around the objects, then send the rectangle to the back. In order to produce a perfect repetitive pattern Fill, the rectangle is aligned with the midpoints and edges of the geometric shapes.*

Figure 10. *A geometric pattern Fill.*

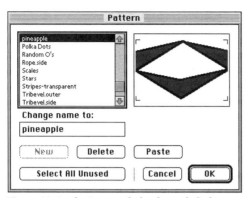

Figure 11. *In the* **Pattern** *dialog box, click the name of the pattern you want to modify, then click* **Paste**.

Figure 12. *A line is added to the pasted pattern.*

Figure 13. *The modified pattern.*

You can modify any pattern, including those supplied with Illustrator. To change an existing pattern, first it must be pasted back into a document. Objects already filled with the pattern in any open documents will be updated automatically.

To modify a pattern:

1. Display a blank area in your document window, then choose Object > Pattern.

2. Click on the name of the pattern you want to modify (**Figure 11**).

3. Click Paste.

4. Click OK. The pattern will be pasted into the center of the document window, and will be selected.

5. Modify the pattern objects (**Figure 12**).

6. Choose the Selection tool.

7. Position the pointer outside all the objects, then press and drag a selection marquee over the bounding rectangle and objects.

8. Choose Object > Pattern.

9. To save over the original pattern, click on its name, then click OK (**Figure 13**).
   or
   To save the modified pattern as a new pattern, click New, enter a name, then click OK.

■ To create a variation of a pattern and preserve the original, follow steps 1–8 above, click New, enter a new name in the "Change name to" field, then click OK.

■ To delete a pattern, click on its name, then click Delete. Objects filled with the pattern will be filled with Black, and the pattern will be deleted from all currently open files in which it was used. (To retrieve a deleted pattern after clicking OK in the Pattern dialog box, choose Edit > Undo.)

Modify a Pattern

123

Path Patterns

The Path Pattern filter renders patterns along the edge of a closed or open path, and can be used to create custom frames, borders, or other decorative shapes. You can use up to three diferent-shaped tile pieces when you create a path pattern — a Side tile, an Outer Corner tile and an Inner Corner tile — which will adapt to fit on the straight segment, curve, or corner part of the path contour. You can design your own tiles or use the pattern tiles that are supplied with Illustrator. **Path pattern objects can be modified, even after they're applied to a path.**

To place a pattern along the edge of a path:

1. Select the object to which you'd like to apply the pattern.

2. Apply a Fill of None and a Stroke color or Stroke of None. You can recolor the object after applying the pattern.

3. Choose Filter > Stylize > Path Pattern.

4. Click the Sides icon (**Figure 14**).

5. Choose a pattern name from the scroll list. For a round object, proceed to step 10. (See our tip regarding accessing pattern files and libraries.)

6. Click the Outer Corner icon.

7. Choose the same pattern name again or choose a different pattern name from the scroll list. Choose None from the list if you don't want the pattern to appear on the corners of the path.

8. Click the Inner Corner icon.

9. Choose the same pattern name again or choose a different pattern name from the scroll list.

10. *Optional:* Enter a new number in the Tile size: Width or Height field to change the size of the pattern tile. The opposite dimension box will adjust automatically.

Diane Margolin

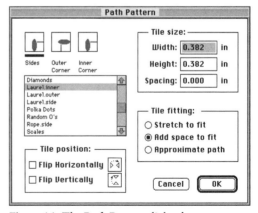

Figure 14. *The Path Pattern dialog box.*

Figure 15. *To create this pattern, Diane Margolin turned on the "Stretch to fit" option, and used Side, Outer Corner, and Inner Corner tile shapes.*

Diane Margolin

11. *Optional:* To add blank space between pattern tiles, enter an amount in the Tile size: Spacing field.

12. To adjust how the pattern tiles fit on the path, click "Stretch to fit" to have Illustrator to lengthen the tiles, where necessary, to fit on the path.
or
Click "Add space to fit" to have Illustrator add blank space between tiles, where necessary, to fit the pattern along the path, factoring in the Tile size: Spacing amount, if one was entered. Choose this option if you want the original path's Stroke color (or subsequently applied Fill color) to show through blank spaces in the pattern.
or
For a rectangular path, you can click "Approximate path" to have the pattern tiles be applied evenly inside or outside the path.

13. *Optional:* To flip the pattern, check the Flip Horizontally and/or Flip Vertically box. This may not work for all pattern tiles.

14. Click OK or press Return. The path pattern will appear on top of the original path, and will be separate from that path. You can recolor the original path, though in order to select it you may have to move the path pattern or send it to the back.

■ If you open a file that contains patterns that are not in your current file, they will appear on both the current document's pattern list in the Path Pattern dialog box and on the Paint Style palette. A folder of path patterns is supplied with Illustrator. You'll find it in the Sample Files folder.

To manually resize selective path pattern tiles:

1. Follow steps 1–14 on the previous two pages.
2. With the path pattern selected, choose Arrange > Ungroup.
3. Deselect the path pattern.
4. Select any tile on the path.
5. Double-click the Scale tool, enter % values for the new tile size, then click OK.
6. Repeat step 5 for any other tiles you want to resize.
7. Choose the Selection tool.
8. Reselect the whole path pattern.
9. Choose Arrange > Group.

A

B

You can create your own pattern tiles for the Path Pattern filter by creating shapes and then placing them on the pattern list using the Pattern dialog box. You can also use any already applied path pattern as a starting point for a new pattern tile.

To create pattern tiles to use with the Path Pattern filter:

1. Draw shapes for the side pattern tile.

Because the Path Pattern filter places side tiles perpendicular to the path, you should rotate any design that is taller than it is wider by following these steps:

2. Choose the Selection tool, then select the shapes.
3. Double-click the Rotate tool.
4. Enter 90 in the Angle box, then click OK.
5. Draw separate shapes for the corner tiles, if necessary, to finish the design.

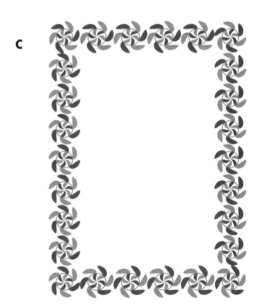

C

Figure 16. *A path pattern tile was applied to a circle (**A**). The width & height values were scaled to the diameter of the circle (**B**). And then the resulting circle path pattern was selected, made into a pattern tile, and applied via the Path Pattern filter to a rectangular path (**C**).*

Path Patterns

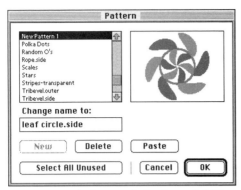

Figure 17. *In the* **Pattern** *dialog box, click* **New** *and enter a name in the* **Change name to** *field. Include the word "side" or "outer" to identify the pattern's function.*

6. Choose the Selection tool, then select the side tile shapes.

7. Choose Object > Pattern.

8. Click New (**Figure 17**). The side tile shapes will display in the preview box.

9. Enter a name in the "Change name to" field. For clarity, type "side" after the name.

10. Click OK or press Return.

11 Repeat steps 6 through 9 for the corner tile shapes. You can type "outer" after the corner tile name.

12. Follow the steps on pages 124–125 to apply the new tiles to a path.

■ You don't need to use a bounding rectangle behind the shapes when you create path pattern tiles — unlike Fill pattern tiles. You can include a rectangle with Fill and/or Stroke colors as part of the tile, but it won't act as a cropping device.

■ Non-square corner tiles will be rotated 90° for each corner of the path, starting from the upper left corner.

■ Try to limit your tiles to about an inch wide — two inches at the most — and resize them if you need to using the Path Pattern dialog box.

■ Use custom colors for Fill and Stroke colors in the tile shapes, and name them appropriately so they can be readily associated with the tile. The tiles can then be recolored quickly by changing the custom colors. You can also use the Adjust Color filter to adjust colors on the applied path pattern.

■ Try applying the Roughen filter with low settings to make geometric shapes look more hand drawn.

Path Patterns

Path Patterns

Have you created something unusual or
beautiful using the Path Pattern filter? We'd
like to see it, and we'd also like to know
how you did it. Send us a laser print at the
address listed at the bottom of page 263.

IMAGES

Nancy Stahl, **Flying Hats**

Nancy Stahl, **Cable Man**

IMAGES

Michael Bartalos, for Mohawk Paper Mills, Inc.

Michael Bartalos, **Tropical Beat***, CD gift box design for Koolwraps*

Michael Bartalos, **Jazzmatazz***, CD gift box design for Koolwraps*

John Hersey, **Cross Swatchbook Cover**

John Hersey, **Dazed**,
T-shirt for Fisher Bicycles

Chris Spollen, **Internet Theft**

John Hersey, illustration for Walldata Corporation

Chris Spollen, **Message from Cyberspace**

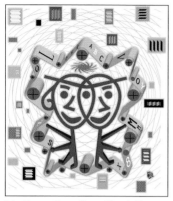

John Hersey, **Cross Swatchbook Cover**

John Hersey, **Dazed**,
T-shirt for Fisher Bicycles

Chris Spollen, **Internet Theft**

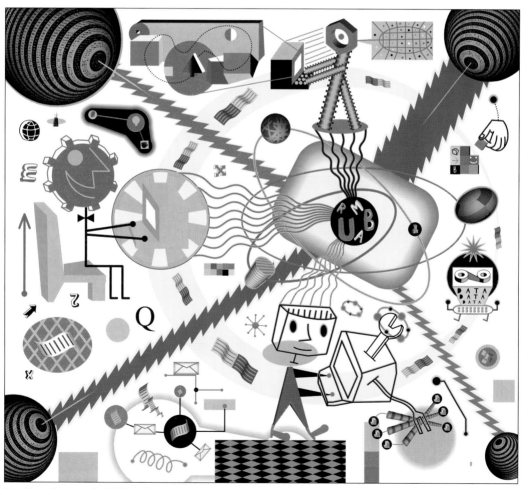

John Hersey, illustration for Walldata Corporation

Chris Spollen, **Message from Cyberspace**

Figure 18. *Choose* **Expand** *from the Object menu.*

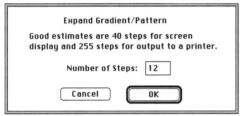

Figure 19. *The Expand dialog box. The **Number of Steps** determines how many individual objects will be created from a gradient Fill only.*

To divide a gradient or pattern Fill into individual objects:

1. Select an object that contains a gradient or pattern Fill.

2. Choose Object > Expand (**Figure 18**).

3. If you're expanding a gradient Fill, enter the desired number of steps (**Figure 19**). A pattern Fill will be divided into the original pattern shapes within the original tiles, not according to the Number of Steps.

4. Click OK or press Return (**Figure 20**). The former gradient or pattern Fill is now a series of separate objects inside a mask. You can now release the mask, alter the mask shape, or just delete the mask altogether.

■ If you want to apply the Transform Each command with its Random option to an expanded pattern (**Figure 21**), first choose Objects > Mask > Release.

Expand a Gradient or a Pattern

Figure 20. *The original pattern.*

A detail of the pattern expanded (Artwork view).

Diane Margolin

Figure 21. *After applying the Expand command, releasing the mask, and applying the Transform Each command (moved .3" horizontally and -.3" vertically, rotated 17°, Random).*

Printing and Transforming Patterns

About printing patterns

For a pattern to preview and print, the "Preview and print patterns" box must be checked in the Document Setup dialog box (File menu). Patterns can slow down screen redraw and printing, though, so uncheck this option when you don't need to preview or print your patterns.

If a document containing a pattern fails to print altogether, try printing it with the Preview and print patterns box unchecked to see if the pattern is the culprit. If it is, try simplifying the pattern or grouping or uniting objects of the same color within the pattern. A document containing multiple patterns may be particularly problematic.

Patterns and the transformation tools

If you transform (Rotate, Scale, Reflect, Shear, or Blend) an object that contains a pattern Fill, you can selectively transform the pattern when you transform the object by checking the Pattern tiles box in the transformation tool's dialog box (**Figures 22–23c**) or always transform by checking the "Transform pattern tiles" box in the General Preferences dialog box (File menu). Path patterns automatically transform.

To transform the pattern but not the object, uncheck the Objects box in the transformation tool's dialog box. Or, choose the transformation tool, click to establish a point of origin, then hold down "P" and press and drag.

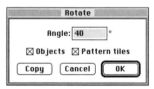

Figure 22. *Check or uncheck the* **Pattern tiles** *box in any transformation tool dialog box.*

Figure 23a. *The original pattern.*

Figure 23b. *The pattern rotated without rotating the object.*

Figure 23c. *The object and pattern sheared.*

LAYERS 12

Each new object you draw in an illustration is automatically positioned on top of the previous object. This positioning is called the stacking order (Figure 1). By default, all new objects are stacked on a single layer. Using the Layers palette, you can add new layers to an illustration, each of which can contain a stack of objects. You can change the stacking order of objects within a layer, and you can reorder whole layers. You can also group objects together so they can be moved as a unit. If you place objects on separate layers, you can selectively display, edit, and print them.

In this chapter you will learn to group and ungroup objects and to restack objects. Using the Layers palette, you will learn to create and reorder layers, move an object to a different layer, hide/show, lock/unlock, and print individual layers, and delete layers.

Figure 1. *Imagine your illustration is built on transparent modular shelves. You can rearrange (restack) objects on an individual shelf (layer), move an object to a different shelf, or rearrange the order of the shelves (layers).*

If you group objects together, you can easily select, cut, copy, paste, transform, recolor, or move them as a unit. When you group objects, they are automatically placed on the same layer (the layer of the frontmost object in the group). You can then apply Layers palette hide/show, lock/unlock, preview, and print options to the whole group.

To group objects:

1. Choose the Selection tool.
2. Hold down Shift and click on each of the objects to be grouped (**Figures 2a–b**).
   or
   Position the pointer outside all the objects, then press and drag a marquee diagonally across them.
3. Choose Arrange > Group (⌘-G) (**Figure 3**).

To ungroup objects:

1. Choose the Selection tool.
2. Click on a group.
3. Choose Arrange > Ungroup (⌘-U).

Figure 2a. *An object is selected.*

Figure 2b. *Additional objects are selected with Shift held down.*

Arrange	
Repeat Transform	⌘D
Move...	⌘⇧M
Bring To Front	⌘=
Send To Back	⌘-
Transform Each...	
Group	⌘G
Ungroup	⌘U
Lock	⌘1
Unlock All	⌘2
Hide	⌘3
Show All	⌘4

Figure 3. *Choose **Group** from the **Arrange** menu.*

Group; Ungroup

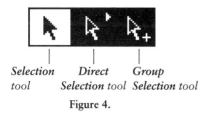

Selection tool   *Direct Selection tool*   *Group Selection tool*

Figure 4.

To select grouped objects:

To select an entire group, click on any item in the group with the **Selection** tool (**Figure 4**).

or

To select individual anchor points or segments of an object within a group, use the **Direct Selection** tool.

or

To select multiple groups within a larger group in the order in which they were added to the group, use the **Group Selection** tool. Click once to select an object in a group (**Figure 5a**); click again on the same object to select the group that object is part of (**Figure 5b**); click again on the object to select the next larger group the first group is part of (**Figure 5c**), etc.

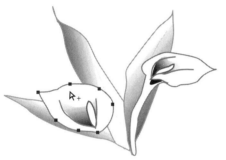

Figure 5a. *Click once with the **Group Selection** tool to select an individual object.*

Figure 5b. *Click a second time with the **Group Selection** tool to select the group that object is a member of.*

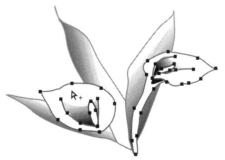

Figure 5c. *Click a third time with the **Group Selection** tool to select the next larger group the first group is a part of.*

Select Grouped Objects

133

Use the Bring To Front or Send To Back command to move an object or a group to the front or the back of its stack within its layer.

To place an object on the bottom of its stack:

1. Choose the Selection tool (**Figure 4**).

2. Click on the object or group.

3. Choose Arrange > Send To Back (⌘--) (**Figures 6–7b**).

■ If you select only a portion of a path (a point or a segment), and change its stacking position, the entire object will move.

Figure 6. *Choose Send To Back from the Arrange menu.*

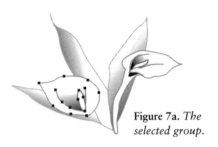

Figure 7a. *The selected group.*

Figure 7b. *After applying the Send To Back command.*

To place an object on the top of its stack:

1. Choose the Selection tool.

2. Click on the object or group.

3. Choose Arrange > Bring To Front (⌘-+) (**Figure 8**). The selected object or group will be placed on the top of its stack within the same layer.

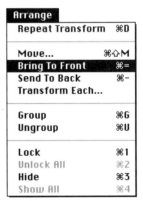

Figure 8. *Choose Bring To Front from the Arrange menu.*

Restack an Object

Figure 9. *The dark gray object was selected and then placed on the Clipboard via the Cut command.*

Edit	
Undo Move	⌘Z
Redo	⌘⇧Z
Cut	⌘X
Copy	⌘C
Paste	⌘V
Clear	
Select All	⌘A
Select None	⌘⇧A
Paste In Front	**⌘F**
Paste In Back	⌘B
Publishing	▶
Show Clipboard	

Figure 10. *Choose* **Paste In Front** *or* **Paste In Back** *from the* **Edit** *menu.*

Figure 11. *The inner flower shape is selected. Paste In Back (Edit menu) is chosen to place the gray object behind the inner flower shape.*

The Paste In Front and Paste In Back commands paste the Clipboard contents just in front of or just behind the currently selected object within the selected object's layer, in the same horizontal and vertical position from which they were cut.

To restack an object in front of or behind another object:

1. Choose the Selection tool.
2. Click on an object (**Figure 9**).
3. Choose Edit > Cut (⌘-X) to place the object on the Clipboard.
4. Click on an object that you wish to paste just in front of or just behind.
5. Choose Edit > Paste In Front (⌘-F).
   or
   Choose Edit > Paste In Back (⌘-B) (**Figures 10–11**).

■ To restack part of an object, use the Direct Selection tool to select the part before choosing Cut.

■ If no object is selected when you choose Paste In Front or Paste In Back, the object on the Clipboard will paste on the top or bottom, respectively, of the stack within the currently active layer (the highlighted layer on the Layers palette).

■ You can use the Paste In Front and Paste In Back commands to stack type outlines. For example, you can copy and Paste in Back a type outline with a Stroke color and a Fill of None, and then apply a wider Stroke of a different color to the copy.

■ If you Paste In Front of or Paste In Back of an object in a group, the pasted object will be added to the group.

Restack an Object

Create a Layer; Reorder Layers

To open or close the layers palette ——
Choose Window > Show Layers (⌘-Control-L).

To activate an individual layer to work on, simply click its name on the Layers palette. You can also reorder layers and lock, hide, or print individual layers. **Any new object you create will be placed on the currently selected layer.**

Figure 12. *Choose* **New Layer** *from the* **Layers** *palette pop-up menu.*

To create a new layer:
1. Choose New Layer from the Layers palette command menu (**Figure 12**).
2. Enter a name for the new layer (**Figure 13**).
3. *Optional:* Choose a different selection color for items on that layer from the Selection color pop-up menu.
4. *Optional:* Choose other layer options (see page 118).
5. Click OK or press Return.

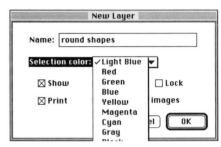

Figure 13. *In the* **New Layer** *dialog box, enter a* **Name** *and choose a* **Selection color.**

- ◼ To insert the new layer directly above the currently highlighted layer, hold down Option when you choose New Layer from the palette command menu.

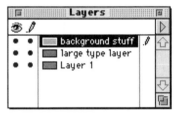

Figure 14a. *Press and drag a layer name up or down.*

The order of names on the Layers palette matches the front-to-back order of layers in the illustration.

To reorder layers:
Press and drag a layer name up or down (the pointer will turn into a fist icon). Release the mouse when the small arrowhead points to the desired position (**Figures 14a–c**). The illustration will redraw.

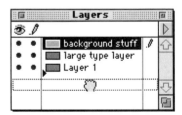

Figure 14b. *Release the mouse when the arrowhead points to the desired position.*

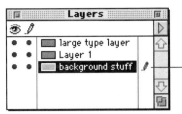

The tiny colored square indicates which layer the currently selected object is on.

Figure 14c. *The newly moved layer is now on the bottom, and objects on that layer are now in the back of the illustration.*

Figure 15. *The topmost leaf is selected.*

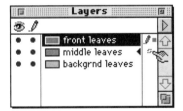

Figure 16. *Move the little square for the selected object. Release the mouse when the arrowhead points to the desired layer name.*

Figure 17. *The object is on a different layer.*

You can move an object to a different layer using just the Layers palette (method 1) or using the Clipboard and the Layers palette (method 2).

To move an object to a different layer (method 1):

1. Choose any selection tool, then click on the object or group you want to move (**Figure 15**). The object's current layer will be highlighted on the Layers palette.

2. Drag the tiny colored square next to the highlighted layer name up or down (the pointer will turn into a pointing hand icon) (**Figure 16**), then release the mouse when the arrowhead points to the name of the layer you want to move the object to. The illustration will redraw with the object in the new layer (**Figure 17**).

To move an object to a different layer (method 2):

1. Choose the Selection tool, then click on the object you wish to move.

2. Choose Edit > Cut.

3. Click on the name of the layer on the Layers palette that you want to move the object to.
   or
   Select an object on the target layer.

4. Choose Edit > Paste. The object will be placed at the top of the stack within the layer you highlighted.
   or
   If an object is selected, choose Edit > Paste in Front or Edit > Paste in Back to paste the object directly in front of or behind the selected object.

■ If the object moves to the top of its stack rather than to a different layer, choose Paste Remembers Layers from the Layers palette command menu to uncheck this option. Paste Remembers Layers can also be turned on or off in the General Preferences dialog box.

The following options affect all the objects on the currently selected layer.

To choose other layer options:

1. Double-click a layer name on the Layers palette.
   or
   Click on a layer name on the Layers palette, then choose "Layer Options for "[layer name]" from the Layers palette command menu.

2. Check **Show** to display the layer; uncheck to hide it (**Figure 18**).

   Check **Preview** to display the layer in Preview view; uncheck to display the layer in Artwork view.

   Check **Lock** to prevent all the objects on that layer from being selected; uncheck to allow objects to be selected.

   Check to **Print;** uncheck to prevent all the objects on that layer from printing.

   Check **Dim placed images** to dim any placed EPS images on that layer (use for tracing); uncheck to display placed images normally.

■ You can use the Layers palette to show/hide or lock/unlock all the objects on an individual layer. To quickly hide or lock one item at a time, you can choose Arrange > Hide or Arrange > Lock. However, you cannot unlock or show individual items using the Arrange menu; choosing Unlock All or Show All will affect all locked or hidden objects in the illustration.

   Choosing the Layers palette option will not affect the status of the menu command, and vice versa. For example, choosing Lock from the Arrange menu will not cause the Lock option box in the Layers Option dialog box to be checked.

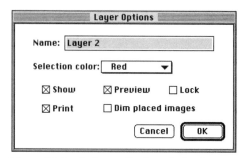

Figure 18. *In the Layer Options dialog box, check the* **Show, Preview, Lock, Print,** *or* **Dim placed images** *boxes on or off.*

CREATE TYPE

In this chapter you will learn how to create type on its own, inside an object, and on a path. You'll also learn how to import type from another application, how to link type, how to copy type or a type object, and how to convert type into graphic outlines. Typographic attributes are modified using the Character and Paragraph palettes, which are covered in Chapter 14, along with methods for selecting type.

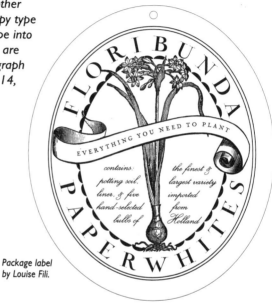

*Package label
by Louise Fili.*

The Type Tools

There are three type tools — the Type tool, the Area Type tool, and the Path Type tool — and they produce different kinds of type objects.

The **Type** tool creates blocks of type consisting of one line or several lines. You can create a free-floating block of type with the Type tool that is not associated with an object, called **point** type; you can draw a rectangle with it, then enter text inside the rectangle; and you can use the Type tool to enter type on the outside edge of an open path or inside a closed path.

The **Area Type** tool is used to create type inside an open or closed path. Lines of type created with the Area Type tool automatically wrap inside the object.

The **Path Type** tool is used to enter a line of type on the outside edge of an open or closed path.

You can also convert a type object into **outlines.** Outline "characters" look like letters, but they have anchor points and segments and they function like graphic objects. You can use this feature to design your own characters or logos.

A few things you should know about fonts

- Make sure Adobe Type Manager (ATM), the utility that smooths font rendering, is installed and is turned on before you launch Illustrator (Figure 1). See the Illustrator Getting Started guide for more information about ATM.

- To convert type into outlines, the screen and printer fonts for the font you are using and Adobe Type Manager must be installed in the system.

- If you open a document containing type styled in a font whose suitcase is closed or not available, the font will not display on screen. If you open a font suitcase using a utility, such as Suitcase, after launching Illustrator, the font will reappear on Illustrator's font list and the type should display correctly. If it doesn't, choose View > Artwork and then choose View > Preview to force the screen to redraw.

If you like to choose character and paragraph attributes before you create type, use the Character and Paragraph palettes. They're discussed on pages 154–162.

Figure 1. *ATM on...*

...and ATM off: jaggies!

Point type is type that stands by itself — it isn't inside an object or along a path.

To create point type:

1. Choose the Type tool (**Figure 2**).
2. Click on a blank area of the Artboard where you wish the type to start. A flashing insertion marker will appear.
3. Enter type. Press Return when you want to start a new line (**Figure 3**).
4. Choose a selection tool and click away from the type block to deselect it.
   or
   Click the Type tool again to complete the block of type and start a new one.

Figure 2. *Type tool.*

'It spoils people's clothes to squeeze under a gate; the proper way to get in, is to climb down a pear tree.'
– Beatrix Potter

Figure 3. *Type created using the Type tool.*

TYPE OBJECTS VS. GRAPHIC OBJECTS —

- When type is entered inside an object or on a path, the object is Filled and Stroked with None. You can reapply Fill and/or Stroke colors to the object if you select it first with the Direct Selection tool.

- Once you place type on or inside a graphic object, it becomes a type object, and it cannot be converted back into a graphic object. To preserve the original graphic object, make a copy of it and convert the copy into a type path.

- You can't enter type into a compound path or a mask object, and you cannot make a mask or compound path out of a text object.

'It spoils people's clothes to squeeze under a gate; the proper way to get in, is to climb down a pear tree.'

*Figure 4. Press and drag with the **Type** tool to create a rectangle, then enter type. The edges of the rectangle will be visible in **Artwork** view.*

'It spoils people's clothes to squeeze under a gate; the proper way to get in, is to climb down a pear tree.'

*Figure 5. The type rectangle reshaped using the **Direct Selection** tool. The edges of the rectangle will be hidden in **Preview** view.*

To create a type rectangle:

1. Choose the Type tool (**Figure 2**).

2. Press and drag to create a rectangle. When you release the mouse, a flashing insertion marker will appear in the upper left corner of the rectangle.

3. Enter type. Press Return when you need to create a new paragraph. The type will automatically conform to the rectangle (**Figure 4**).

4. Choose a selection tool and click away from the type block to deselect it.
   or
   Click the Type tool again to complete the type object and start a new one.

- If your illustration is in Artwork view, the edges of the rectangle will be displayed as you enter type. If your illustration is in Preview view, the type rectangle will only be displayed if you select it.

- You can reshape a type rectangle using the Direct Selection tool. The type will reflow to fit the new shape (**Figure 5**).

- To turn an object created with the Rectangle tool into a type rectangle, click on the edge of the path with the Type tool or the Area Type tool, then enter text.

You can import text into a type rectangle or any other type shape from another application, such as Microsoft Word, WordPerfect or MacWrite.

To import type into an object:

1. Choose the Type tool (**Figure 6**), then press and drag to create a type rectangle.
   or
   Choose the Area Type tool (**Figure 7**), then click on the edge of a graphic object to create a flashing insertion marker (**Figure 8**).

2. Choose File > Import Text.

3. Highlight the name of the text file you want to import (**Figure 9**).

4. Click Import. The text file will flow into the object (**Figure 10**).

■ If you click with the Type tool to create an insertion point rather than press and drag to create a rectangle, each paragraph of the imported text will appear on a separate, single line, and it may be difficult to work with.

■ If fewer than nine file formats are listed on the Show pop-up menu in the Import Text dialog box, do a Custom installation from the Illustrator Installer disk. Select the Claris Translators and the Claris XTND System files.

Import Type

If you create and style text in a layout program and then save the file in Acrobat **PDF** format, you can then open the PDF file using Illustrator's Open command and use it as you would any text in Illustrator. Illustrator will create a new point-text block everywhere a style change occurred in the original text.

Figure 6.
Type tool.

Figure 7.
Area Type tool.

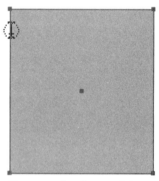
Figure 8. *The object will lose its Fill and Stroke colors as soon as you click on its edge with the Area Type tool.*

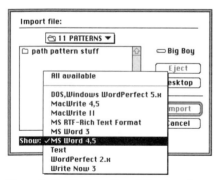
Figure 9. *To display a list of files in only one format, choose that format from the Show pop-up menu.*

Here was peace. She pulled in her horizon like a great fishnet. Pulled it from around the waist of the world and draped it over her shoulder.

Figure 10. *Text appears in the object.*

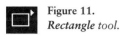

Figure 11.
Rectangle tool.

Here was peace. She pulled in her horizon like a great fish-net. Pulled it from around the waist of the world and draped it over

Figure 12. *The overflow symbol.*

Create a new rectangle.

Figure 13. *Choose* **Link Blocks** *from the Type menu.*

Here was peace. She pulled in her horizon like a great fish-net. Pulled it from around the waist of the world and draped it over

her shoulder. So much of life in its meshes! She called in her soul to come and see.

Figure 14. *Type flows from the first object into the second object.*

If a type rectangle isn't large enough to display all the type inside it, you can enlarge the type rectangle, of course (use the Direct Selection tool with Shift held down), or you can flow the hidden overflow type into a new object. Follow the instructions on this page to flow type into a standard rectangle. Follow the instructions on the next page to flow type into a copy of a non-standard type object.

To link overflow type to a rectangle:

1. Choose the Rectangle tool (**Figure 11**).

2. Press and drag diagonally to create a new rectangle (**Figure 12**).

3. Choose the Selection tool.

4. Hold down Shift and click on both rectangles.
   or
   Drag a marquee across both rectangles.

5. Choose Type > Link Blocks (⌘-Shift-G) (**Figure 13**). Overflow type from the first rectangle will flow into the new rectangle (**Figure 14**).

■ To unlink type objects, choose the Selection tool, click on one of the objects (all the linked objects will be selected), then choose Type > Unlink Blocks (⌘-Shift-U). Each block of type will now be in a separate object.

■ To remove one type object from a series of linked objects, choose the Group Selection tool or the Direct Selection tool, click on the edge of the object to be removed (the type shouldn't be underlined), then press Delete. The type will reflow into the remaining objects.

Link Type

To link overflow type to a copy of an existing object:

1. Choose View > Artwork (⌘-E).

2. Choose the Direct Selection tool (**Figure 15**).

3. Click away from the type object to deselect it.

4. Click on the edge of the type object. The type should not be underlined after you click.

5. Hold down Option and drag a copy of the type object away from the original object. To constrain the movement to a horizontal or vertical axis, hold down Option and Shift while dragging.

6. Release the mouse, then release Option (and Shift, if used). The over-flow type will appear inside the new object (**Figure 16**).

7. *Optional:* Choose Arrange > Repeat Transform (⌘-D) to create additional linked boxes.

■ If both the type and the type object are selected when you drag, a copy of the object will be created, but it will not be linked to the first object.

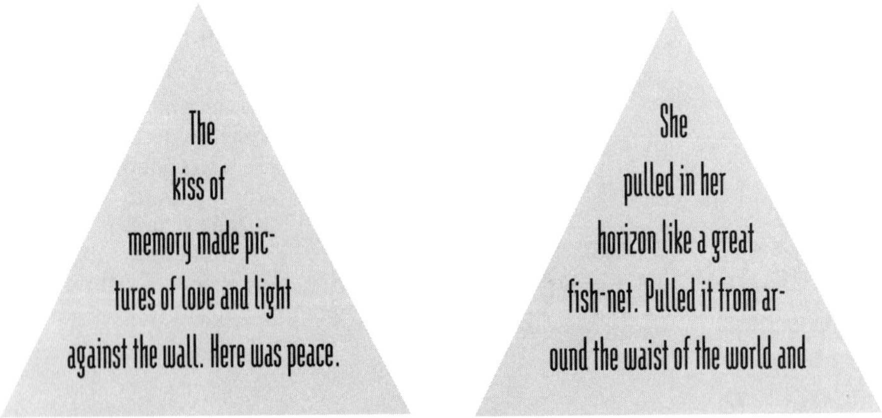

Figure 15. *Direct Selection tool.*

Link Type

The kiss of memory made pic-tures of love and light against the wall. Here was peace.

She pulled in her horizon like a great fish-net. Pulled it from ar-ound the waist of the world and

Figure 16. *Overflow type from the first object appears in a copy of the object. (A Paragraph indent was applied to the type to move it away from the edge of the objects.)*

Use the **Area Type** tool to place type inside a rectangle, an irregularly shaped object, or an open path. The object you use will turn into a type path. You must click precisely on the edge of an object in order to enter type inside it.

To enter type inside an object:

1. Choose the Type tool, or choose the Area Type tool if the object is a filled, open path.

2. Click on the edge of an object. A flashing insertion marker will appear.

3. Enter type. It will wrap inside the object (**Figures 17–18**).

4. Choose a selection tool and click away from the type object to deselect it.
   or
   Click the Area Type tool again to complete the type object and start a new one.

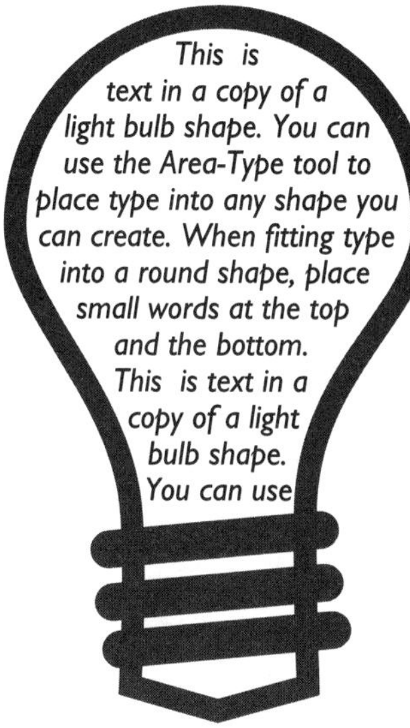

This is text in a copy of a light bulb shape. You can use the Area-Type tool to place type into any shape you can create. When fitting type into a round shape, place small words at the top and the bottom. This is text in a copy of a light bulb shape. You can use

Figure 17. *Area type.*

The kiss of memory made pictures of love and light against the wall. Here was peace. She pulled in her horizon like a great fish-net. Pulled it from around the waist of the world and draped it over her shoulder. So much of life in its meshes! She called in her soul to come and see.
ZORA NEALE HURSTON

Figure 18. *Type in a circle.*

Use the **Path Type** tool to place type on the inside or outside edge of an object. Type cannot be positioned on both sides of a path, but it can be moved from one side to the other after it is created *(see the next set of instructions)*. Only one line of type can be created per path.

To place type on an object's path:

1. Choose the Path Type tool (**Figure 19**).
2. Click on the top or bottom edge of an object. A flashing insertion marker will appear.
3. Enter type. Do not press Return. The type will appear along the edge of the object (**Figures 20a–b**), and the object's Fill and Stroke will revert to None.
4. Choose a selection tool and click away from the type object to deselect it.
   or
   Click the Path Type tool again to complete the type object and start a new one.

To reposition path type:

1. Choose the Selection tool.
2. Click on the path type object.
3. Press and drag the I-beam marker left or right along the edge of the object, move it inside the path, or move it around to the other side of the path.

■ To shift the characters slightly upward or downward on the same side of the path, choose the Type tool, highlight the type, then enter a higher or lower number in the Baseline shift field on the extended Character palette (**Figure 21**).

Figure 19.
Path Type tool.

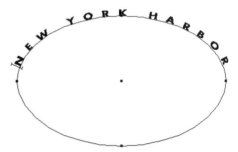

Figure 20a. *Type entered on the edge of an oval.*

Figure 20b. *Path type.*

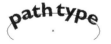 

Figure 21. *Path type —*   *Path type — baseline*
default baseline position. *shifted downward.*

Peter Fahrni

To move or copy type with or without its object, use the Clipboard, a temporary storage area in memory. The Clipboard commands are Cut, Copy, and Paste. *Note:* If you are using System 7.5 or later, you can use the drag-and-drop method to move a type object (see page 69).

To copy a type object from one document to another:

1. Choose the Selection tool.
2. Click on the edge of the object or the baseline of the type.
3. Choose Edit > Copy (⌘-C) (**Figure 22**).
4. Click in another document window.
5. Choose Edit > Paste (⌘-V). The type object will reappear.

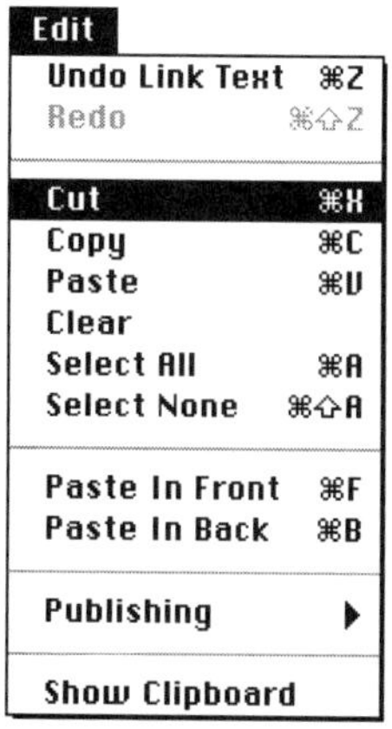

Edit

Undo Link Text	⌘Z
Redo	⌘⇧Z
Cut	⌘H
Copy	⌘C
Paste	⌘U
Clear	
Select All	⌘A
Select None	⌘⇧A
Paste In Front	⌘F
Paste In Back	⌘B
Publishing	▶
Show Clipboard	

Figure 22. *Choose* **Cut** *or* **Copy** *from the* **Edit** *menu, then later choose* **Paste.**

To move type from one type object to another:

1. Choose the Type tool.
2. Highlight the type.
3. Choose Edit > Cut (⌘-X) (**Figure 22**).
4. In the other type object, click to create a flashing insertion marker where you wish the type to reappear (as point type or in another line of type).
5. Choose Edit > Paste (⌘-V).

The **Create Outlines** command converts type into graphic objects. As outlines, the "characters" can be reshaped, transformed, used in a compound or a mask, or filled with a gradient or pattern. Once type is converted into outlines, it can't be converted back into type again and its typeface can't be changed. One great advantage of converting type into outlines is that if you import them into another application, like QuarkXPress, you won't need the printer fonts for the "characters" to print properly.

To create type outlines:

1. Create type using any type tool.

2. Choose the Selection tool.

3. If the type isn't already selected, click on the "x" or on the object's edge.

4. Choose Type > Create Outlines (**Figures 23–24b**). All the characters in the type object or on the path will be converted into outlines. The characters' original Paint Style attributes will be preserved.

■ To create outlines, the Type 1 font (screen font and printer outlines) or TrueType font for the typeface you are using must be installed in your system.

■ Group multiple outline "characters" together using the Group command so they're easier to select and move.

■ If the original character had an interior counter — like in an "A" or a "P" — the character parts will become a compound path after converting to outlines. Choose Object > Compound Paths > Release if you want to divide the inside and outside parts of the type outline into separate objects. To reassemble the two pieces, select them both, then choose Object > Compound Paths > Make *(see Figures 8a–b on page 193).*

Figure 23. *The original type.*

Figure 24a. *Type converted into* **outlines** *(Artwork view).*

Figure 24b. *Type converted into* **outlines** *(Preview view).*

Create Type Outlines

In this chapter you will learn how to select type, how to apply character-based typographical attributes (font, size, leading, baseline shift, tracking, and horizontal scale) using the Character palette, and how to apply paragraph-based attributes (alignment, indentation, and inter-paragraph spacing) using the Paragraph palette. You'll also learn to use Illustrator's word processing features to change case, check spelling, export text, find and replace fonts or text, create columns and rows, apply professional typesetter's marks, auto hyphenate, and apply tabs.

Before you can modify type, you must select it. If you use the **Selection tool**, both the type and its object will be selected (**Figure 1**). If you use the **Direct Selection tool**, you can select just the type object or the type object and the type (**Figure 2**). If you use **a type tool**, only the type itself will be selected, not the type object (**Figure 3**).

If you select point type (not on or inside a type object) with the Selection or Direct Selection tool, the block will have a solid anchor point before the first character and every line of type will be underlined.

If we
shadows
have
offended,
Think but
this —
and all is
mended —

Figure 1. *Type and type object selected with the* **Selection** *tool.*

If we
shadows
have
offended,
Think but
this —
and all is
mended —

Figure 2. *Type object selected with the* **Direction Selection** *tool.*

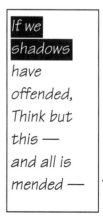

If we
shadows
have
offended,
Think but
this —
and all is
mended —

Shakespeare

Figure 3. *Type selected with the* **Type** *tool.*

Use this selection method if you want to move, transform, restyle, or recolor a whole type block. To recolor or reshape a type object, use the selection method described at the bottom of this page. To edit type or to restyle or recolor part of a type block, use the selection method described on the next page.

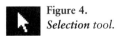

Figure 4. *Selection tool.*

To select type and its object:

1. Choose the Selection tool (**Figure 4**).
2. Click on the **edge** of the type object. This may be easiest to do in Artwork view.
   or
   For point type, with your illustration in Artwork view, you can click on the little "**x**" before the first character (**Figures 5–6**)
   or
   Click on the **baseline** of any character in the type object in any view.

■ To modify the paint attributes of type, use the Paint Style palette *(see Chapter 9)*.

Think but this — and all
is mended —

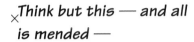

Figure 5. *For* ***point*** *type in* ***Artwork*** *view, click on the "x."*

Think but this — and all
is mended —

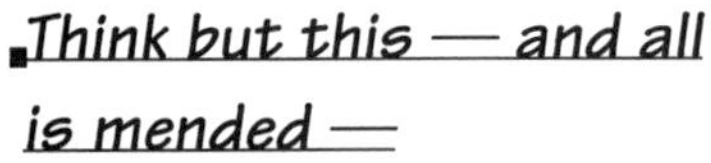

Figure 6. *The* ***type*** *and* ***type object*** *are selected.*

Use this selection method if you want to reshape a type object (and thus reflow the type) or recolor a type object.

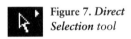

Figure 7. ***Direct Selection*** *tool*

To select a type object and not the type:

1. Choose the Direct Selection tool (**Figure 7**).
2. Click on the **edge** of the type object. This may be easiest to do in Artwork view (**Figure 8**).

   Modifications you make will affect only the type object, and not the type.

Think but this — and
all is mended —

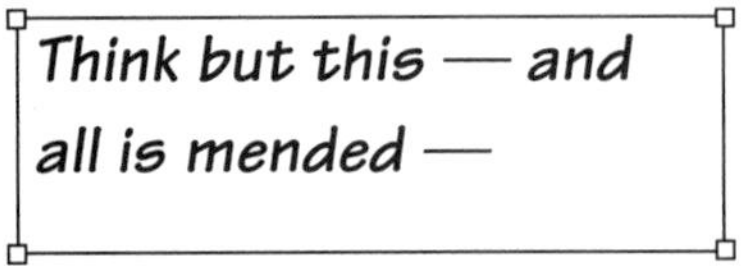

Figure 8. *The* ***type object*** *is selected.*

Use this selection method if you want to edit all or a portion of a type block, or change its character or paragraph specifications or paint style.

To select type and not its object:

1. Choose any type tool.

2. Drag horizontally to select a word or a line of type (the pointer will turn into an I-beam) (**Figures 9–10**).
   or
   Drag vertically to select lines of type.
   or
   Double-click to select a word.
   or
   Triple-click to select a paragraph.
   or
   Click in the text block, then choose Edit > Select All (⌘-A) to select all the type in the block or on the path, including any type it is linked to.
   or
   Click where you want the selection to start, then Shift-click where you want the selection to end. (You can also extend a selection by Shift-clicking.)

3. After modifiying the type, click on the selected type to deselect it but keep the flashing insertion marker in the type block for further editing.
   or
   Choose a selection tool and click away from the type object to deselect it.

x*My line drawing is the purest and most direct translation of my emotion.*

Henri Matisse

Figure 9. *The Type tool pointer will have a dotted outline until it is moved over type.*

x*My line drawing is the purest and most direct* translation of *my emotion.*

Figure 10. *Two words are selected. Note the I-beam pointer.*

Select Type

The Character and Paragraph palettes

Use the **Character** palette (**Figure 11**) to modify type size, font, leading, tracking/kerning, baseline shift and horizontal scale.

Use the **Paragraph** palette (**Figure 12**) to modify paragraph alignment, indentation, or leading, or turn on auto hyphention. (A paragraph is created when the Return key is pressed within a type block. There is no on-screen character symbol for a Return in Illustrator.)

The **Info** palette displays the font name, size, and tracking values of type if it is selected with a type tool. Choose Window > Show Info to open the Info palette. Attributes cannot be changed using this palette; it is for information only (**Figure 15**).

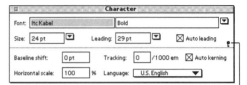

Figure 11. *The Character palette.*

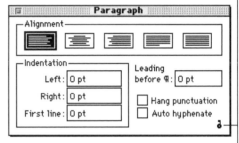

Figure 12. *The Paragraph palette.*

To open or close the bottom panel of the Character or Paragraph palette, click the **palette display lever**.

TO OPEN THE PARAGRAPH PALETTE

Choose Type > Paragraph.
or
Choose Window > Show Paragraph.
or
Hold down Command (⌘) and Shift and press "P".

TO OPEN THE CHARACTER PALETTE

Choose Type > Character.
or
Choose Window > Show Character.
or
Hold down Command (⌘) and press "T".

Figure 13. *Choose Character or Paragraph from the Type menu.*

Figure 14. *Or choose Show Character or Show Paragraph from the Window menu.*

Make sure no fields are highlighted on the Character and Paragraph palettes when you use any of the keyboard shortcuts for changing character or paragraph specifications that are mentioned throughout this chapter.

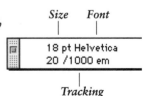

Figure 15. *The Info palette when type is selected.*

Character and Paragraph Palettes

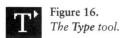

Figure 16.
The Type tool.

To choose a font:

1. Choose the Type tool (**Figure 16**).

2. Select the type you want to modify (**Figure 17**).

3. On the Character palette, choose a font from the Font pop-up menu (**Figure 18a**). Choose from a submenu if the font name has an arrowhead next to it (**Figure 18b**).
   or
   Type the name of a font and the name of a style in the Font fields, then press Return. You need only enter the first few letters of the font name or style; the name or style with the closest spelling match will appear in the field (**Figure 19**).

■ You can also choose a font from the Font menu.

Art, like morality, consists of drawing the line somewhere.

Figure 17. *Select the type you want to modify.*

*Enter a **font name** and **style**.   Or choose from the Font pop-up menu.*

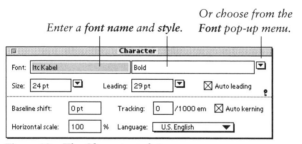

Figure 18a. *The **Character** palette.*

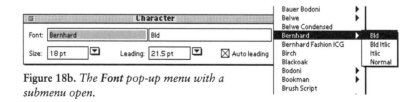

Figure 18b. *The **Font** pop-up menu with a submenu open.*

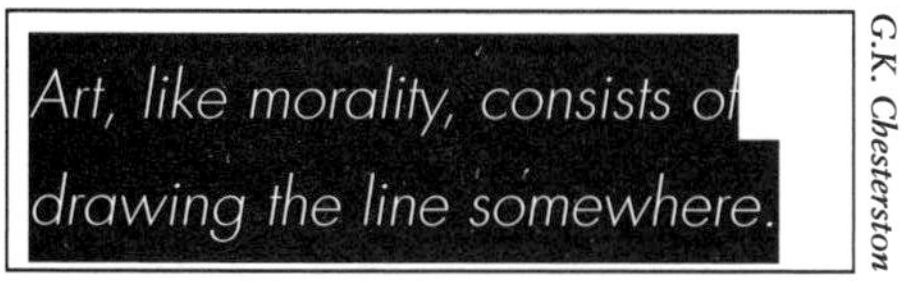

Art, like morality, consists of drawing the line somewhere.

G.K. Chesterston

Figure 19. *The font is changed from Tekton Oblique to Futura Light Oblique.*

To resize type:

1. Select the type you want to modify.

2. On the Character palette, enter a point size between .1 and 1296 in the Size field (⌘-Shift-S to highlight the field), then press Return (or press Tab if you want to highlight the next field) (**Figure 20**). You don't need to reenter the unit of measure. If the highlighted type contains more than one point size, the Size field will be blank, but go ahead and enter the desired size.

   or

   Choose a preset size from the Size pop-up menu.

   or

   To resize type via the keyboard, hold down Command (⌘) and Shift and press ">" to enlarge or "<" to reduce. The increment the type resizes each time you use this shortcut is specified in the Size/leading field in the General Preferences dialog box (File menu).

■ You can also choose a preset size from the Size submenu under the Type menu. To choose a custom size, choose Other from the same submenu. The Character palette will open (if it isn't already open) and the Size field on the palette will automatically highlight. Enter a size, then press Return or Tab.

■ You can scale a selected type object using the Scale tool. Both the object and the type will resize. To scale type uniformly without condensing or extending it, click, then drag using the Scale tool with Shift held down.

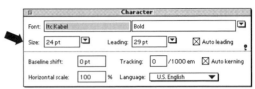

Figure 20. *On the Character palette, enter a number in the Size field or choose a preset size from the pop-up menu.*

TO FIT TYPE TO ITS CONTAINER —
To stretch type to the edges of a text rectangle or type container, choose the Type tool or the Area type tool, highlight a one-line paragraph, then choose Type > Fit Headline (Figures 21a–b).

Figure 21a. *The original, selected characters.*

Figure 21b. *After applying the Fit Headline command.*

Resize Type

*Figure 22. On the **Character** palette, enter a number in points in the **Leading** field, or choose a preset leading amount from the pop-up menu, or check the **Auto leading** box.*

ACT III.

Scene I.

The Wood. The Queen of Fairies *lying*

asleep.

Enter QUINCE, SNUG, BOTTOM, FLUTE,
SNOUT, *and* STARVELING.

Bot. Are we all met?

Quin. Pat, pat; and here is a marvel-lous convenient place for our rehearsal. This green plot shall be our stage, this hawthorn brake our tiring-house; and we will do it in action, as we will do it before the duke.

--- *"Loose"* ***Leading*** *(8-point type; 12 point leading)*

Figure 23.

ACT III.

Scene I.

The Wood. The Queen of Fairies *lying*

asleep.

Enter QUINCE, SNUG, BOTTOM, FLUTE,
SNOUT, *and* STARVELING.

Bot. Are we all met?
Quin. Pat, pat; and here is a marvel-lous convenient place for our rehearsal. This green plot shall be our stage, this hawthorn brake our tiring-house; and we will do it in action, as we will do it before the duke.

--- *"Tight"* ***Leading*** *(8-point type; 8.75 point leading)*

Figure 24.

Leading is the distance, measured in points, from baseline to baseline between lines of type. Each line of type in a block can have a different leading amount. *(To add space between paragraphs, follow the instructions on page 162)*

To change leading:

1. Select the type you want to modify.

2. On the Character palette:

   Enter a number in the Leading field (press Return or Tab) (**Figures 22–24**).
   or
   Choose a preset leading amount from the Leading pop-up menu.
   or
   Check the Auto leading box to set the leading to 120% of the largest type size on each line.

■ You can choose a preset Leading amount from the Leading submenu under the Type menu. To choose a custom leading amount, choose Other from the same submenu. The Character palette will open (if it is not already open) and the Leading field on the Character palette will automatically highlight. Enter a leading amount, then press Return or Tab.

■ Hold down Option and press the up arrow on the keyboard to decrease leading in selected text or the down arrow to increase leading. The incre-ment the leading changes each time you use this shortcut is specified in the Size/leading field in the General Preferences dialog box (File menu).

Leading

Kerning is the adjustment of space between a pair of characters. The cursor must be inserted between a pair of characters in order to kern them.

Tracking is the adjustment of space to the right of one or more highlighted characters. To track type, first select one or more characters with the Type tool or select an entire type block with the Selection tool.

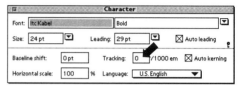

Figure 25. *Enter a number in the **Tracking/Kerning** field on the **Character** palette.*

To kern or track type:

1. Select the type you want to modify.

2. If the bottom of the Character palette is not open, click the palette display lever.

3. In the Tracking/Kerning field on the Character palette (⌘-Shift-K to highlight the field), enter a positive number to add space between characters or a negative number to remove space, then press Return or Tab (**Figures 25–28**).
   or
   Check the Auto kerning box to use the font's built-in kerning values.
   or

■ Hold down Option and press the right arrow on the keyboard to add space between letters or the left arrow to decrease space between letters. The amount of space that is added or removed each time you press an arrow is specified in the Tracking/Kerning field in the General Preferences dialog box (File menu).

Figure 26. *Normal type.*

Figure 27. *Space added between the first two characters.*

Figure 28. *Space removed between the last five characters.*

Kerning and Tracking

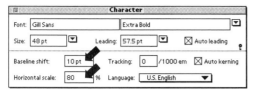

*Figure 29. Enter a number in the **Baseline shift** field or in the **Horizontal scale** field on the Character palette. (If the bottom of the Character palette isn't open, click the palette display lever.)*

Figure 30. Characters on a path, baseline shifted downward.

Figure 31. The "A" baseline shifted 9 points downward.

DANIELLE

Figure 32. Normal type.

DANIELLE

Figure 33. Type condensed 25%.

DANIELLE

Figure 34. Type extended 25%.

The **Baseline shift** command repositions characters above or below the baseline. You can use this command to offset curved path type from its path, to create superscript or subscript characters (there is no superscript or subscript type style in Illustrator), or to create logos.

To baseline shift type:

1. Select the type you want to modify.
2. In the Baseline shift field on the Character palette, enter a positive number to baseline shift characters upward or a negative number to baseline shift characters downward (press Return or Tab) (**Figures 29–31**).
   or
   Hold down Option and Shift and press the up arrow to shift selected characters upward, or the down arrow to shift characters downward. The amount type shifts each time you press an arrow is specified in the Baseline shift field in the General Preferences dialog box (File menu).

The **Horizontal scale** command extends characters (makes them wider) or condenses characters (makes them narrower). The default horizontal scale is 100%. Some designers like to stylize type this way; other designers think it's a sacrilege. You decide.

To horizontally scale type:

1. Select the type you want to modify.
2. In the Horizontal scale field on the Character palette, enter a number above 100 to extend the type or a number below 100 to condense it (press Return or Tab) (**Figures 32–34**).
   ■ You can also horizontally scale a selected type block using the Scale dialog box. Double-click the Scale tool, enter a number other than 100 in the Horizontal field and enter 100 in the Vertical field.

Baseline Shift

Alignment, indent, and leading values affect whole paragraphs. To create a new paragraph in a text block, press Return. Type preceding a Return is part of one paragraph; type following a Return is part of the next paragraph. Type that wraps automatically is part of the same paragraph. To create a line break within a paragraph in non-tabular text, press Tab until the text is forced to the next line.

To change paragraph alignment:

1. Select the paragraph or paragraphs you want to modify.

2. On the Paragraph palette, click the Left, Center, Right, Justify, or Justify Last Line Alignment icon (**Figures 35–37**).

■ The Justify and Justify Last Line alignment options cannot be applied to path type or to point type (type not in a box or in a block), because there is no container to justify the edges to.

■ You can also choose an alignment option from the Alignment submenu under the Type menu.

Paragraph alignment shortcuts

Left	⌘-Shift-L
Center	⌘-Shift-C
Right	⌘-Shift-R
Justify	⌘-Shift-J
Justify last line	⌘-Shift-B

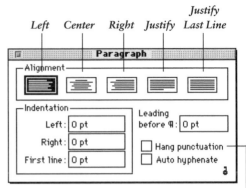

Justify
Left   Center   Right   Justify   Last Line

Figure 35. *Click one of the five **Alignment** icons on the **Paragraph** palette.*

Hanging punctuation looks classy.

Hanging punctuation   *Left Alignment*

'Lo! all these trophies of affections hot,
Of pensiv'd and subdued desires the tender,
Nature hath charg'd me that I hoard them not,
But yield them up where I myself must render,
That is, to you, my origin and ender:
For these, of force, must your oblations be,
Since I their altar, you enpatron me.

Shakespeare

Figure 36.

ACT III.

Scene I.

The Wood. The Queen of Fairies *lying asleep.*

Enter QUINCE, SNUG, BOTTOM, FLUTE, SNOUT, *and* STARVELING.

Center Alignment

Bot. Are we all met?
Quin. Pat, pat; and here is a marvellous convenient place for our rehearsal. This green plot shall be our stage, this hawthorn brake our tiring-house; and we will do it in action, as we will do it before the duke.

Justify Alignment

Shakespeare.

Figure 37.

Right Alignment

To select paragraphs for modification —
If you want to change paragraph attributes of *all* the text in type object or on a path, select the object or path with the Selection tool. To isolate a paragraph or series of paragraphs of any kind of type, use the Type tool.

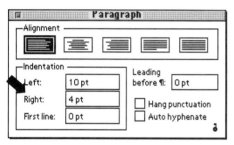

Figure 38. *The Indentation fields on the Paragraph palette.*

Left and Right **Indentation** values can be applied to a paragraph within a type rectangle. Only a Left Indentation value can be applied to point type.

To change paragraph indentation:

1. Select the paragraph or paragraphs you want to modify.

2. Enter new numbers in the Left and/or Right Indentation fields on the Paragraph palette (**Figure 38**).
   or
   To indent only the first line of each paragraph, enter a number in the "First line" field.

3. Press Return or Tab (**Figure 39**).

■ You can enter negative values in the Left or First line Indentation field to move the type to the left. If it is pushed outside the type rectangle or object, it will still display and print.

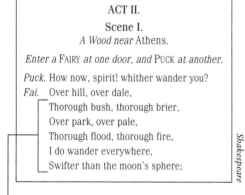

ACT II.

Scene I.

A Wood near Athens.

Enter a FAIRY *at one door, and* PUCK *at another.*

Puck. How now, spirit! whither wander you?
Fai. Over hill, over dale,
Thorough bush, thorough brier,
Over park, over pale,
Thorough flood, thorough fire,
I do wander everywhere,
Swifter than the moon's sphere;

Shakespeare

Figure 39. *Left Indentation.*

ACT III.

Scene I.

The Wood. The Queen of Fairies *lying asleep.*

Enter QUINCE, SNUG, BOTTOM, FLUTE, SNOUT, *and* STARVELING.

Bot. Are we all met?
Quin. Pat, pat; and here is a marvellous convenient place for our rehearsal. This green plot shall be our stage, this hawthorn brake our tiring-house; and we will do it in action, as we will do it before the duke.

Shakespeare

Figure 40. *To create **hanging indentation**, as in this illustration, enter a number in the **Left Indentation** field and the same number with a minus sign in front of it in the **First line Indentation** field.*

Paragraph Indentation

Use the **Leading before ¶** field on the Paragraph palette to add or reduce space between paragraphs. Point type cannot be modified using this feature.

(To adjust the space between lines of type within a paragraph, follow the instructions on page 157)

To adjust spacing between paragraphs:

1. Select the type you want to modify. To modify the leading before only one paragraph in a type block, select the paragraph with the Type tool.

2. Enter a number in the "Leading before ¶" field on the Paragraph palette (**Figure 41**).

3. Press Return or Tab (**Figure 42**).

■ To create a new paragraph, press Return. To create a line break within a paragraph, press Tab.

■ To move paragraphs close together, enter a negative number in the "Leading before ¶" field.

■ To change the horizontal word or letter spacing for justified paragraphs, add higher or lower numbers in the Word spacing: Minimum, Desired, or Maximum fields on the Paragraph palette (click the palette display lever to display the bottom panel). For non-justified type, you can enter values only in the Desired fields.

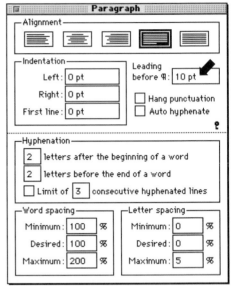

Figure 41. *The **Leading before ¶** field on the **Paragraph** palette.*

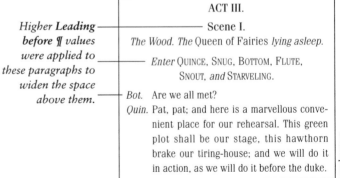

*Higher **Leading before ¶** values were applied to these paragraphs to widen the space above them.*

Figure 42.

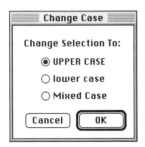

Figure 43. *Click an option in the* Change Case *dialog box.*

The **Change Case** command changes selected text to all UPPER CASE, all lower case, or Mixed Case (initial capitals).

To change case:

1. Select text with a type tool.
2. Choose Type > Change Case.
3. Click Upper case, lower case, or Mixed Case (**Figure 43**).
4. Click OK or press Return.

The **Check Spelling** command checks spelling in your entire illustration using a built-in dictionary. You can also create and edit your own word list.

To check spelling:

1. Choose Type > Check Spelling (**Figure 1**). Words not found in the application or user dictionary will appear on the Misspelled Words list.
2. Leave the currently highlighted Misspelled Word selected or click a different word on the list (**Figure 3**). The misspelled word will be highlighted in your illustration.
3. *Optional:* Check the Case Sensitive box to display the Misspelled Word separately if it appears in different cases (such as *Spelle* and *spelle*).
4. To correct a word with one keystroke: Press Return to replace the first instance of the word with the currently highlighted Suggested Correction.
   or
   Double-click a word on the Suggested Corrections scroll list. If no Suggested Correction appears, there is no similar word in the dictionary.

To correct a word using more than one keystroke:
Click a word on the Suggested Corrections scroll list (**Figure 44**).
or
Type the correct word in the entry field. As you type, words starting

(Continued on the next page)

TO SPELLCHECK USING A FOREIGN LANGUAGE DICTIONARY ————
Click Language in the Check Spelling dialog box, highlight the dictionary you want to use in the Text folder in the Plug-ins folder in the Adobe Illustrator 6.0 folder, then click Open.

Change Case; Check Spelling

with those letters will display on the Suggested Corrections scroll list. You can continue to type the whole word yourself or you can click on any Suggested Correction.

Then:

Click **Change** to change only the first occurrence of the Misspelled Word to the currently highlighted Suggested Correction.

or

Click **Change All** to change all occurrences of the Misspelled Word.

or

Click **Skip** to leave the current Misspelled Word unchanged.

or

Click **Skip All** to leave all occurrences of the Misspelled Word unchanged.

5. *Optional:* Click Learn to add the currently highlighted Misspelled Word or Words to the Learned Words list (the AI User Dictionary file in the Text folder inside the Plug-ins folder) (**Figure 45**). To add more than one word at a time, hold down Command (⌘) while clicking on the words, then click Learn.

6. If you spell-check all the Misspelled Words, you'll get a prompt. Click OK. (Click Done in the dialog box to stop spell-checking.)

■ To modify the Learned Words list (user-defined dictionary), click Edit List in the Check Spelling dialog box, click on a word, retype it, then click Change; or click on a word, then click Remove; or type a new word, then click Add. Hyphenated words are permitted.

■ There is a bug in this feature: the corrected word will take on the styling of the text preceding it and lose its original styling.

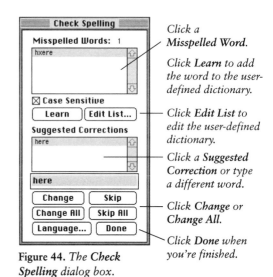

Click a Misspelled Word.

Click Learn to add the word to the user-defined dictionary.

Click Edit List to edit the user-defined dictionary.

Click a Suggested Correction or type a different word.

Click Change or Change All.

Click Done when you're finished.

Figure 44. *The Check Spelling dialog box.*

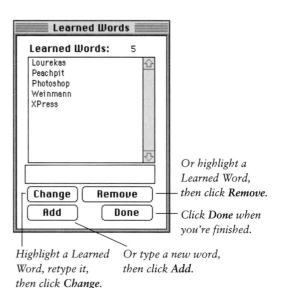

Or highlight a Learned Word, then click Remove.

Click Done when you're finished.

Highlight a Learned Word, retype it, then click Change.

Or type a new word, then click Add.

Figure 45. *Create your own word list using the Learned Words dialog box.*

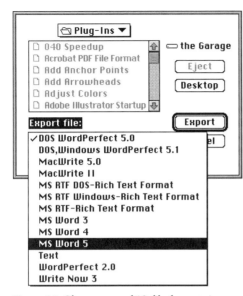

Figure 46. *Choose one of 13 file formats in which to save your selected text from the **Export file** pop-up menu.*

Use the **Export** command to save Illustrator text in a format that can be imported into another application. *Note:* The Claris XTND utility must be installed to access the Export command.

To export text:

1. Highlight the text you wish to export with the Text tool.

2. Choose Type > Export.

3. Choose a drive and folder in which to save the text file (**Figure 46**).

4. Choose a format from the "Export file" pop-up menu.

5. Enter a name for the new file.

6. Click Export.

Use the **Find Font** command to generate a list of the fonts currently being used in an illustration, or use it to replace fonts.

To find and replace a font:

1. Choose Type > Find Font.

2. Check one or more of the Multiple Master, Standard, Type 1 Fonts, or TrueType boxes to selectively display only fonts of those types on the scroll lists. For Multiple Master fonts, you must also check the Type 1 Fonts box.

3. Leave the Document List button highlighted to display on the Replace Fonts list only fonts currently being used in your document of the types checked in Step 3.
   or
   Click System List to display on the Replace Fonts list all the fonts currently available in your system. (To stop the list from displaying, click the Document List button.)

4. Click a font to search for on the Find Fonts in Document scroll list (**Figure 47**).

(Continued on the following page)

Export Text; Find and Replace Fonts

5. Click a replacement font on the Replace Fonts scroll list.

6. Click Find Next or Skip to skip over that occurrence of the font.
or
Click Change to change only the current occurrence of the "Find Font."
or
Click Change All to change all occurrences of the "Find Font."

7. *Optional:* To save a list of the fonts currently being used in the illustration as a SimpleText document, click Save, enter a name, choose a location in which to save the file, then click Save. The SimpleText document can later be opened directly from the Finder.

8. Click Done.

■ To compose a document list before opening the Find Font dialog box, create text in your illustration and apply the desired fonts to it. Or, Copy a text object containing the fonts you wish to add from another document, then Paste it into your document.

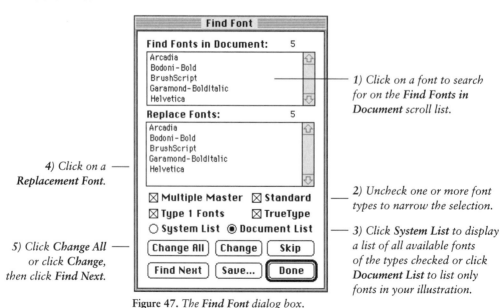

Figure 47. *The Find Font dialog box.*

Find and Replace Fonts

Use the **Find** dialog box to search for and replace characters without changing their paint or typographic attributes.

To find and replace text:

1. *Optional:* Click with the Type tool to create an insertion point to search from that location. If no text object is selected in your document, the search will begin from the most recently created object.

2. Choose Type > Find.

3. Enter a word or phrase to search for in the "Find what" field (**Figure 48**).

4. Enter a replacement word or phrase in the "Replace with" field. Leave the "Replace with" field blank to delete occurrences of the "Find what" text altogether.

Steps 5–8 are optional:

5. Check the Whole Word box to find the "Find what" letters only if they appear as a complete word — not as part of a larger word.

6. Check the Case Sensitive box to find only those occurrences that match the exact uppercase/lowercase configuration of the "Find what" text.

7. Check the Wrap Around box to search from the current cursor position to the end of the text object or string of linked objects and then continue the search from the most recently created object. With Wrap Around unchecked, the search will proceed only from the current cursor position forward.

8. Check the Search Backward box to search backward.

9. Click **Find Next** to search for the first occurrence of the "Find what" word or phrase.

10. Click **Replace** to replace only the currently found occurrence of the "Find what" text.
    or
    Click **Replace, then Find** to replace the first occurrence and search for the next occurrence.
    or
    Click **Replace All** to replace all occurrences at once.

11. Click Done.

■ There is a bug in this feature: the replacement word will take on the font of the word space preceding it.

Find and Replace Text

Figure 48. *In the* **Text Find** *dialog box, enter text you wish to search for in the* **Find what** *field and text you wish to change it to in the* **Replace with** *field. Click* **Find Next,** *then click* **Replace, then Find,** *or click* **Replace,** *or click* **Replace All.**

The **Rows & Columns** command arranges text into columns and/or rows.

To create linked text rows and columns:

1. Select a text object with the Selection tool.

2. Choose Type > Rows & Columns.

3. Check the Preview box to apply changes immediately (**Figure 49**).

4. Click the left/right arrows or enter values in the fields to choose:

   The total number of Columns and Rows to be produced.
   and
   The Width of each Column and the Height of each Row.
   and
   The Gutter (space) between each Column and each Row.
   and
   The Total Width and Total Height of the entire block of Columns and Rows.

5. Click the Text Flow icon to have text flow from column to column (vertically) or from row to row (horizontally).

6. *Optional:* Check the Add Guides box to display a grid around the text blocks.

7. Click OK or press Return (**Figures 50a–b**).

▪ If you select the entire block of rows and columns with the Selection tool and then reopen the Rows & Columns dialog box, the current settings for that block will be displayed.

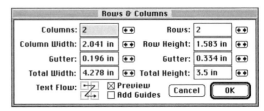

Figure 49. *The Rows & Columns dialog box.*

HERE is some *text* to *arrange* with the Rows & Columns **filter** in the **new** 6.0 illustrator. Notice how **the** text flows from box to box automatically.

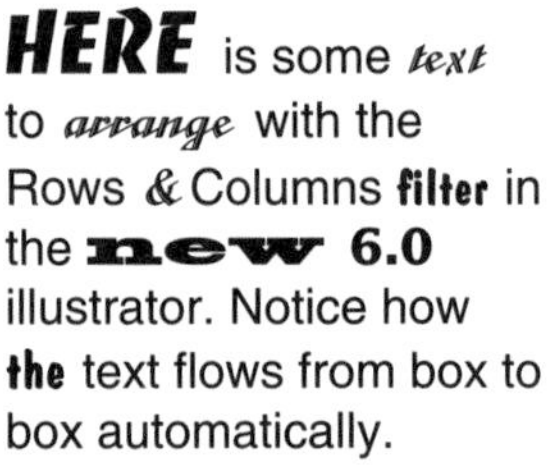

Figure 50a. *One text object...*

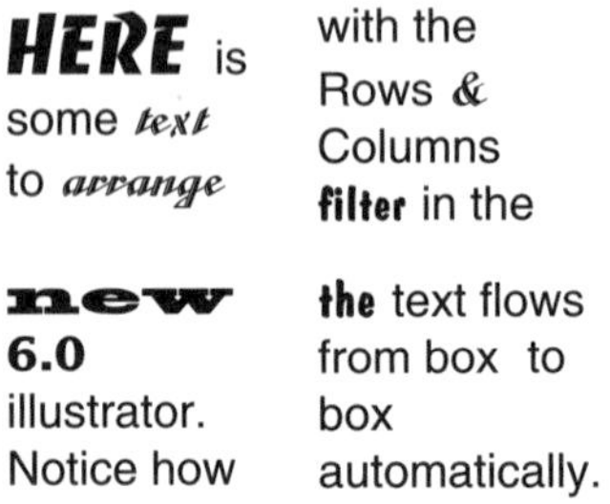

HERE is some *text* to *arrange* | with the Rows & Columns **filter** in the

new 6.0 illustrator. Notice how | **the** text flows from box to box automatically.

Figure 50b. *...converted into two columns and two rows.*

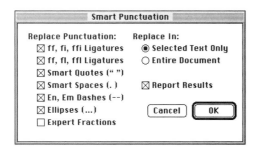

Figure 51. *Check Replace Punctuation options in the Smart Punctuation dialog box.*

DIALOG BOX OPTION	KEYBOARD	SMART PUNCTUATION
ff, fi, ffi Ligatures	ff, fi, ffi	ff, fi, ffi
ff, fi, ffl Ligatures	ff, fi, ffl	ff, fi, ffl
Smart Quotes	' "	' " " '
Smart Spaces (one space after a period)	. T	. T
En, Em Dashes	--	–
	---	—
Ellipses	...	...
Expert Fractions	1/2	½

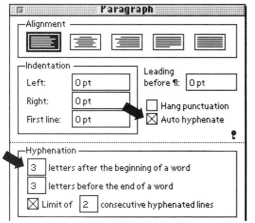

Figure 52. *Choose Hyphenation options on the Paragraph palette.*

To hyphenate a word manually ———

Click with the Type tool where you want the hyphen to appear, then hold down Command (⌘) and Shift and press "-".

The **Smart Punctuation** command converts keyboard punctuation into professional typesetting marks.

To create smart punctuation:

1. *Optional:* Select text with the Type tool to smart-punctuate that text only.
2. Choose Type > Smart Punctuation.
3. Check any of the Replace Punctuation boxes (**Figure 51**).
4. Click Replace In: Selected Text Only (if you selected text) or Entire Document.
5. *Optional:* Check Report Results to display a list of your changes.
6. Click OK or press Return.

■ To apply Ligatures and Expert Fractions, the Adobe Expert font set for the font you are using must be available in your System.

Note: Turning **Auto hyphenation** on or off affects selected or subsequently created text only.

To turn on auto hyphenation:

1. Check the Auto hyphenate box on the Paragraph palette (**Figure 52**).
2. In the "letters after the beginning of a word" field, enter the minimum number of characters to precede any hyphen. Fewer than three letters before or after a hyphen can make text difficult to read.
3. In the "letters before the end of a word" field, enter the minimum number of characters to carry over onto the next line following a hyphen.
4. *Optional:* Check the "Limit of [ ] consecutive hyphenated lines" box and enter a maximum number. More than a couple of hyphens in a row diminishes readability.

■ To hyphenate using a different language dictionary, choose from the Language pop-up menu on the Character palette, then press Return.

Smart Punctuation; Hyphenation

Tabs are used to align columns of text. Default tab stops are half an inch apart. The Tabs palette is used to set custom tab stops.

To insert tabs into text:

Press Tab as you input copy before typing each new column. The cursor will jump to the next tab stop.

or

To add a tab to already inputted text, click just to the left of the text that is to start a new column, then press Tab.

To set custom tab stops:

1. Choose the Selection tool, then select a text object that contains tab characters.

   or

   Choose the Text tool and select text that contains tab characters.

2. Choose Window > Show Tab Ruler (⌘-Shift-T).

3. Click in the tabs ruler where the tab stop or stops are to occur. Text will align to the new stop immediately (**Figure 53**).

4. Click the Left, Center, Right, or Decimal tab alignment button on the left side of the palette (**Figure 54**).

■ To delete a tab stop, drag the tab marker up and out of the ruler. As you drag it, the word *delete* will display on the palette.

■ Hold down Shift and drag a marker to move all the markers to the right of it along with it.

Basic Plaid Country Club

	Front 9	*Back 9*	*Total*
Annie	*38*	*44*	*82*
Jack	*34*	*36*	*70*
Lee	*42*	*48*	*90*
Hubie	*34*	*35*	*69*

Figure 53. *Text aligned using custom tab stops.*

*Check the **Snap** box to have a tab marker snap to the nearest ruler tick mark as you insert it or drag it. Or, to temporarily turn on the Snap feature when the Snap box is unchecked, hold down **Control** as you drag a marker. Ruler increments will display in the currently chosen Ruler units (Document Setup).*

The location of the currently highlighted tab marker.

*Click the **Left, Center, Right,** or **Decimal** Alignment button.*

*Click the **Alignment** box to align the tabs ruler with the left margin of the selected text.*

A left align tab marker. To move a tab stop, drag the marker left or right.

*A selected **right align tab marker.***

*Drag the **Extend Tab ruler** box to the right to widen the ruler.*

Figure 54. *The **Tab Ruler.***

PLAY WITH TYPE | 15

Having learned how to create type (Chapter 13) and style type (Chapter 14), you might like to try some of the simple type exercises in this chapter. There are instructions for creating slanted type, shadow type, and type on a circle, and for wrapping type around an object.

Daniel Pelavin, **After Hours**, logo for Ziff-Davis

To slant a block of type:

1. Choose the Rectangle tool, then draw a rectangle.

2. Choose the Area Type tool.

3. Click on the edge of the rectangle, then enter type (**Figure 2**).

4. With the rectangle still selected, double-click the Rotation tool.

5. Enter 30 in the Angle field.

6. Click OK or press Return (**Figure 3**).

7. Choose View > Artwork to display the rectangle's segments (or hold down Option and click on the dot in the Eye column for the highlighted layer on the Layers palette).

8. Choose the Direct Selection tool.

9. Drag the top segment diagonally to the right until the side segments are vertical (**Figure 4**).

10. *Optional:* Drag the right segment of the rectangle a little to the right to enlarge the object and reflow the type.

11. Choose View > Preview (**Figure 5**).

■ You can also use the Shear tool to slant a block of type (**Figures 1a–b**).

Figure 1a. *The original type block.*

Figure 1b. *Select the type, click with the **Shear** tool on the center of the type, then drag upward or downward from the edge of the type block.*

PEACHPIT PRESS
2414 Sixth Street
Berkeley, CA 94710
800 283-9444
510 548-4393

Figure 2. *The original type object.*

Figure 3. *Rotate the type 30°.*

Figure 4. *Drag the top segment diagonally to the right.*

Figure 5. *The reshaped type object (Preview view).*

Slanted Type

the bakery

Figure 6. *Select a type block.*

the bakery

Figure 7. *Position the shadow close to the original type. Leave the lighter type in front...*

the bakery

Figure 8. *...or send it to the back.*

To create type with a shadow:

1. Create point type *(see page 142)* (**Figure 6**).

2. *Optional:* Select the type with the Type tool, then track the characters out *(see page 158)*.

3. Choose the Selection tool.

4. Click on the type block.

5. Choose View > Preview.

6. Apply a dark Fill color and a Stroke of None.

7. Hold down Option and drag the type block by its baseline or its anchor point slightly to the right and downward. Release the mouse, then release Option.

8. With the copy of the type block still selected, apply a lighter shade of the original type (**Figure 7**).

9. *Optional:* Choose Arrange > Send To Back (**Figure 8**).

10. Reposition either type block — press any arrow key to move it in small increments.

■   To create an even more three-dimensional effect, as in **Figure 9**, duplicate the type block again, then apply the background Fill color to the middle type block.

Peter Fahrni

Figure 9. *Three layers of type. The type on the top layer has a White Fill and a Black Stroke, the type on the middle layer has a 50% Black Fill to match the background, and the type on the bottom has a 100% Black Fill.*

Shadow Type

To create type with a slanting shadow:

1. Follow the steps on the previous page.
2. Choose the Selection tool.
3. Click on the baseline or anchor point of the shadow type.
4. Double-click the Scale tool (**Figure 10**).
5. Click Non-uniform (**Figure 11**).
6. Enter 100 in the Horizontal field.
7. Enter 60 in the Vertical field.
8. Click OK.
9. With the shadow type still selected, double-click the Shear tool (**Figure 10**).
10. Enter 45 in the Angle field (**Figure 12**).
11. Click Horizontal Axis.
12. Click OK or press Return.
13. Use the arrow keys to move the baseline of the shadow text so it aligns with the baseline of the original text (**Figure 14**).

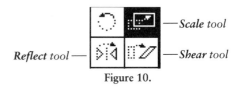

Reflect tool — — *Scale tool*

— *Shear tool*

Figure 10.

Figure 11. *Scale dialog box.*

Figure 12. *Shear dialog box.*

Shadow slant variation:

1. Follow all the steps above.
2. Choose the Selection tool.
3. Click on the shadow type.
4. Double-click the Reflect tool (**Figure 10**).
5. Click Horizontal axis.
6. Click OK or press Return.
7. Move the shadow block down so it aligns with the baselines of the two blocks of letters (**Figure 15**).

■ If you cannot select the shadow type layer in back, select the original type first, press the up arrow key to move it upward, then click on the baseline or anchor point of the shadow type.

Figure 13. *The original type.*

Figure 14. *Reduce the shadow type, then Shear it.*

Figure 15. *After reflecting the shadow.*

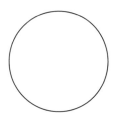

Figure 16. *Create a 3–inch circle.*

Figure 17. *Path Type tool*

Figure 18. *Create path type on the top of the first circle.*

Figure 19. *Create path type on the bottom of the second circle.*

Figure 20. *Drag the path type inside the circle.*

Exercise

Create a logo — type on a circle.

1. Open the Layers, Character, and Paint Style palettes.

2. Choose File > Preferences > General Preferences, then choose Inches from the Ruler units pop-up menu.

3. Double-click Layer 1 on the Layers palette, then rename it "Circle type."

4. Choose the Oval tool, then click on the Artboard (don't drag).

5. Enter "3" in the Width field and click the word "Height."

6. Click OK (**Figure 16**).

7. On the Character palette, enter 24 in the Size field, then press Return.

8. Choose the Path-Type tool (**Figure 17**).

9. Click on the top of the circle.

10. Type "Type & Design" (**Figure 18**).

11. Choose the Selection tool.

12. Drag the I–beam to the left.

13. Choose the Oval tool, then click on the Artboard.

14. Click OK. (Don't change the dimensions in the Oval dialog box.)

15. Choose Path-Type tool.

16. Click on the bottom of new circle.

17. Enter the text "Form & Function" (**Figure 19**).

18. Choose the Selection tool.

19. Drag the I–beam icon inside the circle (**Figure 20**).

20. On the Character palette, enter –24 in the Baseline Shift field, then press Return.

21. Move the path type to the left (move the I–beam icon) (**Figure 21**). Do not cross over the edge of the circle.

22. Apply a Fill color.

23. Apply a Stroke of None.

(Continued on the following page)

Type Exercise

24. Apply the same Fill color to the other type block.

25. Choose the Selection tool.

26. Choose View > Artwork.

27. Drag one circle over the other until the centers perfectly align. Press the arrow keys for precision (**Figure 22**).

28. Choose View > Preview.

29. Choose the Selection tool.

30. Drag a marquee around both circles.

31. Choose Arrange > Group.

32. Double-click the Scale tool.

33. Click Uniform.

34. Enter 125 in the Uniform field.

35. Click OK.

36. Choose Arrange > Repeat Transform.

37. Save the document.

Figure 21. *Baseline shift the path type on the second circle downward, and center it on the circle.*

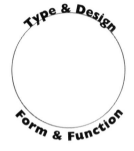

Figure 22. *Drag one circle over the other, then group both circles together.*

To create point type for the "Art & Industry" logo:

1. Create a new layer called "Type Block" using the Layers palette.

2. Select the Type tool.

3. Type "Art," press Return, type "&," press Return, then type "Industry" (**Figure 23**).

4. Use the Type tool to select the type.

5. Choose Type > Alignment > Center.

6. Choose a font, point size, leading, and horizontal scale. Enter a Baseline shift value of 0.

7. Select the "A," choose a different font and size, and change the Fill color.

8. Select the "I," then change the font and size, and the Fill color (**Figure 24**).

9. Select "rt" and Baseline shift it upward.

10. Select "ndustry" and Baseline shift it upward (**Figure 25**).

Art
&
Industry

Figure 23. *The original plain type.*

Figure 24. *The type centered, repainted, and restyled.*

Figure 25. *The small characters baseline shifted upward.*

Type Exercise

Figure 26. *The ampersand Cut and Pasted into a separate type block, then resized and restyled. Place with the other type block.*

Figure 27. *The final type block.*

Figure 28. *The type blocks moved inside the circle. Scale the type block, if necessary.*

To make the "&" into a separate type block so you can resize, restack or reposition it easily:

1. Choose the Type tool, then Select the "&".
2. Choose Edit > Cut .
3. Click the Type tool.
4. Click on the page to create an insertion point.
5. Choose Edit > Paste.
6. Choose the Selection tool, then select the "&".
7. Choose a font, Horizontal scale, Fill color, and large point size (**Figure 26**).
8. Drag the "&" into position with the other type block.
9. With the "&" still selected, choose Arrange > Send to Back (**Figure 27**).
10. Select the "&" and the type block.
11. Choose Arrange > Group.
12. Save the document.

To combine the type blocks for the logo:

1. Choose the Selection tool.
2. Move the "ART" type block inside the circles.

To resize the type block:

1. Select the "ART" type.
2. Double-click the Scale tool.
3. Enter numbers in the Uniform or Non-uniform fields to enlarge or reduce the type block to fit nicely inside the circle.
4. Choose the Selection tool and adjust the position of the type block.
5. Save the document (**Figure 28**).

Type Exercise

To add a backdrop to the logo:

1. Choose New Layer from the Layers palette pop-up menu, enter the name "Gradient," choose a Selection color, then click OK.

2. On the Layers palette, drag the "Gradient" layer name below the other two layers.

3. Choose the Oval tool.

4. Hold down Option and click on the center of the circles.

5. Enter 4.3 (inches) in the Width and Height fields.

6. Click the Gradient color selection method icon on the Paint Style palette.

7. Choose a gradient.

8. Choose the Gradient tool.

9. Drag diagonally across the circle (**Figure 29**).

Figure 29. *Further developed logo, with a radial gradient Fill and a linear gradient Fill.*

To wrap type around an object:

1. Create area type inside an object.

2. Choose the Selection tool.

3. Select the object the type is to wrap around (**Figure 30**).

4. Choose Arrange > Bring To Front.

5. Drag a marquee around both objects.

6. Choose Type > Make Wrap (**Figure 31**).

■   Use the Direct Selection tool to move the object the type is wrapping around. To move multiple objects, first click on each one with Shift held down.

■   To move the type away from the edge of the wrap object, enter values in the Left or Right Indentation fields on the Paragraph palette.

■   To undo the type wrap, choose Type > Release Wrap.

For fine dining, try the food at the Eaterie. Sample our fine wines, extraordinary entrees, and extravagant desserts — it's a true dining pleasure! For fine dining, try the food at the Eaterie. Sample fine wines, extraordinary and extravagant desserts true dining pleasure! For ing, try the food at the Sample our fine wines, e nary entrees, and extravaga serts — it's a true dining pleas For fine dining, try the food at the

Figure 30. *Select a type object and the object the type is to wrap around.*

For fine dining, try the food at the Eaterie. Sample our fine wines, extraordinary entrees, and extravagant desserts — it's a true dining pleasure! For fine dining, try the food at the Eaterie. Sample our fine wines, extraordinary entrees, and extravagant desserts — it's a true dining pleasure! For fine dining, try the food at the Eaterie. Sample our fine wines, extraordinary entrees, and

Figure 31. *The type wrap in Preview view.*

TRANSFORM

This chapter covers the five transformation tools: Scale, Rotate, Reflect, Shear, and Blend.

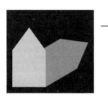 — The **Rotate** tool rotates an object around its center or around a specified point.

 — The **Scale** tool enlarges or reduces the size of an object proportionately or non-proportionately.

 — The **Reflect** tool creates a mirror image of an object across a specified axis.

 — The **Shear** tool slants an object in a specified direction.

 The **Blend** tool transforms one object into another by creating a multi-step progression between them.

HOW TO USE THE TRANSFORMATION TOOLS

A point of origin must be established before you can transform an object (**Figures 1a–c**).

Dialog box method

Select the object, then double-click the tool to open the tool dialog box. The object's center point will be the point of origin.

To use a point of origin other than the object's center point, select the object, choose the transformation tool, hold down Option and click to establish a point of origin, then enter numbers in the tool dialog box.

Press-and-drag method

Select the object, choose the tool, click to establish a point of origin, release and reposition the mouse, then press and drag away from, around, or toward the point of origin.

Or, to use the object's center point as the point of origin, select the object, choose the tool, position the pointer outside the object, then press and drag immediately. The further you drag, the greater the transformation.

Press-and-drag method tips

If you use either drag method, after the point of origin is established, the mouse pointer turns into an arrowhead. For optimal control, position the arrowhead a few inches away from the point of origin before dragging.

To choose a different point of origin, click again to redisplay the crosshair pointer, then follow the remaining instruction steps.

Hold down Option while dragging to transform a copy of the original. Release the mouse, then release Option.

To repeat a transformation

Once you have transformed an object, you can transform it again or transform another selected object by choosing Arrange > Repeat Transform (⌘-D). If you transform and copy an object and then choose Repeat Transform, another copy of the original object will be produced.

Figure 1a. *Click to establish a point of origin.*

Figure 1b. *Reposition the mouse.*

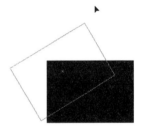

Figure 1c. *Press and drag to transform.*

To learn how to scale or rotate an object using the **Control** palette, see page 233.

To transform type, see pages 172 and 174.

To learn about transforming patterns, see page 130.

Transformation Tool Methods

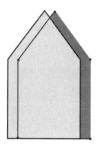

Figure 2. *The shadow object is selected.*

Figure 3. *Rotate tool.*

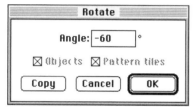

Figure 4. *Enter a number in the* **Angle** *field in the* **Rotate** *dialog box. Click* **Copy** *to rotate a copy of the object.*

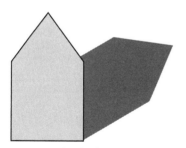

Figure 5. *The shadow was rotated –60°, then moved.*

To rotate an object (dialog box method):

1. Select an object (or objects) (**Figure 2**).
2. Double-click the Rotate tool to rotate the object from its center (**Figure 3**).
   or
   Click the Rotate tool, then hold down Option and click to establish a point of origin.
3. Enter a number between 360 and –360 in the Angle field. Enter a positive number to rotate the object counterclockwise or a negative number to rotate the object clockwise (**Figure 4**).
4. *Optional:* If the object contains a Fill pattern and you check the "Pattern tiles" box, the pattern will rotate with the object. (This option can also be turned on or off in the General Preferences dialog box.)
5. *Optional:* Click Copy to rotate a copy of the original (not the original object) and close the dialog box.
6. Click OK or press Return (**Figure 5**).

To rotate an object by dragging:

1. Select an object.
2. Click the Rotate tool (**Figure 3**).
3. Click to establish a point of origin (the pointer will turn into an arrowhead), release and reposition the mouse, then drag to rotate the object (**Figures 1a–c**). Hold down Option while dragging to rotate a copy of the object.
   or
   Without clicking first, press and drag immediately around the object to use the object's center as the point of origin.

■ Hold down Shift while dragging to rotate in 45° increments. Release the mouse before you release Shift.

Rotate

To scale an object (dialog box method):

1. Select an object.

2. To scale the object from its center, double-click the Scale tool (**Figure 6**).
or
Choose the Scale tool, then hold down Option and click to establish a point of origin.

3. To scale the object **proportionately:**
Click **Uniform** (**Figure 7**).
and
In the Uniform field, enter a number above 100 to enlarge the object or a number below 100 to shrink it.

Optional: Check the "Scale line weight" box to scale the Stroke thickness proportionately.

To scale the object **non-proportionately**, in the Horizontal and/or Vertical fields, enter a number above 100 or below 100 to enlarge or reduce that dimension (**Figure 8**). Enter 100 to leave the dimension unchanged. Line weights won't transform.

4. *Optional:* Click Copy to scale a copy of the original (not the original object) and close the dialog box.

5. *Optional:* If the object contains a Fill pattern and you check the "Pattern tiles" box, the pattern will rescale with the object.

6. Click OK or press Return (**Figures 9a–c**).

Figure 6.
Scale tool.

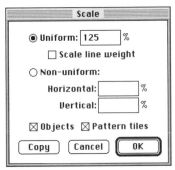
Figure 7. *In the Scale dialog box, click **Uniform** to scale proportionately, and enter a percentage.*

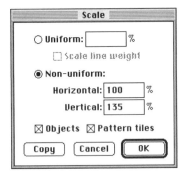
Figure 8. *To scale non-proportionately, enter **Horizontal** and **Vertical** percentages.*

Figure 9a.
The original object.

Figure 9b. *The object and the pattern scaled **Uniformly** (125%).*

Figure 9c. *The object and pattern scaled **Nonuniformly** (100% Horizontal, 135% Vertical).*

Scale

To scale an object by dragging:

1. Select an object.

2. Click the Scale tool (**Figure 6**).

3. Click to establish a point of origin (**Figure 10**) (the pointer will turn into an arrowhead), release and reposition the mouse (**Figure 11**), then drag away from the object to enlarge it or drag toward the object to shrink it (**Figure 12**). Hold down Option while dragging to scale a copy of the object. The object will remain selected when you release the mouse (**Figure 13**).

   or

   To scale from the object's center, without clicking first, press and drag away from or toward the object.

■ Hold down Shift while dragging diagonally to scale the object proportionately. Release the mouse before you release Shift.

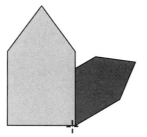

Figure 10. *Click to establish a point of origin.*

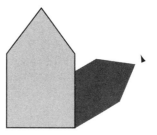

Figure 11. *Release and reposition the mouse.*

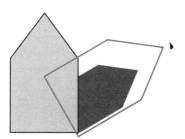

Figure 12. *Press and drag away from the object.*

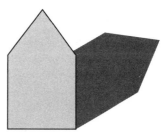

Figure 13. *The shadow object is enlarged.*

To reflect (flip) an object (dialog box method):

1. Select an object.
2. To reflect from the object's center, double-click the Reflect tool (**Figure 14**).
   or
   Choose the Reflect tool, then hold down Option and click to establish a point of origin.
3. Click the Horizontal or Vertical button (the axis the mirror image will flip across) (**Figure 15**).
   or
   Enter a number between 180 and −180 in the Angle field. Enter a positive number to rotate the object counterclockwise or a negative number to rotate the object clockwise. The angle is measured from the horizontal (*x*) axis.
4. *Optional:* If the object contains a Fill pattern and you check the "Pattern tiles" box, the pattern will reflect with the object.
5. *Optional:* Click Copy to reflect a copy of the original (not the original object) and close the dialog box.
6. Click OK or press Return (**Figures 16–17**).

To reflect an object by dragging:

1. Select an object.
2. Choose the Reflect tool (**Figure 14**).
3. Click to establish a point of origin (the pointer will turn into an arrowhead).
4. Release and reposition the mouse, then press and drag. The object will flip across the axis you create by dragging. (Hold down Option to reflect a copy of the object.)
- Hold down Shift while dragging to mirror the object in 45° increments. Release the mouse before you release Shift.

Figure 14.
Reflect tool.

Figure 15. *In the Reflect dialog box, click Horizontal or Vertical, or enter a number in the Angle field.*

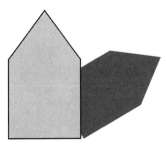

Figure 16. *The original objects.*

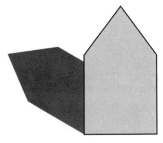

Figure 17. *The shadow reflected along the Vertical Axis.*

Reflect

Figure 18. *The shadow object is selected.*

Figure 19. *Shear tool*

Figure 20. *In the Shear dialog box, enter an Angle, then click an Axis button.*

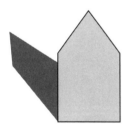

Figure 21. *The shadow object sheared at a −35° Angle on the Horizontal Axis.*

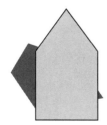

Figure 22. *The shadow object sheared at a −35° Angle on a 35° Axis Angle.*

To shear (slant) an object (dialog box method):

1. Select an object (**Figure 18**).
2. To shear the object from its center, double-click the Shear tool (**Figure 19**).
   or
   Choose the Shear tool, then hold down Option and click to establish a point of origin.
3. Enter a number between 360 and −360 in the Angle field (**Figure 20**).
4. Click the Horizontal or Vertical button (the Axis along which the object will be sheared) (**Figure 21**).
   or
   Click the Axis: Angle button, then enter a number in the Axis: Angle field (the angle will be calculated relative to the horizontal (x) axis) (**Figure 22**).
5. *Optional:* Check the "Pattern tiles" box to shear a pattern Fill with the object.
6. *Optional:* Click Copy to shear a copy of the original (not the original object) and close the dialog box.
7. Click OK or press Return. The object will shear from its center.

To shear an object by dragging:

1. Select an object.
2. Click the Shear tool (**Figure 19**).
3. Click to establish a point of origin, release and reposition the mouse, then drag. Hold down Option while dragging to shear a copy of the object.
   or
   Without clicking, position the pointer outside the object, then press and drag away from the object. The object will slant from its center along the line that you drag.

■ Start dragging, then hold down Shift to shear the object in 45° increments. Release the mouse, then release Shift.

Shear

185

Blend

The **Blend** tool creates a multi-step progression between two objects. The objects can have different shapes and can have different Fills and Strokes. You can blend two open paths — like lines — or two closed paths, but you can't blend an open and a closed path.

To blend (transform) one object into another:

1. Move two open or two closed objects apart to allow room for the transition objects that will appear between them.

2. Choose the Selection tool.

3. Marquee both objects.

4. Choose the Blend tool (**Figure 23**).

5. Click on a point on the first object.

6. Click on a corresponding point on the second object (**Figure 24**). For example, if you clicked on the top left corner of the first object, click on the top left corner of the second object. If the objects are open paths, click an endpoint on each.

7. Enter a number in the Steps field (**Figure 25**). The fewer the steps and the farther apart the original objects are, the less the transition objects will overlap. Try a low number first. *(See the box at right)*

8. Click OK or press Return. A series of transition objects will appear between the first and last objects. Only the transition objects will be selected, and they will be grouped (**Figure 26**).

ABOUT BLEND STEPS ──────────

■ Illustrator automatically inserts a suggested number of steps in the Blend dialog box based on the difference in CMYK percentages between the two objects and the assumption that the output device will be high-resolution (1200 dpi or higher). To produce a smooth transition between objects, use the suggested step number. To output on a lower resolution printer or to produce a noticeable, banded transition, enter a lower number.

■ Illustrator's Gradient feature may produce smoother color blends than the Blend tool. Gradients are designed for high-resolution printing.

■ If you create a color blend across a wide distance (more than seven inches), banding may result. Use Adobe Photoshop to produce a wide color blend.

Figure 23.
Blend tool.

Figure 24. *Click on corresponding points on two objects.*

Figure 25. *In the **Blend** dialog box, enter a number of transition **Steps** for the blend.*

To blend only colors between objects — not object shapes — use one of the Blend filters, which are covered on page 112.

■ After producing a blend, group the original objects and the transition objects together so you can select and move them easily.

■ If you don't like the blend, press Delete while the transition objects are still selected. The original objects won't be deleted. Select the original objects again and redo the blend, if you like.

■ If one of the original objects contains a process color and the other object contains a spot color, the transition objects will be painted with process colors. If you blend two tints of the same spot color, the transition objects will be painted with graduated tints of that color. To blend between a spot color and white, repaint the white object with 0% of the spot color.

■ If you click with the Blend tool on non-corresponding points of similar objects (such as the top of one shape and the bottom of the other), the transition objects will be "twisted."

■ If one object has more points than the other, rather than selecting the whole objects, as in step 3 on the previous page, you can use the Direct Selection tool to select the same number of similarly located points on each object.

■ If the original objects have a Stroke color, the transition objects will be clearly delineated.

Blend

Figure 26. *A military plane transformed into a bird.*

To make the edge of an object look three-dimensional:

1. Select an object (**Figure 27**).

2. Apply a Fill color and a Stroke of None.

3. Double-click the Scale tool.

4. Click Uniform.

5. Enter a number between 60 and 80 in the Percentage field.

6. Click Copy.

7. With the copy still selected, choose a lighter or darker variation of the original Fill color (**Figure 28**). For a process color, you can hold down Shift and drag a process color slider on the Paint Style palette.

8. Choose the Selection tool.

9. Marquee both objects, or hold down Shift and click on both objects.

10. Click the Blend tool.

11. Click on a point on one object.

12. Click on a similarly located point on the other object.

13. Enter a number between 30 and 60 in the Steps field (**Figure 29**).
 or
 Leave the suggested number as is.

14. Click OK or press Return (**Figure 30**).

■ Make sure the smaller object is in front of the larger object before blending them.

■ If the objects have many points, click on non-similar points on the first and last objects to produce a different-looking blend.

Figure 27. *The original object.*

Figure 28. *A reduced-size copy of the object is created, and a darker Fill color is applied.*

Figure 29. *In the Blend dialog box, enter a number of transition Steps.*

Figure 30. *The two objects are blended together.*

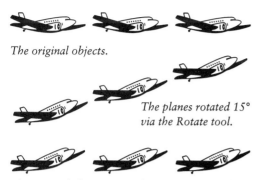

The original objects.

*The planes rotated 15°
via the Rotate tool.*

*The original objects rotated 15° via the Transform
Each command.*

Figure 31.

Arrange
Repeat Transform	⌘D
Moue...	⌘⇧M
Bring To Front	⌘=
Send To Back	⌘-
Transform Each...	
Group	⌘G
Ungroup	⌘U
Lock	⌘1
Unlock All	⌘2
Hide	⌘3
Show All	⌘4

Figure 32. *Choose
Transform Each
from the Arrange
menu.*

Transform Each

Scale
Horizontal: 150 %
Vertical: 100 %

Move
Horizontal: 0 pt
Vertical: 0 pt

Rotate
Angle: 106 °

☐ Random ☒ Preview
Copy Cancel OK

Figure 33. *The Transform Each dialog box.*

The Transform Each command modifies one or more selected objects relative to their individual center points. The transformation tools, in contrast, transform multiple objects relative to a single, common center point (**Figure 31**). To make your illustration look more irregular and hand drawn, apply the Transform Each command to multiple objects with the Random box checked.

To apply several transformation commands at once:

1. Select one or more objects.
2. Choose Arrange > Transform Each (**Figure 32**).
3. Check the Preview box (**Figure 33**).
4. Move the Scale sliders to change the object's horizontal and/or vertical dimensions.
5. Choose a higher Horizontal Move amount to move the object to the right (or vice versa), or higher Vertical Move amount to move the object upward (or vice versa).
6. Enter a number in the Rotate Angle field, or move the dial in the circle.
7. *Optional:* Check the Random box to have Illustrator apply random transformations within the range of the slider values you've chosen. For example, if you set Rotation Angle to 35°, Illustrator will pick a different number between 0 and 35 for each selected object.
8. Click OK or press Return (**Figures 34a–b**).

■ Hold down Option and click Reset to restore the original dialog box values. The Preview box will uncheck.

■ Objects are scaled horizontally or vertically relative to the objects' current horizontal and vertical axes.

Transform Each

(Illustrations on the next page)

Transform Each

Figure 34a. *The original objects.*

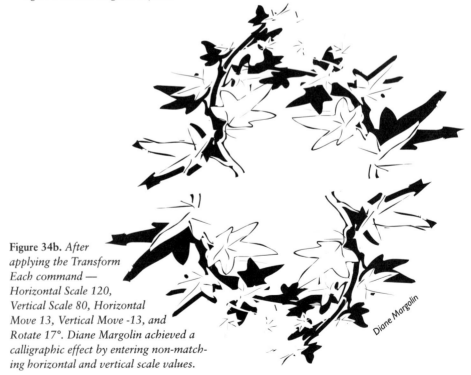

Figure 34b. *After applying the Transform Each command — Horizontal Scale 120, Vertical Scale 80, Horizontal Move 13, Vertical Move -13, and Rotate 17°. Diane Margolin achieved a calligraphic effect by entering non-matching horizontal and vertical scale values.*

Diane Margolin

COMPOUNDS 17

The compound path command joins two or more objects into one object. Where the original objects overlapped, a transparent "hole" is created, through which shapes or patterns behind the object are revealed.

In this chapter, you will learn to create a compound path using the Make Compound Paths command or the Minus Front filter, to release a compound path, and to recolor parts of a compound path. The Divide filter is also discussed because it can be used to create "cutouts" or translucent effects.

Figure 1. *Several objects are placed on top of a larger object, and all the objects are selected.*

Regardless of their original paint attributes, all the objects in a compound path are painted with the attributes of the backmost object, and they're grouped.

To create a compound path:

1. Arrange the objects you want to see through in front of a larger shape (**Figure 1**). (For these instructions, you might want to display the illustration in two windows: one in Artwork view and the other in Preview view.)

2. Choose the Selection tool.

3. Marquee all the objects, or hold down Shift and click on all the objects.

4. Choose Object > Compound Paths > Make (⌘-8) (**Figure 2**). The frontmost objects will "cut" through the backmost object (**Figures 3–4**).

■ Areas where the original frontmost objects overlap each other, and parts of the original frontmost objects that extend beyond the edge of the backmost object, will be painted with the color of the backmost object.

■ Use the Selection tool to select and move a whole compound path; use the Direct Selection tool to select and move a part of a compound path.

■ Regardless of the layers the original objects were on, the final compound path will be placed on the frontmost object's layer.

■ Only one Fill color can be applied to a compound path.

■ To add an object to a compound path, select the compound path and the object you wish to add to it, then choose Object > Compound Path > Make.

Figure 2. *Choose Make from the Compound Paths submenu under the Object menu.*

Figure 3. *The objects converted into a compound path.*

Figure 4. *A background object is placed behind the compound path. (And a white Stroke is applied.)*

Figure 5. *Click on the compound path.*

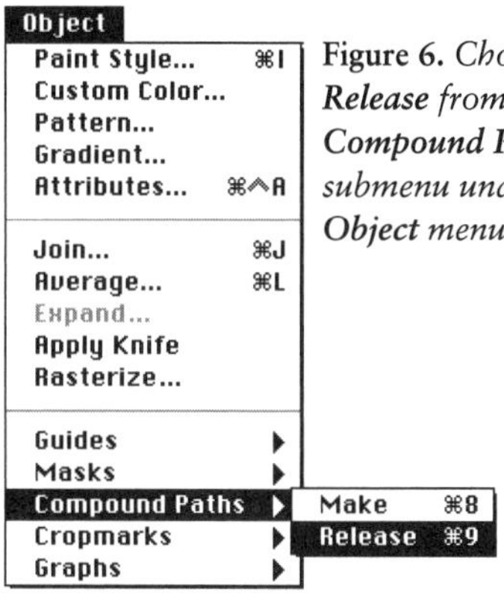

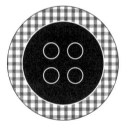

Figure 6. *Choose* **Release** *from the* **Compound Paths** *submenu under the Object menu.*

Figure 7. *The released compound path. The button-holes are no longer transparent.*

Figure 8a. *Type out-lines (a compound path).*

Figure 8b. *The compound path released into separate objects. (The counter of the "P" was moved for illustration purposes.)*

You can revert a compound path back into individual objects.

To release a compound path:

1. Choose the Selection tool.
2. Click on the compound path (**Figure 5**).
3. Choose Object > Compound Paths > Release (⌘-9) (**Figure 6**). All the objects will be selected and painted with the attributes from the compound path (**Figure 7**).

■ If you release a type outline compound path that has a counter (interior shape), the counter will become a separate shape with the same paint attributes as the outer part of the let-terform (**Figures 8a–b**).

■ To remove an object from a compound path without releasing the compound, select the object with the Direct Selection tool, then press Delete. Or, Cut and Paste the object if you want to save it.

■ All objects released from a compound path will have the same Stroke and Fill, not their pre-compound colors. It may be difficult to distinguish over-lapping objects if your illustration is in Preview view; they will be easier to distinguish in Artwork view. The objects will also stay on the same layer, regardless of which layer they were on before being assembled into a compound.

Release a Compound Path

The paint colors in areas that are "cut out" in a compound path can be reversed.

To reverse the Fill of an object in a compound path:

1. Choose Direct Selection tool.

2. Click on the object in the compound path you wish to modify (**Figure 9**).

3. Choose Object > Attributes (⌘-Control-A) (**Figure 10**).

4. If the "Reverse path direction" box is checked, uncheck it, or vice versa (**Figure 11**).

5. Click OK. The selected path will now have the opposite Fill (the compound path Fill Color or a Fill of None) (**Figure 12**).

■ If the Reverse path direction box is gray, you have selected the whole compound path. Be sure to select one path within the compound instead.

Figure 9. *Click on an object in the compound path.*

Figure 10. *Choose **Attributes** from the **Object** menu.*

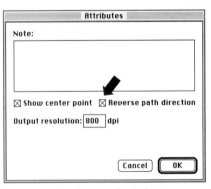

Figure 11. *Check or uncheck the **Reverse path direction** box in the **Attributes** dialog box.*

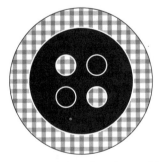

Figure 12. *The color of two of the buttonholes has been reversed.*

Figure 13. *The front-most object does not extend beyond the edge of the black square.*

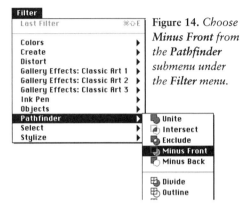

Figure 14. *Choose* **Minus Front** *from the* **Pathfinder** *submenu under the* **Filter** *menu.*

Figure 15. *The box is a compound path.*

Figure 16a. *The lines extend beyond the box.*

Figure 16b. *After applying the Minus Front filter, the box is divided into three separate objects, and is* **not** *a compound path.*

To create a compound path using the Minus Front filter:

1. Arrange the objects you wish to use in the compound path. Make sure the frontmost objects do not extend beyond the edge of the backmost object, otherwise you will not create a compound path (**Figure 13**).

2. Choose the Selection tool.

3. Select all the objects.

4. Choose Filter > Pathfinder > Minus Front (**Figure 14**). The frontmost objects will "cut through" the backmost object (**Figure 15**).

■ If objects extend beyond the edge of the backmost object before you apply the Minus Front filter, the backmost object will be divided into separate objects, and the overhanging objects will be deleted (**Figures 16a–b**). The result will not be a compound path, but you can create interesting effects by applying different Fill colors to the separate objects.

■ You can arrange smaller objects behind a larger object and then apply the Minus Back filter. The smaller objects will "cut" through the frontmost object.

■ If the frontmost object is a line, choose Filter > Objects > Outline Path to convert it into a closed path before applying the Minus Front filter. Using a line in a compound path may produce irregular cutout shapes.

The **Divide** filter does not create a compound path, but it can be used to create compound-like effects, illusions of translucency, or cutouts.

To apply the Divide filter:

1. Arrange objects so they at least partially overlap (**Figure 17**).

2. Choose the Selection tool.

3. Marquee all the objects.

4. Choose Filter > Pathfinder > Divide (**Figure 18**). Each area where the original objects overlapped will become a separate object.

5. Click away from all objects to deselect them.

6. Choose the Direct Selection tool.

7. Click on any of the objects and apply new Fill colors or apply a Fill of None to make an object transparent (**Figure 19**). Or move or remove individual objects to create cutouts.

■ The Divide filter will remove any Stroke color from the original objects. You can reapply a Stroke color to any object after applying the filter.

Figure 17. *The original objects. The type was converted into outlines.*

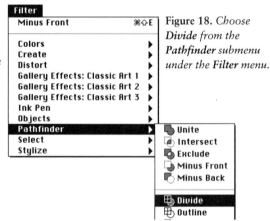

Figure 18. *Choose **Divide** from the **Pathfinder** submenu under the **Filter** menu.*

Figure 19. *After applying the Divide filter. Unlike in a compound path, the areas where the original objects overlapped are now separate objects. Different Fill colors were applied to parts of the letters.*

Divide Filter

MASKS | 18

A mask is also called a clipping path, because it "clips" away the parts of other shapes that extend beyond its border. Only parts of objects that are within the confines of the mask will show. Masked objects can be moved, restacked, reshaped, or repainted. In this chapter you will learn how to create a mask, how to restack, add, delete, or repaint masked objects, how to unmask an object, and how to release a mask.

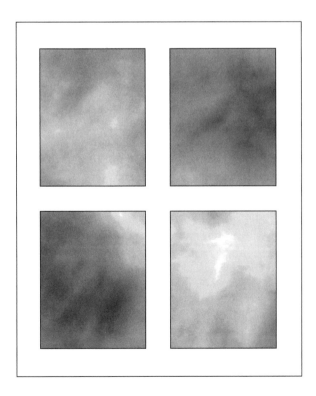

Note: To use a group of objects or use type outlines as a mask, you must first convert them into a compound path (choose Object > Compound Paths > Make).

To create a mask:

1. *Optional:* Follow the instructions on the next page to place the masking object and the objects to be masked on one layer before you create the mask so you can easily reposition them using the Layers palette.

2. Arrange the objects to be masked (**Figure 1**). The masking object can be an open or closed path.

3. Select the masking object, then choose Arrange > Bring to Front or move the object to the top layer using Layers palette (**Figure 2**).

4. Choose the Selection tool.

5. Select all the objects, including the masking object.

6. Choose Object > Masks > Make (**Figure 3**). The mask will have a Stroke and Fill of None and all the objects will be selected. You can move masked objects individually using the Selection or Direct Selection tool.

■ If the mask is too complex, it may not print. Don't make a mask out of a complex shape with hundreds of points or out of an intricate compound path. Don't use more than seven or eight type outline characters per mask.

■ If you want to copy a masked object, use the Copy and Paste commands rather than the Option–drag shortcut.

Figure 1. *Arrange the objects to be masked.*

Figure 2. *Place the masking object in front of the other objects.*

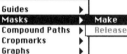

Figure 3. *Choose* Make *from the* Masks *submenu under the* Object *menu.*

Figure 4. *A Stroke color was applied to the mask in this illustration.*

Create a Mask

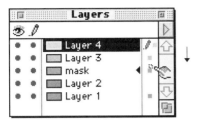

Figure 5a. *The little square from* **Layer 4** *being moved down to the layer called* "**mask**."

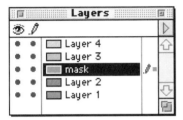

Figure 5b.

Any objects on the same layer as, and in front of an object that is selected to be masked, or on a layer in between the layers of objects to be masked, will also be masked. You can prevent this problem by following these steps.

To position the objects to be masked on one layer:

1. If the Layers palette is not displayed, choose Window > Show Layers.

2. Choose New Layer from the Layers palette pop-up menu, enter a name, then click OK.

3. Choose the Selection tool.

4. Hold down Shift and click on the masking object and the objects to be masked.

5. On the Layers palette, drag the little square in the rightmost column up or down to the new layer (**Figures 5a–b**).

6. Follow the instructions on the previous page to create a mask.

■ You can also select all the objects (step 3) and then group them, which will automatically put them on one layer.

Figure 6. *Choose* **Bring To Front** *or* **Send To Back** *from the* **Arrange** *menu.*

Stacking is explained in Chapter 10.

To restack a masked object:

1. Choose the Selection tool.

2. Select the object to be restacked.

3. Choose Arrange > Bring To Front or Arrange > Send To Back (**Figure 6**).
   or
   Choose Edit > Cut, select another masked object, then choose Edit > Paste In Front or Edit > Paste In Back.

Re-Layer or Re-Stack Masked Objects

To select mask objects:

To select the mask and the masked objects, choose the **Group Selection** tool, then double-click on any of the objects.

To select one or more **individual masked objects**, use the **Selection** tool.

If you haven't applied a Fill or Stroke color to the mask, it will be invisible in Preview view. To select **only the mask** when your illustration is in **Preview** view, choose the **Selection** tool, then drag across where you think the edge of the mask is. If your illustration is in Artwork view, choose the Selection tool, then click on the edge of the mask.

To **select all the masks in your illustration**, deselect all objects, then choose Filter > Select > Select Masks. Shift-click with the Selection tool on any mask you don't want selected.

To convert a gradient or a pattern into a grouped set of masked objects, select an object that contains a gradient or pattern Fill, then choose Object > Expand.

To add an object to a mask:

1. Choose the Selection tool.
2. Select the object to be added.
3. Move the object over the mask (**Figures 7a**).
4. Choose Edit > Cut.
5. Click on a masked object.
6. Choose Edit > Paste In Front (⌘-F) or Edit > Paste In Back (⌘-B). The new object will be masked and will be stacked in front of or behind the object you selected (**Figure 7b**).

■ Follow the instructions on the previous page if you want to change the stacking position of the newly pasted object.

Figure 7a. *Move the object you want to add over the mask.*

Figure 7b.

Figure 8. *Select the object you want to unmask.*

Edit

Undo Copy	⌘Z
Redo Cut	⌘⇧Z
Cut	**⌘X**
Copy	⌘C
Paste	⌘U
Clear	
Select All	⌘A
Select None	⌘⇧A
Paste In Front	⌘F
Paste In Back	⌘B
Publishing	▶
Show Clipboard	

Figure 9. *Choose* **Cut** *from the* **Edit** *menu, deselect the mask, then choose* **Paste**.

Figure 10. *The object is now unmasked.*

To unmask an object:

1. Choose the Selection tool.
2. Click on the object you want to unmask (**Figure 8**).
3. Choose Edit > Cut (**Figure 9**).
4. *Optional:* If the mask and masked objects are on different layers, highlight a layer on the Layers palette that is above or below those layers.
5. Choose Edit > Paste. The pasted object will now be independent of the mask. Reposition it, if you like (**Figure 10**).

■ To unmask an object another way, select the object, then, on the Layers palette, drag the little square for the selected object to a different layer.

■ To unmask an object and delete it from the illustration, select it, then press Delete.

■ To determine whether an object is being masked, select the object, then choose Object > Attributes (⌘-Control-A). If the object is being masked, you'll see these words: *The current selection is affected by a mask.*

Figure 11. *The mask is released.*

When you release a mask, the complete objects are displayed again.

To release a mask:

1. Choose the Group Selection tool.
2. Double-click on the mask or click on the masking object.
3. Choose Object > Masks > Release (**Figure 11**).

To apply a Fill and/or Stroke color to a mask for the first time, you must use the Paint Style palette and the Fill and Stroke for Mask filter. To choose new Fill or Stroke colors for a masked object, just use the Paint Style palette.

To Fill and/or Stroke a mask:

1. Choose the Selection tool. (Choose the Direct Selection tool if the masked object is part of a group.)

2. In Artwork view, drag over or click on the edge of the mask (**Figure 12**).

3. Choose Preview view, then choose a Fill and/or Stroke color from the Paint Style palette.

4. Choose Filter > Create > Fill & Stroke for Mask (**Figure 13**).

5. Click OK when the prompt appears. The new Stroke and Fill will be separate objects. You can now select either object with the Selection tool and repaint it without having to reapply the Fill & Stroke for Mask filter (**Figures 14–15b**). The Stroke object will be in front of, but not part of, the mask.

   If the masked objects are on the same layer, the Fill object will be masked. If the masked objects are on more than one layer, you can't apply this filter. Place all the objects on one layer (see page 199).

6. *Optional:* To group the Stroke object with the mask, choose the Selection tool, press and drag a marquee across the mask and the Stroke object, then choose Arrange > Group.

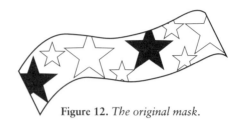

Figure 12. *The original mask.*

Figure 13. *Choose* **Fill & Stroke for Mask** *from the* **Create** *submenu under the* **Filter** *menu.*

Figure 14. *A Black Fill was applied to the mask. The masked objects were also repainted.*

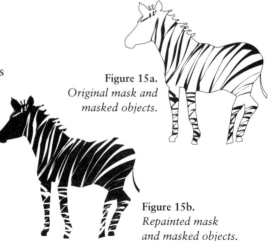

Figure 15a. *Original mask and masked objects.*

Figure 15b. *Repainted mask and masked objects.*

This chapter covers many of Illustrator's powerful and easy-to-use image editing and object reshaping filters.

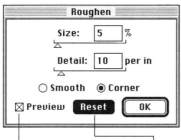

Many filter dialog boxes have a Preview option — turn it on to preview the filter effect in your illustration while the dialog box is open. Press Tab to preview after entering a new amount in an entry field.

In any dialog box with a Preview option and sliders, hold down Option and click Reset to restore the initial dialog box settings.

*The **last used filter** (⌘-Shift-E). Select to reapply the filter with the same settings. (To apply the last used filter using new settings, choose the filter name from the submenu.)*

Figure 1. *The Filter menu.*

Eight filter submenu categories are covered in this book:

Color: Adjust color in one or more objects.

Create: Create an object mosaic, create trim marks, or paint a mask.

Distort: Reshape or stylize objects.

Ink Pen: Create line work textures.

Objects: Convert Strokes into closed objects, add anchor points to an object.

Pathfinder: Unite, divide, merge, crop, or recolor overlapping objects.

Select: Select objects with the same characteristics as the currently selected object.

Stylize: Reshape objects for special effects.

Some filters are applied just by selecting the filter name from a submenu (**Figure 1**). Other filters are applied via a dialog box in which special options are selected.

Note: For a filter to be accessible in Illustrator, it must be in the Plug-ins folder when the application is launched. To access certain Objects filters (Offset Path, Outline Path) and all the Pathfinder filters, a math coprocessor must be installed on your Macintosh.

You can apply Photoshop-compatible filters to placed images and to objects rasterized in Illustrator. To use Photoshop 3.0.4 filters in Illustrator, copy the filters (or aliases of the filters) into a new folder in the Filters folder inside Illustrator's Plug-ins folder.

(Some Illustrator filters are covered in other chapters. See the index for page locations.)

Filters

Object Mosaic Filter

The **Object Mosaic** filter breaks a raster image into little "pixel" squares that are separate objects and can be moved individually. *Note:* This filter can be applied to a rasterized object, a PICT, a TIFF or a parsed EPS, but not to a placed EPS.

To "pixelate" a placed image:

1. Click on a placed image.

2. Choose Filter > Create > Object Mosaic (**Figure 2**).

3. *Optional:* The Current Size field displays the width and height of the image in points (**Figure 3**). Enter new numbers in the New Size: Width and/or Height fields. Or, enter a new Width (or Height), click Lock Width (or Lock Height), then click Use Ratio to have Illustrator automatically calculate the height (or width) proportionate to the original dimensions.

4. Enter the number of tiles to fill the width and height dimensions. If you clicked Use Ratio, the Number of Tiles will be calculated automatically.

5. *Optional:* To add space between each tile, enter numbers in the Tile Spacing Width and Height fields.

6. Click Color or Gray.

7. Click OK or press Return (**Figures 4a–c**).

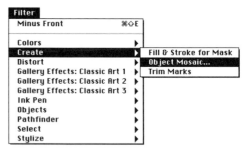

*Figure 2. Choose **Object Mosaic** from the **Create** submenu under the **Filter** menu.*

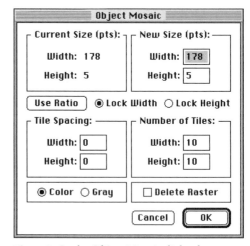

*Figure 3. In the **Object Mosaic** dialog box, enter numbers in the **New Size** and **Number of Tiles** **Width** and **Height** fields.*

Figure 4a. *The original PICT.*

Figure 4b. *The **Object Mosaic** filter applied with no **Width** or **Height** change.*

Figure 4c. *The **Object Mosaic** filter applied, **Use Ratio** option not clicked and the **Height** value changed.*

Figure 5. *The original object.*

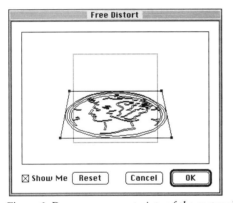

Figure 6. *Drag any corner points of the rectangle in the **Free Distort** dialog box.*

To apply the Free Distort filter:

1. Select an object or objects (**Figure 5**).

2. Choose Filter > Distort > Free Distort.

3. Drag any corner point or points of the rectangle that surrounds the object(s) in the dialog box (**Figure 6**). You can drag it beyond the edges of the dialog box.

4. Check the Show Me box to preview the shape in the dialog box.

5. *Optional:* Click Reset if you want to restore the original object and surrounding rectangle in the Preview window.

6. Click OK or press Return (**Figures 7–8b**).

■ If the object is complex, it may not be drawn accurately in the preview box, but it will be drawn accurately in the illustration.

■ To apply the Free Distort filter to type, you must first convert the type to outlines (choose Type > Create Outlines).

■ The last rectangle shape used in the Free Distort dialog box will be displayed if the dialog box is reopened. Click OK to apply the same distortion to another object or click Reset to restore the rectangle to its normal shape.

Free Distort Filter

Figure 7. *After applying the Free Distort filter.*

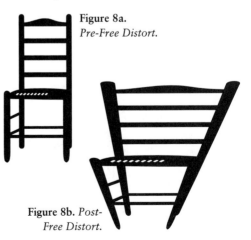

Figure 8a. *Pre-Free Distort.*

Figure 8b. *Post-Free Distort.*

To scribble or tweak:

1. Select an object or objects.

2. Choose Filter > Distort > Scribble and Tweak.

3. Check the Preview box (**Figure 9**).

4. Click Scribble or Tweak. Scribble moves points randomly, Tweak moves points the actual amounts you specify.

5. Choose Horizontal and Vertical amounts (calculated as a percentage of the longest segment of the object) to specify how much an anchor point or a segment can be moved (Scribble) or will actually move (Tweak).

6. Check the Anchor Points, "In" Control Points or "Out" Control Points boxes to choose which points on the path will be moved.

7. Click OK or press Return (**Figures 10–11**). Direction lines will be added automatically to the corner points of paths with straight sides. How these new direction lines are moved depends on the "In" and "Out" options you chose.

■ The greater the number of anchor points on the path, the greater the Scribble filter effect. To add points, apply the Add Anchor Points filter (Objects submenu).

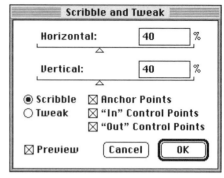

Figure 9. *The Scribble and Tweak dialog box.*

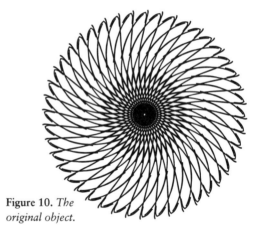

Figure 10. *The original object.*

Figure 11. *After applying the Scribble filter, Horizontal 14.5, Vertical 19.5, "In" and "Out" boxes checked.*

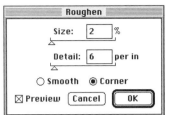

Figure 12. *The Roughen dialog box.*

Figure 13a. *The original object.*

Figure 13b. *After applying the Roughen filter (Size 39, Detail 2, Smooth).*

Figure 13c. *Figure 13a after applying the Roughen filter (Size 30, Detail 3, Corner).*

The **Roughen** filter makes an object look "hand drawn" by adding and then moving anchor points.

To rough up a shape:

1. Select an object or objects, and choose View > Hide Edges (⌘-Shift-H), if you like, to make previewing easier.

2. Choose Filter > Distort > Roughen.

3. Click Preview (**Figure 12**).

4. Enter a number in the Size field (a percentage of the object's longest path segment) to specify how far points can be moved. Try a low number first.

5. Enter a number in the Detail field (how many points will be added to each inch of the path segments).

6. Click Smooth to produce soft edges or click Corner to produce Sharp edges.

7. Click OK or press Return (**Figures 13a–14**).

Figure 14. *Left: the original image; right: after applying the Roughen filter (Size 2, Detail 6, Smooth).*

Figure 15a. *The original objects.*

To twirl path points around an object's center (dialog box method):

1. Select an object or objects (**Figure 15a**). If several objects are selected, they will be twirled together.

2. Choose Filter > Distort > Twirl.

3. Enter a number in the Angle field. Enter a positive number to twirl the paths clockwise; enter a negative number to twirl them counterclockwise.

4. Click OK or press Return (**Figures 15b–c**).

■ To add points to a path and heighten the Twirl filter effect, choose Filter > Objects > Add Anchor Points before applying the Twirl filter.

Figure 15b. *The objects twirled together, Angle 1000°.*

Figure 15c. *Twirl filter applied to Figure 15b, Angle 3000°.*

Roughen and Twirl Filters

207

The Twirl plug-in tool, like the Twirl filter, twirls points around an object's center, but it generally produces more subtle effects.

To twirl points around an object's center (mouse method):

1. Select an object.
2. Choose the Twirl tool from the Plug-in Tools palette (Window > Show Plug-in Tools) (**Figure 16**).
3. Click where you want the center of the object to be.
4. Move the mouse slightly away from the center point, then drag clockwise around the object to twirl it clockwise or drag counterclockwise to twirl the object counterclockwise. Repeat to intensify the twirl effect (**Figures 17a–b**).

■ The angle of twirl that is created by dragging the mouse will be entered automatically in the Twirl filter dialog box (Filter > Distort > Twirl). You can Option-click on the illustration with the Twirl tool to open the Twirl filter dialog box.

■ The Twirl tool and Twirl filter won't change a pattern or gradient Fill; they will twirl only the object's overall path shape. To twirl a pattern or gradient Fill, apply the Object > Expand command to the object first to break the pattern or gradient down into discrete shapes. A document containing numerous expanded and twirled objects will be large in size, though, and may not print easily.

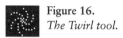

Figure 16.
The Twirl tool.

Figure 17a. *The original*

Figure 17b. *After twirling.*

Twirl Plug-in Tool

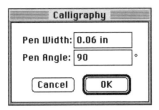

Figure 18. Enter numbers in the Pen Width and Pen Angle fields in the Calligraphy dialog box.

The **Calligraphy** filter produces a thick-and-thin line like the Brush tool produces when used with its Calligraphic option. Unlike the Brush tool, however, the Calligraphy filter can be applied to any existing object except a type object.

To create calligraphic edges:

1. Select an object.
2. Choose Filter > Stylize > Calligraphy.
3. Enter a number in the Pen Width field (the width of the thickest part of the stroke) (**Figure 18**).
4. Enter a number in the Pen Angle field.
5. Click OK or press Return (**Figures 19a–20b**).

■ The Calligraphy filter will convert an open path — like a line — into a closed path. If the object is a filled, closed path, the filter will remove its center area and create a thick-and-thin Fill along its edge, like a ribbon.

Figure 19a. The original object. This flower was drawn with the Freehand tool.

*Figure 19b. After applying the **Calligraphy** filter.*

Figure 20a. The original object, drawn with the Brush tool. Filters > Pathfinder > Unite was applied to remove extraneous angle pieces before applying the Calligraphy filter.

*Figure 20b. After applying the **Calligraphy** filter.*

Calligraphy Filter

209

Drop shadow objects that the **Drop Shadow** filter creates are colored in a darker shade of the object's Fill and Stroke colors. (To produce a shadow by copying an object, see page 173.)

To create a drop shadow:

1. Select one or more objects (**Figure 21**).

2. Choose Filter > Stylize > Drop Shadow.

3. Enter a number in the X Offset field (the horizontal distance between the object and the shadow) and a number in the Y Offset field (the vertical distance) (**Figure 22**).

4. Enter the Percentage of Black to be added to the object's Fill color to produce the shadow color. 100% will produce solid black.

5. *Optional:* Check the "Group shadows" box to group the object with its shadow.

6. Click OK or press Return (**Figure 23**).

■ If the objects are type outlines and you check the Group Shadows box, each character will be grouped individually with its shadow. Instead, you can select the original type shapes with the Selection tool, group them, apply the Drop Shadow filter with the Group Shadows box unchecked, and then group the shadow objects by themselves. (If you drag a type outline with the Direct Selection tool, the outlines will separate from the inside areas.)

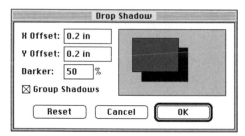

Figure 21. *The original type outlines.*

Drop Shadow

X Offset: 0.2 in
Y Offset: 0.2 in
Darker: 50 %
⊠ Group Shadows

Reset   Cancel   OK

Figure 22. *In the Drop Shaadow dialog box, enter X and Y Offset values and the percentage the shadow color will be Darker than the object's Fill color.*

Figure 23. *After applying the Drop Shadow filter.*

Figure 24. *To texturize your drop shadow like ours, apply the Drop Shadow filter with the "Group shadows box" unchecked. Select the shadow shapes, apply the Object > Rasterize command, and choose Filter > Gallery Effects: Classic Art 2 > Rough Pastels. Click Texture Controls, choose the Sandstone Type, click the upper left Light Position button, and click OK. Move the Stroke Length slider to the three-quarter point, click Preview, then click Apply. Finally, choose Filter > Gallery Effects: Classic Art 3 > Glass, choose a low Smoothness setting (1–2) and a low Distortion setting (1–2), then click Apply. You could also apply a Blur plug-in filter from Photoshop.*

gothic
horror

Figure 25. *The original objects (type outlines).*

Figure 26. *After applying the Punk filter.*

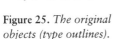

Figure 25. *The original objects (type outlines).*

Figure 26. *After applying the Punk filter.*

To punk or bloat an object:

1. Select an object or objects (**Figure 25**).
2. Choose Filter > Distort > Punk and Bloat.
3. Check the Preview box.
4. Move the slider to the left to Punk (move anchor points outward and curve segments inward, or to the right to Bloat (move anchor points inward and curve segments outward).
5. Click OK or press Return (**Figure 26**).

■ To add points to the path and intensify the Punk or Bloat effect, choose Filter > Objects > Add Anchor Points before applying the filter. See also Figures 15–17 on page 76.

And a couple of third-party filters...

Figure 27a. *A fish is selected.*   Figure 27b. *The **Gefilte** dialog box.*   Figure 27c.

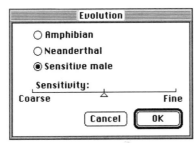

Figure 27d. *An amphibian is selected.*   Figure 27e. *The **Evolution** dialog box.*   Figure 27f. *Sensitive male.*

The **Outline Path** filter should be applied to an open path before applying a Pathfinder filter, or if you want to apply a Gradient to an object's Stroke.

Note: This filter produces the most predictable results when it's applied to an object with wide curves. It may produce odd corner shapes if it's applied to an object with sharp corners. Use Filter > Pathfinder > Unite to eliminate odd corner shapes.

To turn a Stroke or an open path into a closed, filled object:

1. Select an object that has a Stroke color (**Figure 28**).

2. Choose Filter > Objects > Outline Path (**Figure 29**). The width of the new filled object will be the same thickness that the original Stroke was (**Figure 30**).

■ If you apply the Outline Path filter to a closed path to which Fill and Stroke colors have been applied, you'll end up with two separate objects: a Fill object and a compound Stroke object.

Figure 28. *Select an object with a Stroked path. To produce the button shown below, a gradient Fill and a stroke was applied to the object before applying the* **Outline Path** *filter.*

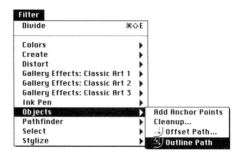

Figure 29. *Choose* **Outline Path** *from the* **Objects** *submenu under the* **Filter** *menu.*

Figure 30. *The* **Outline Path** *filter converted the Stroke into a closed path. To produce this button, the Stroked path was selected with the Selection tool and a gradient Fill was applied to it. Then the Gradient tool was dragged across it to make it contrast with the gradient Fill in the inner circle.*

The thread was created using the Freehand tool. The **Outline Path** *filter was applied to it, and then it was also Filled with a gradient.*

Figure 31a. *The original objects.*

Figure 31b. *Unite filter.*

Figure 32a. *The original objects.*

Figure 32b. *Intersect filter.*

Figure 33a. *The original objects.*

Figure 33b. *Exclude filter.*

Figure 34a. *The original objects. The white circle is placed over the black circle.*

Figure 34b. *Exclude filter. One new object is formed. The "white" area is transparent.*

Figure 35a. *The original objects.*

Figure 35b. *The Exclude filter.*

The Pathfinder filters

The Pathfinder filters are among the most powerful and useful Illustrator features. They create a new, closed object or objects or a compound path (a group of two or more closed shapes) from two or more selected and overlapping objects by joining, splitting, or cropping them. The Pathfinder filters fall into four general categories: combining, dividing, color mixing and trapping.

Note: The Unite, Intersect, Exclude, Minus Front, and Minus Back filters produce unpredictable results when applied to a combination of open and closed paths. For more predictable results, apply Filter > Objects > Outline Path to close your open paths before you apply a Pathfinder filter.

Combining filters

Unite: Joins selected objects into one compound path object. Interior objects are deleted. The paint attributes of the frontmost object are applied to the new object (**Figures 31a–b**) *(see also pages 80–81).*

Intersect: Deletes any non-overlapping areas from overlapping, selected objects. The paint attributes of the frontmost object are applied to the new object (**Figures 32a–b**). The selected objects must partially — not completely — overlap to apply this filter.

Exclude: Makes areas where selected objects overlap transparent. The paint attributes of the frontmost object are applied to the new object (**Figures 33a–35b**).

Combining Filters

Minus Front: The backmost selected object is "cut away" where selected objects overlap it, and objects overlapping the backmost object are deleted. The paint attributes of the backmost object are preserved. This filter works like the Make Compound Paths command if the original frontmost objects do not extend beyond the edge of the backmost object (**Figures 36a–37b**). *(see also page 195)*

Minus Back: The frontmost selected object is "cut away" where selected objects overlap it. Objects overlapping the frontmost object are deleted; the paint attributes of the frontmost object are preserved (**Figures 38a–b**). The selected objects must partially — not completely — overlap to apply this filter.

Figure 36a. *The original objects.*   Figure 36b. *Minus Front filter.*

Figure 37a. *The original objects.*   Figure 37b. *Minus Front filter.*

Figure 38a. *The original objects.*   Figure 38b. *Minus Back filter.*

Dividing filters

These filters divide overlapping areas of selected objects into separate, non-overlapping closed objects (Fills) or lines (Strokes).

Divide: The new objects retain their previous Fill and Gradient colors. Stroke colors are removed (**Figures 39a–40b**). *(see also page 196)*

Figure 39a. *The original objects.*   Figure 39b. *Divide filter (pulled apart for emphasis).*   Figure 40a. *The original objects.*   Figure 40b. *Divide filter (pulled apart for emphasis).*

Figure 41a. *The original objects.*

Figure 41b. *Outline filter (pulled apart for emphasis).*

Figure 42a. *The original objects.*

Figure 42b. *Trim filter (pulled apart for emphasis).*

Figure 43a. *The original objects.*

Figure 43b. *Merge filter (pulled apart for emphasis).*

Figure 44a. *The original objects.*

Figure 44b. *Crop filter.*

Figure 45a. *The original objects.*

Figure 45b. *Crop filter.*

Outline: Objects turn into stroked lines. The Fill colors of the original objects become the Stroke colors, and Fill colors are removed (**Figures 41a–b**). Use this filter to create partial strokes on objects that had no Stroke originally.

Trim: The frontmost object shape is preserved; parts of objects that are behind it and overlap it are deleted. Adjacent or overlapping objects of the same color or shade remain separate (unlike the Merge filter). Objects retain their original solid or gradient Fill colors; Stroke colors are deleted (**Figures 42a–b**).

Merge: The frontmost object shape is preserved; adjacent or overlapping objects of the same color or shade are combined. Objects retain their original solid or gradient Fill colors; Stroke colors are deleted (**Figures 43a–b**).

Crop: The frontmost object "trims" away areas of selected objects that extend beyond its borders. The remaining non-overlapping objects retain only their Fill colors; Stroke colors are removed. The frontmost object is also removed (**Figures 44a–45b**). Unlike a mask, the original objects can't be restored.

Outline, Trim, Merge, and Crop Filters

Color mixing filters

The color mixing filters turn areas where objects overlap into separate objects. The new Fill colors are a mixture of the overlapping colors, and Stroke colors are removed. Both filters have a dialog box option for converting custom colors into process colors.

Hard: Simulates overprinting. The highest CMYK values from each object are mixed in areas where they overlap. The effect is most noticeable where colors differ most (**Figures 46a–b**).

Soft: Creates an illusion of transparency. The higher the Mixing rate you enter in the Pathfinder Soft dialog box, the more transparent the frontmost object will appear (**Figures 47a–48b**). To create a painterly effect, layer three color objects, then apply the Soft filter at about 75%. Or, to lighten the underlying colors, place an object with a white Fill across other filled objects and enter a Mixing rate between 75% and 100%.

Figure 46a. *The original objects.*   Figure 46b. *Hard filter.*

Figure 47a. *The original objects.*   Figure 47b. *Soft filter (90%).*

Figure 48a. *The original objects.*   Figure 48b. *Soft filter (40%).*

Hard and Soft Filters

Exercise
Create a light bulb using filters.

1. *Draw a **circle** and a **rectangle**. Apply a Fill of None and a 2 point gray Stroke to both objects.*

2. *Select the bottom point of the circle with the **Direct Selection** tool. Drag the point downward. Select both objects.*

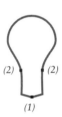

3. *Apply the **Unite** filter (Pathfinder submenu). Use the **Add-anchor-point** tool to add a point on the bottom segment (1), then use the **Direct Selection** tool to drag it downward. Rotate the direction lines upward for the points where the curve meets the straight line segment (2).*

(2)   (2)

(1)

4. *Apply the **Outline Path** filter (Objects submenu).*

5. *Create a rounded rectangle or an oval slightly wider than the base of the bulb. Rotate it using the **Rotation** tool. Option–Shift–drag two copies downward.*

6. *Position the ovals on the bottom of the bulb. Select all four shapes. Apply the **Unite** filter.*

7. *Use the **Star** tool (Plug-in Tools palette) to create a 20 point star (1st radius: .4", 2nd radius: .69"). Apply a gray Fill that is lighter than the Fill on the bulb, and a Stroke of None.*

8. *Position the star over the bulb. Select the Star, then choose **Send to Back** (Edit menu).*

9. *Apply the **Divide** filter to the star and bulb shapes to divide the star. Select and delete the part of the star inside the bulb (use the Direct Selection tool).*

10. *Use the **Freehand** tool to draw a filament line inside the bulb. Apply a Fill of None and a Black Stroke to the filament.*

11. *Bulb variation: Before applying the **Divide** filter (step 9), apply the **Roughen** filter (Distort submenu) to the star (Size: 2, Detail: 10, Jagged).*

217

The **Ink Pen** filter creates an amazing assortment of line work patterns by turning an object into a mask and then creating line work shapes within that mask. You can choose from 25 preset pen patterns — called hatch styles — that you can use as is or further modify using a wide variety of options.

To apply the Ink Pen filter:

1. Select an object.

2. Choose Filter > Ink Pen > Effects.

3. Check the Preview box.

4. Choose a predefined effect from the Settings pop-up menu. If you're satisfied with the pattern, click OK. To further modify it, follow any of the remaining steps.

5. Choose a predefined hatch style from the Hatch pop-up menu.

6. Move the Density slider to adjust the number of hatches in the fill. Move the slider to the right to increase the hatch density.

For steps 7–10, choose an option other than None from the pop-up menu and move one or both of the sliders.

7. Dispersion increases/decreases the amount hatch shapes are scattered.

8. Thickness increases/decreases the line thickness of the hatch shapes. This property is only available for hatch styles that are composed of lines (Cross, Crosshatch 1, Vertical Lines and Worm).

9. Rotation increases/decreases the amount the hatch shapes are rotated.

10. Scale increases/decreases the size of the hatch shapes.

Additional options:

11. From the Hatch Color pop-up menu, choose whether the hatch style retains its original color or matches the currently selected object's Fill color.

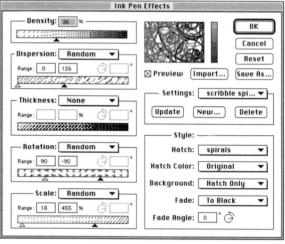

Figure 49. *The **Ink Pen Effects** dialog box showing custom hatch and custom settings.*

THE HATCH STYLE POP-UP MENU OPTIONS

None
No effect.

Constant
Effect repeats without changing across the entire shape.

Linear
Effect changes from one side of the Fill shape to the other in a straight-line progression.

Reflect
Effect changes starting from the center of the Fill shape outward.

Symmetric
Like Linear, but more proportionate and even.

Random
Effect changes in a random, haphazard fashion across the Fill shape.

The Linear, Reflect, Symmetric and Random options have two sliders each, and their position determines the range of choices for that option. The wider the distance between a pair of sliders, the wider the range of possibilities for that option. Enter a value in the Angle box to specify an axis for the change. Press Tab to preview an Angle change.

Ink Pen Fills can be quite complex, and their direction lines and line endpoints may extend way beyond the edge of the original object. To prevent accidentally selecting an Ink Pen Fill, put the Ink Pen object on its own layer and lock the layer.

If your Ink Pen Fill doesn't print, try reducing the object's Output resolution (see page 245). Also, don't apply the Ink Pen filter to an object that already contains an Ink Pen Fill — it will demand too much from your output device.

12. From the Background pop-up menu, choose whether the object will retain its Fill color or will have a Fill of None, with the hatch taking on the current Fill color.

13. From the Fade pop-up menu, choose whether the hatch style will fade To Black or To White across the Fill shape. If the object's Fill was a gradient, choose Use Gradient to color the hatch style with the gradient. If you like, you can enter an angle for the axis along which the fade will occur. Press Tab to preview the angle effect.

14. Click OK or press Return.

■ To save properties or style changes to a separate custom hatch set file, click Save As, enter a name in the Hatch Set Name field, choose a location in which to save the file, then click Save. This file will be available to import into other documents.

■ To import hatch settings, click Import, locate and highlight the hatch file, then click Open.

■ To save any properties and style options changes to a custom settings variation, click New, enter a name in the Settings Name field, then click OK or press Return.

■ Click Delete to delete an existing Settings variation. Warning! This can't be undone by the Undo command or by pressing Cancel in the Ink Pen Effects dialog box.

■ Click Update to save the current property and style options to the current Settings variant. Warning! Update overwrites existing variant settings.

■ To adjust the density of the hatch style a different way, click a different gray on the grayscale bar next to the preview window.

Ink Pen Filter

The hatch is the underlying pattern tile that is used by the Ink Pen filter.

To create a new hatch style pattern:

1. Create a small object or objects to use as the pattern.

2. Select the object or objects.

3. Choose Filter > Ink Pen > Edit.

4. Click New.

5. Enter a name in the Hatch Name field. Click OK or press Return. The new pattern will display in the preview window (check the Preview box).

6. Click OK or press Return to close the Ink Pen Edit dialog box and save the hatch with the current document.

■ Click Delete to remove the currently highlighted hatch style from the Hatch pop-up menu. This can't be undone.

■ Click Save as to save the hatch in a separate file that can be imported into other documents via the Ink Pen Effects dialog box.

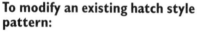

To modify an existing hatch style pattern:

1. Scroll to a blank area of the Artboard, and deselect.

2. Choose Filter > Ink Pen > Edit.

3. Choose the pattern you want to edit from the Hatch Style pop-up menu.

4. Click Paste.

5. Click OK or press Return. The hatch pattern objects will be selected. Zoom in, if you need to.

6. Modify the hatch pattern.

7. Reselect all the hatch pattern objects.

8. Follow steps 3–6 in the previous set of instructions (and read the tips).

Figure 50.

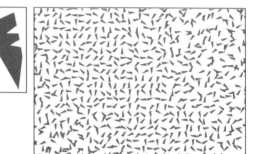

Figure 51.

Figure 52.

Figure 53.

GRAPHS 20

Six different graph styles can be created in Illustrator: grouped column, stacked column, line, pie, area, and scatter. Explaining Illustrator's somewhat difficult-to-use graphing features in depth is beyond the scope of this book. However, this chapter contains learn-by-example instructions for creating a simple grouped column graph and then customizing the graph design. Also included are general guidelines for creating other types of graphs. Alternate design and graph style variations are discussed in the Tips. See the Illustrator User Guide for more information about creating graphs.

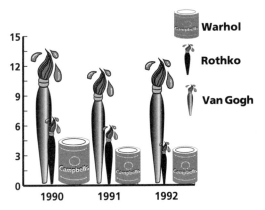

THE BASIC GRAPH-MAKING STEPS

- Define the graph **area**
- Enter graph **data** and **labels**
- Choose **graph style** options
- Add custom **design** elements

A graph created in Illustrator is a group of objects. As long as a graph remains grouped, its data and/or style can be changed. As with any group, individual elements in a graph can be selected using the Direct Selection or Group Selection tool and then modified without having to ungroup the whole graph.

To define the graph area:

Choose the Graph tool (**Figure 1**), then press and drag diagonally.

or

Choose the Graph tool, click on your page, enter numbers in the Width and Height fields, then click OK (**Figure 2**). The Graph data dialog box will open automatically.

■ You can use the Scale tool to resize the whole graph later on.

Figure 1.
Graph tool.

Figure 2. *Enter* **Width** *and* **Height** *dimensions for the graph in the* **Graph** *dialog box.*

The **Graph Data** dialog box is like a worksheet, with rows and columns for entering numbers and labels. Most graphs are created in an *x/y* **axis** formation. The *y*-axis (vertical) is numerical and shows the data in quantities. The *x*-axis (horizontal) represents information categories.

To enter graph data:

1. For this exercise, enter the data shown in **Figure 3** directly into the cells in the Graph data dialog box. Be sure to enter quotation marks with the dates in the first column. Don't enter any non-numerical characters. (For other graphs, you can click Import to import a tab-delineated text file or a file from a spreadsheet application.)

   Press **Tab** to move across a row.
   or
   Press **Return** to move down a column.
   or
   Click on any row or column cell.
   or
   Press any arrow key.

2. On the top row of the worksheet, enter the **labels**. These will appear next to the legend boxes in the graph.

3. Click OK (**Figure 4**).

■ If you make a mistake when entering data, click on the incorrect data cell, correct the error in the highlighted entry line, then press Tab or Return to accept the correction.

Do not enter any data in this first cell for a Column graph.

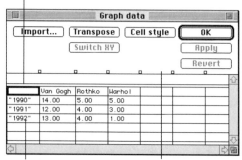

Type these numbers, including the quota-ton marks.

Type onto this entry line to fill the currently highlighted cell.

Figure 3. *The* **Graph data** *dialog box.*

Drag this square to the right to make the second column wider.

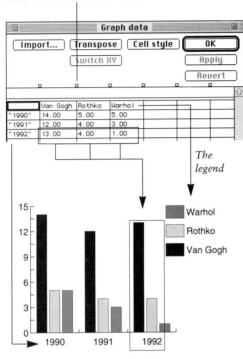

Figure 4. *The relationship between data on the worksheet and the parts of the graph.*

Figure 5. *The Graph Style dialog box.*

■ To make a column wider to accommodate a long label name, drag the small square at the top right of that column to the right.

■ To have a legend name appear on two lines, enter "|" (hold down Shift and press the key just above the Return key) in the entry line where you want the name to break.

■ To preview the new graph while the Graph data dialog box is open, click Apply. Move the dialog box to the side if you need to.

When you click on different graph types in the **Graph Style** dialog box, a thumbnail preview of the graph displays in the dialog box.

To style the graph:

1. Select the whole graph (use the Selection tool), then choose Object > Graphs > Style.

2. For this exercise, click the Grouped column button (**Figure 5**). This graph style is a good choice if you want to compare two or three entities over several time periods.

3. Enter 80 in the Column width field to make the individual columns narrower. With a Cluster width of 80%, the three column shapes will spread across only 80% of the horizontal area allotted for each x-axis category.

4. For this exercise, click the Use left axis button. The Axis options affect how and where the x/y axis appears.

5. To style the axis, click the Left button. For this exercise, leave the default "Calculate axis values from data" button selected (**Figure 6**). Illustrator will scale the y-axis automatically based on the largest and smallest numbers entered on the worksheet. (Select "Use manual axis

(Continued on the following page)

Graphs

values" to enter your own maximum and minimum values for the *y*-axis.)

6. The lower part of the dialog box is used for styling the axis **tick lines** (the small lines perpendicular to the axis lines). For this exercise, click the Short button (the default) and enter 2 in the "Draw... tick marks per tick line" field to add an extra tick mark between each *y*-axis number.

7. Click OK in both dialog boxes (Figure 7).

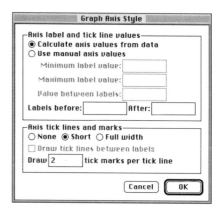

Figure 6. *In the Graph Axis Style dialog box, choose labels for and size of the vertical axis, and choose* **Axis tick lines and marks** *options.*

To Customize the Graph

You can move, transform or modify the Fill and/or Stroke of an individual object in a graph if you select it first with the Group Selection tool.

■ To restack part of a graph, select a whole group (i.e., the bars and their legend or an axis and its tick marks) with the Group Selection tool, then choose Arrange > Bring To Front or Arrange > Send To Back.

To recolor the columns/legends:

(In this "Artists Graph": Warhol, Rothko, Van Gogh)

1. Choose the Group Selection tool.

2. Double-click on a legend rectangle to select the legend and its three related columns.

3. Change the Fill and/or Stroke for the legend and the related column objects (Figure 8).

■ You can also click on a column with the Group Selection tool to select it, click a second time to add its related columns to the selection, and click a third time to add its legend to the selection. Or, use the Direct Selection tool with Option held down instead of using the Group Selection tool.

Tick lines.

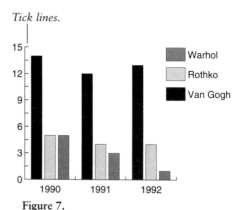

Figure 7.

Figure 8. *To restyle this column graph, new Fill patterns were applied to each legend and related column, a heavier Stroke weight was applied to the axes, and the type in the graph was changed.*

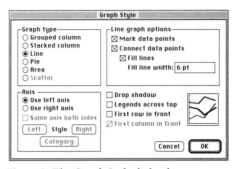

Figure 9. *The Graph Style dialog box.*

To change the type in a graph:

1. Choose the Group Selection tool.
2. Click once on the baseline of a type block to select just that block.
   or
   Click twice to select all the type in the legends or all the labels.
   or
   Click three times to select all the type in the graph.
3. Modify the type as usual (**Figure 9**).

■ To switch the row and column data, choose Object > Graphs > Data, then click Transpose.

To combine different styles in one graph:

1. Choose the Group Selection tool.
2. Click twice on the legend box for the category you wish to have in a new style.
3. Choose Object > Graphs > Style.
4. Click a new Graph type and modify the options for that type. For this exercise, click the **Line** button (**Figure 9**).
5. In the options area, check the "Fill lines" box and enter 6 in the "Fill line width" field.
6. Click the "Use left axis" button.
7. Click OK (**Figure 10**).

■ To select the line bar in the graph, click twice with the Group Selection tool on the small line bar in the legend (not on the small square marker), or click on the line bar segments in the graph.

■ To modify the marker squares (the points on the line), double-click on the marker in the legend with the Group Selection tool.

Click on the line (not the square marker) to select the legend and its line bar.

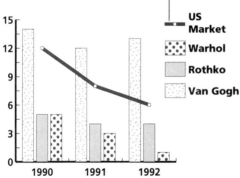

Figure 10. *The Grouped column style and Line style are combined this "Artist's Graph." A new legend name and a column of new data was entered into the Graph data dialog box. The new legend box and its bars were selected, then Line was selected as the Graph type in the Graph Style dialog box. The new line and the legend were selected with the Goup Selection tool (two clicks) and Bring to Front was chosen from the Arrange menu.*

You can replace the rectangles in a graph with graphic objects.

To create a custom graph design:

1. Create a graphic object. Draw a rectangle around the object. Apply a Fill and Stroke of None (unless you want the rectangle to display in the graph). With the rectangle selected, choose Arrange > Send To Back.

2. Choose the Selection tool, and press and drag a marquee over the rectangle and the graphic object.

3. Choose Object > Graphs > Design.

4. Click New (**Figure 12**).

5. Enter a name for the graphic object. For this exercise, enter "Brush," then click OK.

6. Click on a legend box twice with the Group Selection tool (the legend and its bars should be selected).

7. Choose Object > Graphs > Column.

8. Choose a "Column design type" (**Figure 13**). The selected type will preview in a thumbnail. For the "Artists Graph," we chose Uniformly scaled to keep the brush wide and we unchecked the "Rotate legend design" box.

9. Click OK (**Figure 14**).

■ Choose the "Vertically scaled" option to stretch the entire design object.

■ Choose the "Repeating design" option to create a stacked column of design objects. The top of the stack can be scaled or cropped to fit the numeric value of that column. To keep the design object from becoming too small, enter a larger number in the "Each design represents" field.

■ Choose the "Sliding" option to stretch the design object across a section you designate.

■ To append a graph design from another document, see page 94.

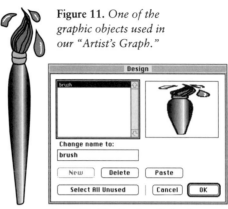

Figure 11. *One of the graphic objects used in our "Artist's Graph."*

Figure 12. *The **Design** dialog box.*

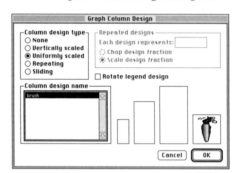

Figure 13. *The **Graph Column Design** dialog box.*

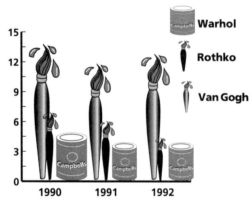

Figure 14. *Custom design elements in a Column graph. Column design type: Uniformly scaled. In the Graph Style dialog box, we increased the Column width value to further widen the brush (we chose 100%). You can also use the Scale tool to resize a selected graph object.*

Graphs

PRECISION TOOLS 21

There are many tools that you can use to position or move objects more precisely. In this chapter you will learn how to use rulers and guides to align and position objects. How to move an object a specified distance via the Move dialog box. How to use the Measure tool to calculate the distance between objects. How to use the Control palette to reposition, resize, rotate, or scale an object. And how to use the Align palette to align or distribute objects.

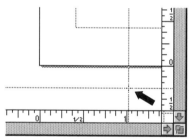

Figure 1a. *Press and drag diagonally away from the intersection of the rulers.*

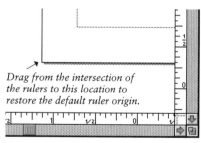

Drag from the intersection of the rulers to this location to restore the default ruler origin.

Figure 1b. *Note the new position of the 0's on the rulers.*

The ruler origin

The rulers are located on the bottom and right edges of the document window. The ruler origin is the point from which all measurements are read — the point where the 0 is on each ruler. By default, the ruler origin is positioned at the lower left corner of the page, but it can be moved to a different location in any individual document.

To move the ruler origin, make sure the rulers are displayed (choose View > Show Rulers or use the Command-R shortcut), then drag the square where the two rulers intersect to a new position (**Figures 1a–b**). To restore the ruler origin to its default position, drag the square where the two rulers intersect back to the lower left corner of the page.

*(**Note:** If you move the ruler origin, the position of a pattern Fill in a selected object may change.)*

227

To change the ruler units for the current document only:

1. Choose File > Document Setup (⌘-Shift-D).

2. Choose Picas/Points, Inches, or Millimeters from the Ruler units pop-up menu (**Figure 2**).

3. Click OK or press Return.

■ To choose a unit of measure for the current *and* future documents, use the General Preferences dialog box (File menu).

■ The Ruler units you choose will also be the unit used in dialog boxes.

■ The larger the view size, the finer the ruler increments. Dotted lines on the rulers indicate the current location of the pointer.

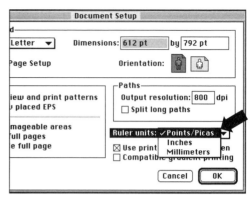

Figure 2. *Choose **Points/Picas, Inches,** or **Millimeters** from the **Ruler units** pop-up menu in the **Document Setup** dialog box.*

Guides are non-printing dotted lines that you can use to mechanically align or arrange objects. If the Snap to point box is checked in the General Preferences dialog box (File menu), as you drag an object within two pixels of a guide, the edge of the object under the pointer will snap to the guide. The pointer will turn white when it's over the guide. You can create a guide by dragging from the horizontal or vertical ruler or you can turn any object into a guide.

To create a ruler guide:

1. *Optional:* Create a new layer for the guide or guides.

2. If the rulers are not displayed, choose View > Show Rulers (⌘-R).

3. Drag a guide from the horizontal or vertical ruler onto your page (**Figure 3**). A newly created guide will be locked.

■ Choose View > Hide Guides or View > Show Guides to hide or display guides.

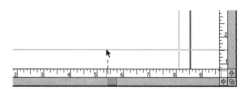

Figure 3. *Press and drag a **guide** from the horizontal or vertical ruler.*

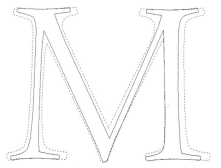

Figure 4. *Typeface designer Jonathan Hoefler uses guides created from outline text characters as a reference for creating new characters. In this example, a character in the text version of the Mazarin typeface that he designed for GQ magazine is turned into guides and serves as a reference for creating a new version of the typeface for larger display sizes.*

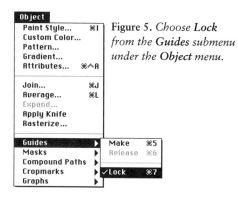

Figure 5. *Choose Lock from the Guides submenu under the Object menu.*

To turn an object into a guide:

1. Select an object or a group.
2. Choose from the Object > Guides > Make (⌘-5). The object will have a dotted border and a Fill and Stroke of None (**Figure 4**).

To unlock guides:

1. Choose Object > Guides > Lock (⌘-7) (to deselect the command) (**Figure 5**). All the guides will unlock.
2. *Optional:* Select any unlocked guide with the Selection tool, then move it or press Delete to remove it.

■ To move a locked guide, choose the Selection tool, then hold down Control and Shift and drag the guide.

To turn a guide back into an object:

1. Choose the Selection tool.
2. Hold down Control and Shift and double-click the dotted border of the guide. The guide will turn into a selected object with its former Fill and Stroke.

■ To unlock multiple guides: If the guides are locked, choose Object > Guides > Lock (to deselect the command), choose the Selection tool, marquee or click on the guides you want to convert, then choose Object > Guides > Release (⌘-6).

To place guides around an object or create evenly spaced guides:

1. Choose the Selection tool, then select an existing rectangle. *Warning:* If you use a non-rectangular shape, the shape will revert to a rectangle!
   or
   Choose the Rectangle tool, then drag a rectangle to define the guide area (**Figure 6**).

2. Choose Type > Rows & Columns.

3. Make sure the Preview box is checked (**Figure 7**).

4. Check the Add Guides box.

5. Choose the desired number of Columns or Rows, Column Width, Row Height, and Gutters. To place guides around the object without dividing it, leave the number of Columns and Rows as 1.

6. Click OK or press Return (**Figure 8**).

7. Choose the Selection tool.

8. Hold down Shift and click on the rectangle or rectangles to deselect them.

9. Choose Object > Guides > Make (**Figure 9**). If you like, you can now delete the rectangles that were used to create the guides.

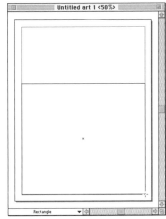

Figure 6. *Drawing a rectangle to define the guide area.*

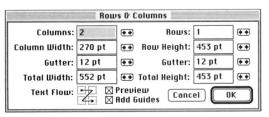

Figure 7.

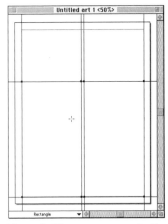

Figure 8. *Lines are automatically created around the rectangles.*

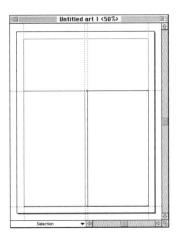

Figure 9. *The lines converted into guides.*

Figure 10. *Choose Move from the Arrange menu.*

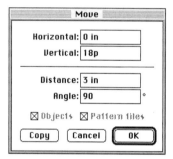

Figure 11. *In the Move dialog box, enter numbers in the Horizontal and Vertical fields, or enter a Distance and Angle you want to move the object.*

You can precisely reposition an object by entering values in the **Move** dialog box. Move dialog box settings remain the same until you change them, move an object using the mouse, or use the Measure tool, so you can repeat the same move as many times as you like using the Repeat Transform shortcut (⌘-D).

To move an object a specified distance:

1. Choose the Selection tool.

2. Select the object you want to move.

3. Choose Arrange > Move (⌘-Shift-M) (**Figure 10**).
   or
   Hold down Option and click the Selection tool.

4. Enter a positive number in the **Horizontal** and/or **Vertical** field to move the object to the right or upward, respectively. Enter a negative number to move the object to the left or downward (**Figure 11**). Enter 0 in either field to keep the object on that axis *(You can use any of these units of measure: "p", "pt", "in", or "cm")*
   or
   Enter a positive **Distance** amount and a positive **Angle** between 0 and 180 to move the object upward. Enter a positive Distance amount and a negative Angle between 0 and –180 to move the object downward. The other fields will change automatically.

5. *Optional:* Click Copy to close the dialog box and move a copy of the object (not the object itself).

6. Click OK or press Return.

■ If you move any object manually or using the Move dialog box that contains a pattern Fill while the Pattern tile box is unchecked in the Move dialog box, the pattern won't move with the object. The Pattern tile box will remain unchecked until you reopen the dialog box and re-check it.

You can use the **Measure** tool to calculate the distance and/or angle between two points in an illustration. When you use the Measure tool, the amounts it calculates are displayed on the **Info** palette, which opens automatically.

Figure 12.
Measure tool.

To measure a distance using the Measure tool:

1. Choose the Measure tool (**Figure 12**).

2. Click the starting and ending points spanning the distance or angle you wish to measure (**Figures 13a–b**).
   or
   Press and drag from the first point to the second point.

   Measurements will be displayed on the Info palette (**Figure 14**).

■ Hold down Shift while clicking or dragging with the Measure tool to constrain the measurement to a horizontal or vertical axis.

■ The distances calculated using the Measure tool, as displayed on the Info palette, become the current values in the Move dialog box, so you can use the Measure tool as a guide to judge how far to move an object first, then open the Move dialog box and click OK.

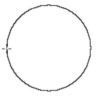 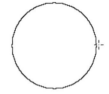

Figure 13a. *Click a starting point. The Info palette will open.*

Figure 13b. *Click an ending point. The distance between clicks will be displayed on the Info palette.*

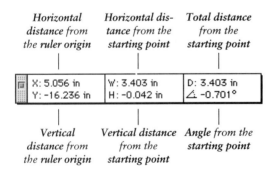

Horizontal distance from the ruler origin — *Horizontal distance from the starting point* — *Total distance from the starting point*

| X: 5.056 in | W: 3.403 in | D: 3.403 in |
| Y: -16.236 in | H: -0.042 in | ∠ -0.701° |

Vertical distance from the ruler origin — *Vertical distance from the starting point* — *Angle from the starting point*

Figure 14. *The Info palette after clicking a starting and ending point with the Measure tool. The x and y positions are measured from the ruler origin.*

Use the Control palette to reposition, resize, scale, or rotate an object or objects based on exact values or percentages.

To reposition, resize, or rotate an object using the Control palette:

1. If the Control palette isn't open, choose Window > Show Control Palette.

2. Select an object or objects.

3. *Optional:* Objects are normally modified relative to their upper left corners. To modify objects relative to a different point, click on the Reference Point Options icon on the left side of the palette (**Figure 15**), then click on any handle.

Press Return or Tab to apply new values entered on the Control palette.

4. To **move** the object horizontally, enter a new value in the X field. (Enter a higher value to move the object rightward.)

   To **move** the object vertically, enter a new value in the Y field. Enter a higher value to move the object upward.

   To change the **width** and/or **height** of the object, enter new values in the W (width) and/or H (height) fields.

   To **scale** the entire object proportionally, enter a higher or lower percentage in the Scale field. *(*The Scale field always reverts to 100%.)

   To **rotate** the object counterclockwise, enter a positive value in the Rotate field. Enter a negative value to rotate it clockwise.

The Reference Point Options icon. The upper left corner of the object is currently highlighted.

The x and y axes location of the currently selected reference point. Enter new values to move the object.

The Width and Height of the selected object.

The Scale field for resizing the object.

The Rotate field for rotating the object.

	Control Palette		
X: 3.667 in	W: 0.667 in		100 %
Y: 7.167 in	H: 0.688 in		0 °

Figure 15. *The* **Control** *palette.*

To align or distribute objects:

1. To align, select two or more objects. To distribute, select three or more objects.

2. Choose Window > Show Align.

3. Click an **Align** icon (**Figure 18**).
   and/or
   Click a **Distribute** icon. Objects will distribute evenly between the two objects that are farthest apart.
   (**Figures 16–17**)

■ If you'd like to apply a different alignment or distribution option, use the Undo command to undo the last one.

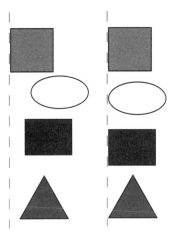

Figure 16. *The original objects.*

The objects aligned horizontally to the leftmost object and distributed vertically from left edges.

Figure 17. *The original objects.*

The objects aligned by centers, horizontally and vertically (the two middle Align icons on the Align palette).

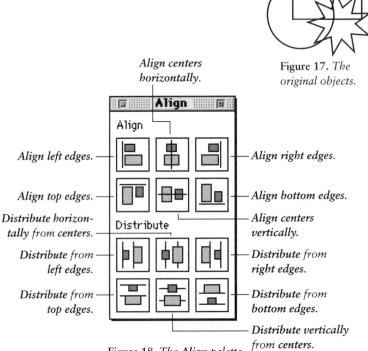

Align centers horizontally.

Align left edges.

Align right edges.

Align top edges.

Align bottom edges.

Distribute horizontally from centers.

Align centers vertically.

Distribute from left edges.

Distribute from right edges.

Distribute from top edges.

Distribute from bottom edges.

Distribute vertically from centers.

Figure 18. *The Align palette.*

(Side tab) **Align or Distribute Objects**

PREFERENCES  22

In this chapter you will learn to choose default settings for many features, tools, and palettes. You can create a startup file with colors, patterns, gradients, and document settings that you work with regularly so they will automatically be part of any new document you create. Using the General Preferences dialog box, you can set Tool Behavior, Keyboard increments, Ruler units, and Edit behavior defaults for the current and future documents. And using the Color Matching dialog box, you can improve, albeit slightly, the accuracy of your color monitor.

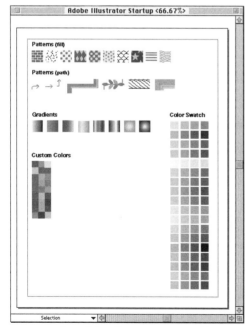

Figure 1. *The Adobe Illustrator Startup file.*

To create a custom startup file:

1. In the Finder, duplicate the existing Adobe Illustrator Startup file (it's in the Plug-ins folder in the Illustrator application folder) and move the copy to another folder.

2. Double-click the original Adobe Illustrator Startup file (**Figure 1**).

3. Create or append colors (see page 104), patterns, or gradients and apply them to individual objects in the file (plain rectangles are fine); choose Document Setup or Page Setup options; choose ruler and page origins; choose a view size; create new view settings; choose a document window size and scroll positions. You can also open files from the Illustrator Sample Files folder and drag-and-drop objects containing colors, gradients, or patterns you want into the Startup file window.

4. Choose File > Save As.

■ A startup file with a lot of custom components may cause Illustrator to launch slowly. To reduce the number of elements in the startup file, delete any extra patterns or gradients that you don't need.

General Preferences

Choose File > Preferences > General

TOOL BEHAVIOR

Constrain angle
The angle for the *x* and *y* axes. The default setting is 0° (parallel to the edges of the document window). Tool and dialog box measurements are calculated relative to the current Constrain angle.

Corner radius
The amount of curvature in the corners of objects drawn with the Rounded Rectangle tool. 0 produces a right angle.

Freehand tolerance
The value (between 0 and 10) that determines whether many or few anchor points will be created when you draw an object using the Freehand tool. 1 will produce many points on a line; 10 will produce fewer points. The Freehand tolerance also affects how many points will be created on a path rendered by the Autotrace tool.

Auto Trace gap
(0–2) how closely the Autotrace tool traces the contour of a PICT template. The lower the gap, the more closely an image will be traced, and the more anchor points will be created.

Snap to point
When checked, the part of an object that is under the pointer will snap to a guide or an anchor point on another object if it is moved within two pixels of it.

Transform pattern tiles
When checked, the transformation tools will modify an object and any pattern fill it may contain. (You can also turn this option on or off for an individual transformation tool in its own dialog box and also in the Move dialog box.)

Scale line weight
Check this box to scale an object's Stroke Weight when you use the Scale tool. (You can also turn this option on or off for the Scale tool in its own dialog box.)

Area select
When checked, if you click with a selection tool on an object's Fill when your illustration is in Preview view, the whole object will be selected.

Use precise cursors
The drawing and editing tool pointers display as a crosshair icon.

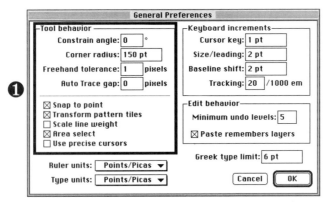

Figure 2. *The Tool behavior section of the General Preferences dialog box.*

General Preferences

RULER UNITS ❷

Ruler units
The unit of measure for the rulers and all dialog boxes for the current document *and* all new documents *(see the instructions on page 228 to change Ruler units for an individual document)*.

Type units
The unit of measure in the type Size, Leading, and Baseline shift fields on the Character palette, and in the Indentation and Leading before ¶ fields on the Paragraph palette.

KEYBOARD INCREMENTS ❸

Cursor key
The distance a selected object moves when a keyboard arrow is pressed.

Size/leading, Baseline shift, Tracking
The amount selected text is altered each time a keyboard shortcut is executed for the respective command.

EDIT BEHAVIOR ❹

Minimum undo levels
You can undo/redo up to 200 operations, depending on available memory. If additional RAM is necessary to perform illustration edits, the number of undos will be reduced to the specified minimum.

Paste remembers layers
Whether an object cut or copied to the Clipboard can be pasted onto a different layer from where it originated (unchecked), or can only be pasted back onto its current layer (checked). Paste remembers layers can also be turned on or off from the Layers palette command menu.

Greek type limit
The point size at which type displays on the screen as gray bars rather than as readable characters. Greeking speeds screen redraw, but it has no effect on how a document prints.

General Preferences

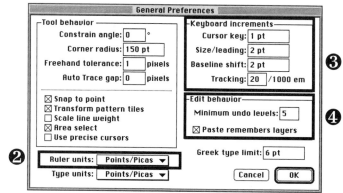

Figure 3. *The Ruler units, Keyboard increments, and Edit behavior sections of the General Preferences dialog box.*

You can enhance the simulation (calibration) of on-screen color using the **Color Matching** dialog box. You'll need to use a printed progressive color bar from your print shop for these instructions.

To calibrate your color monitor:

1. Choose File > Preferences > Color Matching.

2. If you move files between Adobe Photoshop and Adobe Illustrator, check the "CIE calibration" box so Illustrator can match Photoshop's RGB-to-CMYK conversion settings (**Figure 4**).

Follow steps 3–5 if you checked the CIE box.

3. Choose the ink and printer type your final printer will use from the Ink pop-up menu.

4. Choose your monitor type from the Monitor pop-up menu for better translation between on-screen color and printed color.

5. Enter an amount in the Gamma field — the same amount as in Photoshop's Gamma Control Panel (usually 1.8).

Follow steps 6–8 if you didn't check the CIE box.

6. Compare the nine swatches with a printed progressive color bar from your print shop. If a swatch doesn't closely match the color on the printed bar, click on it.

7. In the Apple Color Picker, move the luminosity slider left or right or change any individual Hue Angle, Saturation, or Lightness values to make the new color swatch match the color bar, then click OK (**Figure 5**).

8. Repeat steps 6–7 for any other non-matching swatches.

9. Click OK or press Return.

■ To restore the original Color Matching dialog box settings and swatches, click Use Defaults.

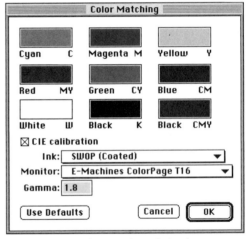

Figure 4. *The Color Matching dialog box.*

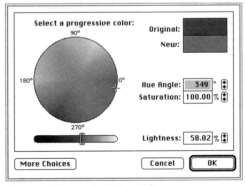

Figure 5. *The Apple Color Picker.*

OUTPUT 23

In Illustrator, objects are described and stored as mathematical commands, but they are rendered as dots when they are printed. The higher the resolution of the output device, the finer and sharper the rendering of lines, curves, gradients, and continuous-tone images. In this chapter you will learn to print an illustration on a PostScript black-and-white or composite color printer, to create crop or trim marks, to print an oversized illustration, and to troubleshoot printing problems. (To produce color separations, read Chapter 24.)

Michael Bartalos, **Downloading Files**, for In Magazine

To print on a black-and-white or a color PostScript printer:

1. Select the Chooser from the Apple menu, click the LaserWriter icon, click on the desired printer name, then close the Chooser.

2. In Illustrator, choose File > Page Setup.

3. Choose a size from the Paper pop-up menu (**Figure 1**).

4. Make sure the correct Orientation icon is selected (to print vertically or horizontally on the paper).

5. Click OK or press Return.

6. Choose File > Print (⌘-P).

7. Enter the desired number of Copies (**Figure 2**).

8. To print a single full page document or a Tile imageable areas document, leave the Pages: All button selected.
   or
   To print selective tiled pages, enter starting and ending page numbers in the From and To fields.

9. Choose Level 1 or Level 2 (depending on your printer and printer driver) from the PostScript® pop-up menu.

10. Click Options, then choose Color/Grayscale so colors will print in color on a color printer or in shades of gray on a black-and-white printer. For a color printer, choose the appropriate color options.

11. Click OK.

12. Click the Destination: Printer button.

13. Click Print or press Return.

■ On a Tile imageable areas document, only tile pages with objects on them will print. If a direction line from a curved anchor point extends onto a blank tile, that page will also print.

PRINTER HALFTONES

If your printer has halftone enhancing software, click Options in the Print dialog box, then choose On or Printer's Default from the PhotoGrade or FinePrint pop-up menu. This will enable the printer's halftone method and disable Illustrator's built-in halftone method.

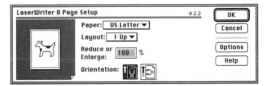

Figure 1. *In the Page Setup dialog box for a black-and-white printer, choose a Paper size.*

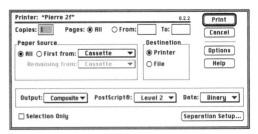

Figure 2. *In the Print dialog box, enter a number of Copies and the Pages you want to print.*

Print Black & White or Color

Figure 3.
Rectangle tool.

Figure 4a. *A rectangle is drawn.*

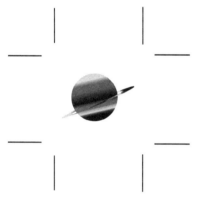

Figure 4b. *After choosing the Make Cropmarks command.*

Crop marks are short perpendicular lines around the edge of a page that a print shop uses as a guide to trim the paper. Illustrator's Cropmarks command creates crop marks around a rectangle that you draw, and they become part of your illustration.

To create crop marks:

1. Choose the Rectangle tool (**Figure 3**).

2. Draw a rectangle to encompass some or all of the objects in the illustration.

3. With the rectangle still selected, choose Object > Cropmarks > Make. The rectangle will disappear, and crop marks will appear where the corners of the rectangle were (**Figures 4a–b**).

- If the Single full page box is checked in the Document Setup dialog box and you don't create a rectangle before choosing the Make Cropmarks command, crop marks will be placed around the full page.

- Only one set of crops can be created per illustration using the Cropmarks command. To create more than one set of crop marks in an illustration, apply the Trim Marks filter *(instructions are on the next page)*.

- If you apply the Make Cropmarks command a second time, new marks will replace the existing one.

To remove crop marks created with the Cropmarks command:

Choose Object > Cropmarks > Release. The selected rectangle will reappear, with a Fill and Stroke of None. You can repaint it or delete it.

- If the crop marks were created for the entire page, the released rectangle will be the same dimensions as the printable page (and the same size as the Artboard, if the Artboard dimensions match the printable page dimensions).

Crop Marks

241

The **Trim Marks** filter places eight trim marks around a selected object or objects. You can create more than one set of Trim Marks in an illustration.

To create trim marks:

1. Select the object or objects to be trimmed.

2. Choose Filter > Create > Trim Marks. Trim marks will surround the smallest rectangle that could be drawn around the object or objects (**Figure 5**).

■ Group the trim marks with the objects they surround so you can move them as a unit.

■ To move or delete trim marks, select them first with the Selection tool.

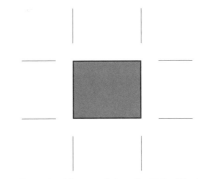

Figure 5. *After applying the* **Trim Marks** *filter.*

To print (tile) an illustration that is larger than the paper size:

1. Choose File > Document Setup.

2. Uncheck the Use Page Setup box (**Figure 6**).

3. Choose the appropriate Artboard Dimensions for the large illustration.

4. Click "Tile imageable areas."

5. Click OK or press Return.

6. Double-click the Hand tool to display the entire Artboard.

7. *Optional:* Change the Orientation in the Page Setup dialog box.

8. *Optional:* Choose the Page tool (**Figure 7**), then press and drag the tile grid so it divides the illustration into better tiling breaks. The grid will redraw (**Figure 8**).

9. Follow steps 1–13 on page 240.

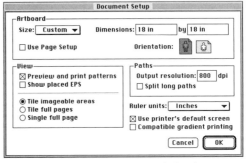

Figure 6. *In the* **Document Setup** *dialog box, uncheck the* **Use Page Setup** *box and click* **Tile imageable areas.**

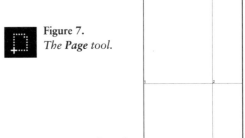

Figure 7.
The **Page** *tool.*

Figure 8. *Tile grid.*

How to solve printing problems

When things don't go as smoothly as you'd like...

Patterns

■ By default, patterns preview and print. If a document containing patterns doesn't print, uncheck the "Preview and print patterns" box in the Document Setup dialog box (File menu) and try printing again. If the document prints, the patterns are the likely culprit.

■ Try to limit the number of pattern Fills in an illustration.

■ Make the original bounding rectangle for the pattern tile no larger than one-inch square.

■ Don't Stroke a path using the Paint Style palette pattern Fill color selection method icon; use the Path Pattern filter instead.

■ Don't apply a pattern Fill to a compound path.

Complex paths

A file containing complex paths with many anchor points may not print — a limitcheck or VM error message may appear in the print progress window. If possible, limit the number of complex objects in your illustration. If you do get such a message, first manually delete excess anchor points from long paths using the Delete-anchor-point tool (**Figure 9**) and try printing again.

If that doesn't work, check the "Split long paths" box in the Document Setup dialog box (**Figure 10**) and try printing again. Complex paths will be split into two or more separate paths without changing the overall path shapes. The "Split long paths" option does not affect stroked paths, compound paths, or masks. You can also split a Stroked path manually using the Scissors tool. (To preserve a copy of the document with its "non-split" paths, before checking the "Split long paths" box, save the document under a new name using Save as.) Choose Filter > Pathfinder > Unite if you want to rejoin split paths.

Figure 9. *Delete-anchor-point tool.*

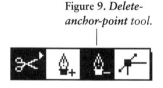

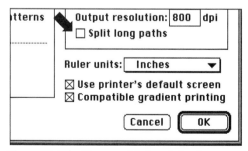

Figure 10. *The Document Setup dialog box.*

Other troubleshooting tips

- Masks may cause printing problems, particularly those created from compound paths. A document containing multiple masks may not print altogether. For a complex mask, consider using the Knife tool to cut all the shapes in half — including the mask object itself — before you create the mask. Select and mask each half separately, and then move them together.

- As a last resort you can lower the output resolution of individual objects to facilitate printing *(see the following page)*.

- Choose Filter > Objects > Cleanup to delete any Unpainted Objects, any Stray Points (inadvertent clicks on the Artboard), and any Empty Text Paths (**Figure 11**).

- Try using fewer fonts in the file if you receive a VM error, or convert large text into outlines (Type > Create Outlines) so fewer fonts need to be downloaded.

- Try using a Pathfinder filter — like Divide or Minus Front — to produce the same effect as a compound.

- On the Layers palette, double-click the name of the layer the object is on, and make sure the Print box is checked.

- To improve gradient Fill printing on a PostScript Level 1 imagesetter and some PostScript clone printers, check the "Compatible gradient printing" box in the Document Setup dialog box, opened from the File menu, then re-save the file. Don't check this option if your gradients are printing well (it may slow printing), or if you're using a PostScript Level 2 imagesetter.

- If you're creating an illustration using complex commands like compounds and masks, print the file in stages as you add complex elements so you'll be able to pinpoint where a problem is if one of the versions doesn't print. Or, place a complex object on its own layer and uncheck the print option for that layer, then try printing again.

- See pages 226–232 of the Adobe Illustrator User Guide for more troubleshooting tips.

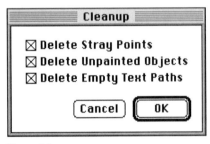

Figure 11.

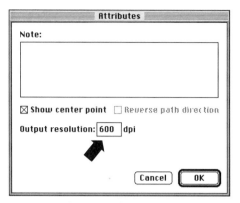

Figure 12. *Change an object's **Output resolution** in the **Attributes** dialog box.*

The degree to which Illustrator renders an object precisely is determined by the object's output resolution. Different objects within an illustration can be rendered at different resolutions. If a complex object doesn't print, lower its output resolution and try printing again.

Note: The Output resolution command replaces the Flatness command found in earlier versions of Illustrator. The higher the Flatness or the lower the output resolution the less precisely a printed curve segment will match the original mathematically defined curve segment.

To lower an object's output resolution to facilitate printing:

1. Choose any selection tool, then click on the object that did not print or you anticipate may not print.

2. Choose Object > Attributes.

3. Enter a lower number in the "Output resolution" field (**Figure 12**).

4. Click OK or press Return. Try printing the file again. If the object prints, but with noticeable jaggedness on its curve segments, its Output resolution is too low. Choose a higher resolution, and try printing again.

■ To reset the Output resolution for all future objects, choose File > Document Setup, then change the number in the Output resolution field. 800 dpi is the default Output resolution.

Output Resolution

Selection Info and Document Info

To display information about a selected object (or objects), choose File > Selection Info. With Objects chosen from the Info pop-up menu, the Selection Info dialog box lists the number of paths, masks, compounds, custom colors, patterns, gradients, fonts, placed EPS images, and raster art images in the object. To view more detailed information on any of these elements, choose from the Info pop-up menu (**Figure 13**). Click Done when you're finished.

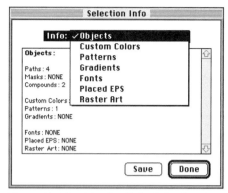

Figure 13. *The Selection Info dialog box (an object is selected in the illustration).*

To display information about the entire illustration, make sure no objects are selected, then choose File > Document Info. The Document Info dialog box displays the current Document Setup dialog box settings (**Figure 14**). You can also choose to display information about all Objects, all Custom Colors, etc.

Click Save to save Document or Selection Info as a SimpleText document. Choose a location in which to save the SimpleText file, rename the file, if desired, then click Save. To open the SimpleText document, double-click the file's icon in the Finder. You can print this file and refer to it when you prepare your document for imagesetting.

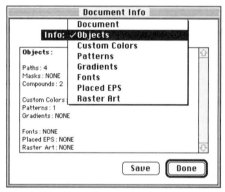

Figure 14. *The Document Info dialog box (no objects are selected).*

TO ACQUIRE AN ILLUSTRATOR OBJECT IN MACROMEDIA DIRECTOR

In Illustrator, hold down Option while choosing Edit > Copy to place the object on the Clipboard. The operating system will rasterize the object. In Director, click on a Cast Member window on the Cast palette and choose Edit > Paste Bitmap. Objects with gradient and pattern Fills and small-sized Illustrator-rasterized objects can be Option-copied into Director.

■ Because Illustrator objects are in CMYK color and Director objects are in RGB color, an Illustrator object Option-copied may be

dithered when it appears in Director. To preserve more of the original color, copy the objects first into Photoshop 3, and then copy from Photoshop 3 into Director.

■ Illustrator type can be Option-copied into Director, and since the Illustrator type is not anti-aliased, the type edges will look crisp in Director. If Illustrator type is copied first into Photoshop 3, use Edit > Paste and make sure to uncheck the Anti-Alias option in the Paste dialog box. Anti-Aliased type will have a white halo along its edges in Director.

Document and Selection Info; MacroMedia Director

SEPARATIONS/TRAPPING

You can produce color separations directly from Illustrator 6.0. This chapter contains a brief introduction to Illustrator's Separation Setup dialog box and an introduction to trapping, which helps compensate for color misregistration on press.

Trapping and color separations are usually handled by a prepress provider — a service bureau or a print shop. Talk with your print shop before producing color separations or building traps. They will tell you what settings to use. Don't guess!

What are color separations?

To print an illustration on press, you need to supply your print shop with paper or film output (color separations) from your Illustrator file — one sheet per process or spot color. If you give your print shop paper, they will have to photograph it to produce film. If you output directly onto film, you will save an intermediary step, and the ultimate print quality will be better. Your print shop will use the film separations to produce plates to use on the press — one plate for each color.

In **process color** printing, four basic ink colors, Cyan (C), Magenta (M), Yellow (Y), and Black (K) are used to produce a multitude of colors. A document that contains color photographs — whether from Illustrator, from a photo manipulation program, or from a layout program (such as QuarkXPress) — must be output as a four-color process job.

In **spot color** printing, a separate plate is produced for each spot color. Pantone inks are commonly used spot color inks. If your illustration contains more than four or five colors, you can lower your expenses if you convert your spot colors into their process color equivalents and run it as a four-color process job; only four sheets of film and only four plates will be required. Pantone colors are usually richer and cleaner looking than process colors, though, and some Pantone colors have no process color equivalents. Using Separation Setup, you can convert spot colors into process colors and you can specify which colors will be output.

To prepare a file for Separation Setup:

1. Calibrate your monitor (*see page 238*).
2. Decide which colors in the illustration you want to Overprint (*see the box at right*).
3. Create traps, if needed (*see pages 253–254*).
4. *Optional:* Place any objects that you don't want to appear on the color separations on a separate layer and uncheck the Print option for that layer, or hide the layer altogether (*see chapter 12 and page 252*).
5. *Optional:* Create cropmarks (*see page 241*).

To use Separation Setup:

1. Choose File > Separation Setup.
2. In the Setup dialog box, you'll see a file preview window on the left and Separation settings on the right (**Figures 1 and 3**). Check the Preview box.
3. To open or change the current PPD file, click the Open PPD button at the top of the dialog box.
4. In the PPD (PostScript Printer Description) file dialog box, locate and highlight the PPD file specified by your service bureau for your target printer or imagesetter, then click Open (**Figure 2**). The PPD files should be in the Printer Description folder in the Extensions folder in the System folder. If they're not there, check the Utilities folder in the Illustrator application folder.
5. *Optional:* The white area in the preview window represents the page size. Separation Setup will automatically choose the default page size for the chosen printer definition. Choose a new size from the Page Size pop-up menu if your print shop requests that you do so.

WHAT IS OVERPRINTING?

Normally, Illustrator automatically knocks out the background color under an object so the object color won't mix with the background color. If you check the Overprint Fill or Stroke box on the Paint Style palette, the Fill or Stroke color will overprint background colors. Where colors overlap, a combination color will be produced. Turn on the Overprint option if you are building traps. You can simulate the mixing of overlapping colors by applying the Filter > Pathfinder > Hard filter (see page 216).

Colors will overprint on a printing press but *not* on a PostScript color composite printer.

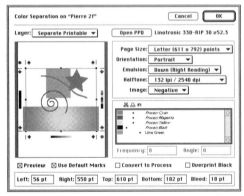

Figure 1. *Locate and Open the EPS illustration you wish to color separate.*

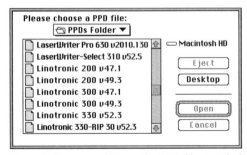

Figure 2. *Locate and Open the PPD file specified by your service bureau.*

Color Separations

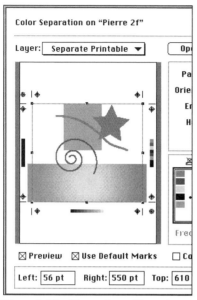

Figure 3. *The illustration will preview on the left side of the **Setup** dialog box.*

6. From the Orientation pop-up menu, Choose **Portrait** to position the image vertically within the imageable area of the separation (**Figure 4**).
   or
   Choose **Landscape** to position the image horizontally within the imageable area of the separation. The orientation of the image on the page will change, but not the orientation of the page on the film.

7. Select Up (Right Reading) or Down (Right Reading) from the Emulsion pop-up menu.

8. Select a combined Halftone screen ruling (lpi)/Device resolution (dpi) from the Halftone pop-up menu.

9. Select Positive or Negative from the Image pop-up menu.

You can click OK at any time to save the current Separation Setup settings and you can reopen the dialog box at a later time to make further changes. When you save your document, separation settings are saved with the document.

Now follow the instructions on pages 250–252.

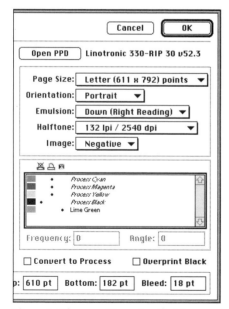

Figure 4. *Choose settings specified by your print shop from the right side of the **Setup** dialog box.*

Color Separations

By default, Illustrator will create and print a separation for each process and custom color used in an illustration. Using the Separation Setup dialog box, you can turn printing on or off for individual colors. You can also convert individual custom colors into process colors.

To choose colors to print and/or convert to process:

1. Choose File > Separation Setup if the dialog box isn't open.

2. In the process and custom colors scroll window, you will see a dot for each color used in the illustration. For each color you want to print, click in its print column to make a dot appear (**Figure 5**).

3. Click in the process color column to make a dot appear for each custom color you want to convert into a process color.
   or
   Check the Convert to Process box to convert all custom colors in the document.

4. Click in a color's don't print column (the crossed-out printer icon) if you don't want it to print.

■ Don't change the settings in the Frequency and Angle columns unless advised to do so by your service bureau.

■ Check the Overprint Black box if you want black fills and strokes to overprint background colors. You don't need to mix a process black (a black made from a mix of C,M,Y, and K) to use this option. When turned on, this option overrides the Overprint Black filter.

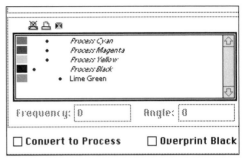

Figure 5. *Move a dot or click to place a dot under the don't print, print, or convert custom color columns in the process and custom color scroll window on the right side of the* **Separation Setup** *dialog box. Note: The file in this example did not contain any black in its colors, so Process Black was automatically set to don't print.*

COLOR PROOFING DEVICES

There are several reasons to proof your computer artwork before it's printed. First, the RGB colors that you see on your computer screen won't match the printed CMYK colors unless your monitor is professionally calibrated. Obtaining a proof will give you an opportunity to correct the color balance or brightness of a picture, or catch output problems like banding in gradations. And most print shops need a proof to refer to so they know what the printed piece should look like. Digital (direct-from-disk) color proofs — like IRIS or 3M prints — are the least expensive color proofs, though they're not perfectly reliable. An advantage of using an IRIS print, though, is that you can color correct your original electronic file and run another IRIS print before you order film. A more accurate but more expensive proof is a Chromalin or Matchprint, which is produced from film (color separations). Matchprint colors may be slightly more saturated than final print colors, though. The most reliable color proof, and by far the most expensive, is a press proof, which is produced in the print shop from your film negatives on the final paper stock.

Color Separations

To create crop marks for separations

If you haven't created crop marks for your document in Illustrator, the Separation Setup feature will, by default, create crop marks at the edge of the illustration's bounding box, which is the smallest rectangle that can encompass all the objects and direction lines in the illustration. It displays as a dotted line rectangle in the preview window. Adobe recommends setting crop marks in Illustrator using the Make Cropmarks command rather than using Separation Setup to set crop marks, so you can control more precisely the exact printable area of your illustration.

Separation Setup regards crop marks created using the Trim Marks filter as artwork. If your document contains Trim Marks, you can uncheck Use Default Marks to remove the default cropmarks. Unfortunately, this will also remove all printer's marks (crop and registration marks and color bars).

The **bounding box** defines the printable area around which Separation Setup places crop marks. You can resize the bounding box in the preview window so it surrounds a different part of the illustration, though it usually does not need to be adjusted. If you move or resize the bounding box, Separation Setup crop marks will move with the bounding box. You might need to move the image and/or resize the bounding box if the illustration contains objects that are outside the Artboard and there are no Illustrator-generated crop marks, because Separation Setup will include off-the-page objects as part of the image to be printed. Follow these instructions if you want to resize the bounding box (and thus re-crop the illustration).

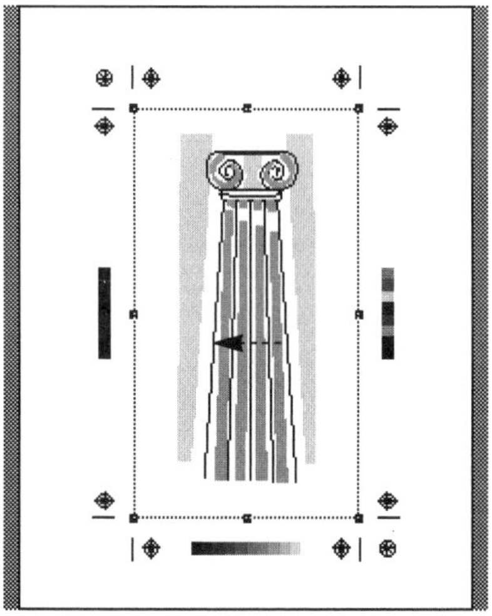

Figure 6. *Moving the image in its bounding box.*

Color Separations

To re-crop the illustration in the bounding box:

To move the illustration relative to the bounding box, position the pointer over the image in the preview window, then press and drag (**Figure 6**).

or

To move the dotted line bounding box itself, position the pointer over any non-handle part of the dotted line and press and drag the box (**Figure 7**).

or

To resize the dotted line bounding box, press and drag any of its four corner or four side handles (**Figure 8**).

- To restore the default bounding box, reenter the original values into the Left, Right, Top and Bottom boxes. You may want to note these values before you re-crop. Or, choose a different size from the Page Size pop-up menu, then choose the desired page size again. The bounding box size will be restored, but you may have to re-center the illustration within the box.

- To restore the default printing marks, choose Settings > Use Default Marks.

To choose which layers in the illustration to separate:

Choose an option from the Layer pop-up menu in the Separation Setup dialog box to control which layers will be color separated (**Figure 9**):

Printable to separate only those layers for which the Print option was turned on. To use this option effectively, place non-printing objects on a special non-print layer; Separation Setup will place the crop marks correctly.

Visible to separate only those layers that aren't hidden.

All to separate all layers.

- To force the preview to redraw, choose a different option and then choose the desired option.

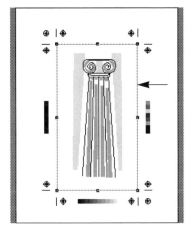

Figure 7. *Drag any non-handle part of the dotted line to move the bounding box and the illustration together.*

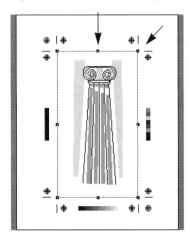

Figure 8. *Drag a side or corner handle to reshape the bounding box.*

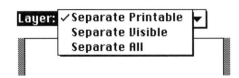

Figure 9. *The **Layer** pop-up menu in the Separation Setup dialog box.*

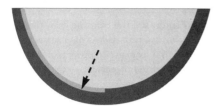

Figure 10. *Spread a lighter color foreground object.*

Figure 11. *Choke a darker color foreground object.*

The arrows above show the effect of reducing the area of the darker object due to the trap.

What is trapping?

Trapping is the extension of a color so it overlaps another color. The purpose of trapping is to compensate for gaps that might appear between colors due to mis-registration on press.

There are two basic kinds of traps. A **Spread** trap extends a lighter color object over a darker background color (**Figure 10**). A **Choke** trap extends a lighter background color over a darker color object (**Figure 11**). In either case, the extending color overprints the object or background color, creating a combination color where they overlap.

In Illustrator, you can build traps automatically or by specifying your own stroke width percentages.

Ask your print shop for advice before building traps into your illustration.

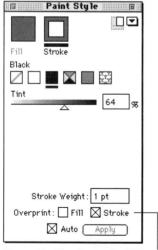

Figure 12. *The **Overprint Fill** and **Stroke** boxes are located on the right side of the **Paint Style** palette.*

To create a spread trap:

1. Select the lighter color foreground object (**Figure 10**).

2. Apply a Stroke in the same color as the object's Fill. The Stroke Weight should be **twice** the trap width suggested by your print shop for this object.

3. Check the Overprint Stroke box (**Figure 12**).

   The foreground object will overlap the background object by half the thickness of the new Stroke. The new Stroke will blend with the background color via the Overprint option. The Stroke will extend halfway inside and halfway outside its object's edge.

To create a choke trap:

1. Select the darker color foreground object (**Figure 11**).

2. Apply a Stroke in the same color as the lighter background object's Fill. Choose a Stroke Weight that is **twice** the trap width suggested by your print shop for this object.

3. Check the Overprint Stroke box (**Figure 12**).

   The lighter background color will now overlap the dark foreground object by half the width of the new Stroke.

■ A choke trap reduces the area of the darker object by a half the Stroke Weight. Be careful if you choke small type!

To trap a line:

1. Apply a Stroke color and Weight (**Figure 13**).

2. Choose Filter > Objects > Outline Path (**Figure 14**). The line will become a filled object, the same width as the original Stroke.

3. Apply a Stroke to the modified line. If the line is lighter than the background color, apply the same color as the Fill of the line. Otherwise, apply the lighter background color. Choose a Stroke Weight that is **twice** the trap width suggested by your print shop for this object.

4. Check the Overprint Stroke box (**Figure 12**).

   The line will now overlap the background color by half the width of the new Stroke. The Stroke will blend with the background color when it overprints.

Trapping tip

If you apply automatic trapping and then change an object's size, the trap width will change, so it's best to apply automatic trapping after you finalize the size of the objects.

Figure 13. *Stroke a line.*

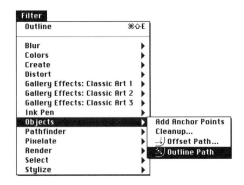

Figure 14. *Choose* **Outline Path** *from the* **Objects** *submenu under the* **Filter** *menu.*

Bug alert

In the first release of Illustrator 6.0, only one specific percentage of black can be specified for overprinting, instead of a percentage-or-higher range. According to Adobe, this bug will be fixed shortly. These instructions apply to the bug-free version.

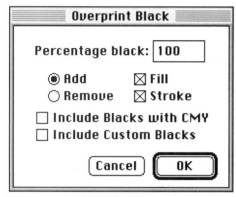

Figure 15. *The Overprint Black dialog box.*

Normally, in PostScript color separations, objects on top *knock out* the color of objects underneath them so inks don't mix with each other on press. When a color *overprints*, it prints right on top of the color beneath it and mixes with that color. Black is sometimes printed this way to eliminate the need for trapping. Using the **Overprint Black** filter, you can specify which Black areas will overprint. **CONSULT WITH YOUR PRINT SHOP BEFORE USING THIS FEATURE.**

To overprint black:

1. Select an object or objects containing black.
2. Choose Filter > Colors > Overprint Black.
3. Click Add to turn the Overprint option on for the specified "Percentage black" you will enter (**Figure 15**).
4. Enter an amount in the "Percentage black" field. Objects containing this black percentage or higher (to 100%) will overprint.
5. Check Fill to overprint black Fills; check Stroke to overprint black Strokes.
6. Check the "Include Blacks with CMY" box to have any CMYK mixture containing the percentage black (or higher) overprint.
7. Check the "Include Custom Blacks" box to have any custom color containing the percentage black (or higher) overprint.
8. Click OK or press Return.

■ If you select more than one black object and then apply the Overprint Black filter, the filter will affect only those objects containing the Percentage black (or higher). The objects will remain selected after using the filter.

■ The Separation Setup overprinting black option will override the Overprint Black filter. Use this filter to selectively separate black objects.

Overprint Black

The **Trap** filter creates traps automatically by determining which color object is lighter, and then spreading that color into the darker object. *Note:* The Trap filter won't trap an object containing a gradient Fill, a pattern Fill, or placed art, or an object with a Stroke color but no Fill color.

Want to avoid trapping altogether? Make sure all your colors share at least one component color in common (Cyan, Magenta, Yellow, or Black).

To create traps automatically:

1. Select two or more objects.
2. Choose Filter > Pathfinder > Trap.
3. Enter the Thickness amount specified by your print shop for the trap (**Figure 16**).

ASK YOUR PRINT SHOP ABOUT OPTIONAL STEPS 4–6.

4. Enter a value in the Height/width field to counter paper stretch on press.
5. Enter a value in the Tint reduction field to prevent trap areas between light colors from printing too dark.
6. Check "Convert custom colors to process" to convert custom colors in the selected objects into process colors.
7. Check Reverse traps to have darker colors trap into lighter colors.
8. Click OK or press Return.

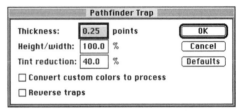

Figure 16. *Enter a trap* Thickness *in the* Pathfinder Trap *dialog box.*

The Trap filter doesn't take into account the Stroke color of underlying objects. To overcome this limitation, convert the Stroke into a filled object.

To create a trap on top of a Fill and a Stroke (a workaround):

1. Choose the Selection tool, then click on the background object that has a Fill and Stroke.
2. Choose Filter > Objects > Outline Path.
3. Deselect both objects, choose the Direct Selection tool, then click on the outermost object (the "Stroke").
4. Choose Filter > Pathfinder > Unite to remove any excess points from the outline path object.
5. Apply the Trap filter *(instructions above)*.

Automatic Trapping

Appendix A: **Keyboard Shortcuts**

KEY: ↖ *Click*   ↖↖ *Double-click*   ┈↖ *Press and drag*

FILES

New dialog box (without template)	⌘ N
New dialog box (with template)	⌘ Option N
Open dialog box	⌘ O
Close	⌘ W
Save	⌘ S
Document Setup dialog box	⌘ Shift D
General Preferences dialog box	⌘ K
Print dialog box	⌘ P
Quit Illustrator	⌘ Q

DIALOG BOXES

Highlight next field/option	Tab
Highlight previous field/option	Shift Tab
Select all characters in field	⌘ A
Delete all characters in field	⌘ A, then Delete
Cancel	⌘ . (Period key)
Reset dialog box with a preview box and sliders	Option ↖ Reset
OK	Return
None	⌘ N

Open/Save dialog boxes (System 7.x)

Desktop	⌘ D
Up one folder level	⌘ Up Arrow
Open file	↖↖ file name

PALETTES

Show/Hide all palettes	Tab
Show/Hide Paint Style	⌘ I
Show/Hide Toolbox	⌘ Control T
Reset Toolbox to default settings	⌘ Shift ↖↖ any tool
Reset current tool to default setting	Shift ↖↖ tool

Show/Hide Layers	⌘ Control L
Show/Hide Info	⌘ Control I
Show/Hide Character	⌘ T
Show/Hide Paragraph	⌘ Shift P
Show/Hide Tabs palette	⌘ Shift T

UNDO/REDO

Undo last operation	⌘ Z
Redo last undone operation	⌘ Shift Z

DISPLAY

Preview View	⌘ Y
Artview View	⌘ E
Preview Selection	⌘ Option Y
Crosshair pointer	Caps lock
Display entire Artboard	⬥⬥ Hand tool
Fit in Window	⌘ M
Actual size (100%)	⬥⬥ Zoom tool -or- ⌘ H
Zoom out (Zoom tool selected)	Option ⬥
Zoom in (any tool selected)	⌘ Spacebar ⬥ -or- ⌘]
Zoom out (any tool selected)	⌘ Option Spacebar ⬥ -or- ⌘ [
Zoom in from center (Zoom tool selected)	Control ⋯⬥
Use Hand tool (any tool selected)	Spacebar
Show/Hide Rulers	⌘ R
Show/Hide Edges	⌘ Shift H
New View dialog box	⌘ Control V
Hide template	⌘ Shift W
Hide a selected object	⌘ 3
Hide all unselected objects	⌘ Option 3
Show All	⌘ 4

CREATE OBJECTS

Create object from center using Rectangle, Rounded Rectangle or Oval tool	Option ⋯⬥
Toggle between Rectangle, Rounded Rectangle, or Oval tool's draw-from-center option	⬥⬥ tool
Create circle or square using Rectangle, Rounded Rectangle or Oval tool	Shift ⋯⬥

PLUG-IN TOOLS

Move object as you draw with Polygon, Star, or Spiral tool	Space bar
Constrain orientation as you draw with Polygon, Star, or Spiral tool	Shift
Add or subtract sides as you draw with Polygon tool, points as you draw with the Star tool, or segments as you draw with the Spiral tool	Up or down arrow
Align shoulders as you draw with Star tool	Option
Increase or decrease outer radius as you draw with Star tool or decay as you draw with Spiral tool	Control

SELECT

Use the last used selection tool	⌘
Toggle between Selection or Group Selection tool and Direct Selection tool	⌘ Tab
Toggle between Group Selection tool and Direct Selection tool	Option
Selection marquee (any selection tool)	····▶
Select All	⌘ A
Select None	⌘ Shift A

MOVE

Move dialog box	⌘ Shift M (with object selected) -or- Option ▶ Selection tool
Drag a copy of object	Option ····▶
Move selected object in current Cursor key increments (General Preferences)	Arrow keys
Constrain movement to 45°, 90°, 135°, or 180°	Shift

PATHS

Use Add-anchor-point tool (Pen tool selected)	Control (over segment)
Use Delete-anchor-point tool (Pen tool selected)	Control (over point)
Toggle between Add-anchor-point tool and Delete-anchor-point tool (either selected)	Option
Use Convert-direction-point tool (Pen tool selected)	Control Option
Use Convert-direction-point tool (any selection tool selected)	Control

Keyboard Shortcuts

Use Convert-direction-point tool (Freehand tool selected)	⌘ Option Control
Use Rotate direction line (Pen tool selected)	Control Option ⌁
Constrain angle of direction line to 45°, 90°, 135°, or 180° (Direct Selection tool or Convert-direction-point tool selected)	Shift ⌁
Convert a smooth point into a corner point using Direct Selection tool	Control ⌁
Convert a smooth point into a corner point using Pen tool	Control Option ⌁
Convert a non-continuous curve into a continuous curve using Direct Selection tool	Control ⌁ (on direction point)
Use Pen tool (Freehand tool selected)	Control
Use Add-anchor-point tool (Freehand tool selected, over segment)	⌘ Control
Use Delete-anchor-point tool (Freehand tool selected, over point)	⌘ Control
Use Convert-direction-point tool (Freehand tool selected)	⌘ Option Control
Erase while drawing with Freehand tool	⌘ ⌁ (on new path)
Use Pen tool (Autotrace tool selected)	Control
Join two selected endpoints	⌘ J
Average two selected points	⌘ L
Average and Join two selected endpoints	⌘ Option J

PAINT

Toggle between Eyedropper tool and Paint Bucket tool (either selected)	Option

RESTACK

Bring To Front	⌘ = (Equal key)
Send To Back	⌘ – (Minus key)
Paste In Front	⌘ F
Paste In Back	⌘ B

TYPE

Use Area Type tool (Type tool selected, over open path)	Option
Use Path Type tool (Type tool selected, over closed path)	Option
Use Type tool (Area Type or Path Type tool selected)	Control Option
Select a word	⌁⌁

Select a paragraph	🠕🠕🠕
Select all type	⌘ A
Hard Return	Enter
Link Blocks	⌘ Shift G
Unlink Blocks	⌘ Shift U
Align left	⌘ Shift L
Align center	⌘ Shift C
Align right	⌘ Shift R
Justify	⌘ Shift J
Justify last line	⌘ Shift B
Size field on Character palette	⌘ Shift S
Increase point size	⌘ Shift >
Decrease point size	⌘ Shift <
Increase leading	Option Down Arrow
Decrease leading	Option Up Arrow
Tracking field on Character palette	⌘ Shift K
Increase kerning/tracking	Option Right Arrow
Decrease kerning/tracking	Option Left Arrow
Increase kerning/tracking 5x	⌘ Option Right Arrow
Decrease kerning/tracking 5x	⌘ Option Left Arrow
Increase baseline shift	Option Shift Up Arrow
Decrease baseline shift	Option Shift Down Arrow
Force hyphenate a word	⌘ Shift – (Hyphen key)

Curly quotes

'	Option Shift]
'	Option]
"	Option Shift [
"	Option [

TRANSFORM

Transformation tool dialog box (any transformation tool selected)	Option 🠕
Transform object along nearest 45° angle (Shear or Reflect tool)	Shift ⁻⁻⁻🠕
Rotate object in 45° increments (Rotate tool)	Shift ⁻⁻⁻🠕
Scale object uniformly (Scale tool)	Shift ⁻⁻⁻🠕
Scale object along nearest 45° angle (Scale tool)	Shift ⁻⁻⁻🠕
Repeat transformation	⌘ D

Keyboard Shortcuts

Transform Pattern Fill only (after clicking
with transformation tool)   P ····➤

Transform copy of object (after clicking
with transformation tool)   Option ····➤

COMPOUNDS

Make Compound Path   ⌘ 8

Release Compound Path   ⌘ 9

CLIPBOARD

Cut   ⌘ X

Copy   ⌘ C

Paste   ⌘ V

PRECISION TOOLS

Make Guides   ⌘ 5

Release Guides   ⌘ 6

Lock/Unlock Guides   ⌘ 7

Constrain Measure tool to nearest 45° angle   Shift ➤ or ➤➤

Lock (selected object)   ⌘ 1

Lock all unselected objects   ⌘ Option 1

Unlock All   ⌘ 2

MISC.

Attributes dialog box   ⌘ Control A

Group   ⌘ G

Ungroup   ⌘ U

Last used filter   ⌘ Shift E

Keyboard Shortcuts

Appendix B: **The Artists**

Michael Bartalos
30 Ramona No. 2
San Francisco, CA 94103-2292
Voice 415-863-4569
Fax 415-252-7252
xi, 239, color section

Peter Fahrni
Voice 212-472-7126
81, 85, 118, 148, 173

Louise Fili
Louise Fili Ltd.
71 Fifth Avenue
New York, NY 10003
Voice 212-989-9153
Fax 212-989-1453
141

John Hersey
Voice 415-927-2091
Fax 415-927-2092
ultraduc@linex.com
thingbat@aol.com
color section

Jonathan Hoefler
The Hoefler Type Foundry
611 Broadway, Suite 815
New York, NY 10012-2608
Voice 212-777-6640
Fax 212-777-6684
info@typography.com
http://www.typography.com
229

Diane Margolin
41 Perry Street
New York, NY 10014
212-691-9537
*52, 53, 55, 61, 76, 88, 109,
110, 124, 125, 190, 206*

Daniel Pelavin
80 Varick Street
New York, NY 10013
Voice 212-941-7418
Fax 212-431-7138
dpelavin@inch.com
dpelavin@aol.com
http://www.inch.com/~dpelavin
47, 171

Miriam Schaer
199 Eighth Avenue, A3
Brooklyn, NY 11215
Voice/Fax 718-788-2029
74777.1534@compuserve.com
54, 92, 264

Chris Spollen
Moonlight Press Studio
362 Cromwell Avenue
Ocean Breeze, NY 10305
Voice 718-979-9695
cjspollen@aol.com
http://www.inch.com/~cspollen/
*xii, 1, 48, 91, 99, 113, 114,
color section*

Nancy Stahl
470 West End Avenue, 8G
New York, NY 10024
Voice 212-362-8779
Fax 212-362-7511
NStahl@aol.com
color section

Calling all Illustrators, Photoshoppers, and Painters

If you'd like to submit artwork for future editions of this book or our Photoshop, Painter, or QuarkXPress QuickStart Guides, please mail your paper output to Peter Lourekas, c/o Communication Design Dept., Parsons School of Design, 66 Fifth Avenue, New York, NY 10011. We will review every submission very carefully and thoughtfully. Paper output only, please!

We'd love to see...

Imaginative typography, maps, images created with the Ink Pen or Path Pattern filter, photorealistic images, patterns, masks, graphs, or anything else you'd like to impress us with.

Our Thanks

Special Thanks

Miriam Schaer

to

All the artists listed on the previous page. Their generous contributions of artwork really jazzed up this edition, and they're certain to inspire our readers.

and

Patricia Pane at Adobe Systems, Inc. for leading us to all the right people at Adobe. And Eric Hess at Adobe for patiently and thoroughly answering our many technical questions about the 6.0 upgrade.

and

Ted Nace and all the Peachpitters — always a pleasure to work with.

and

Johanna Gillman for screen grabbing all the new menus and dialog boxes.

and

Stephen "eagle-eyes" Caratzas, for his proofreading services.

Index

Index

Index

Index

Index